A Prosentential Theory of Truth

A
Prosentential
Theory
of
Truth

D O R O T H Y   G R O V E R

PRINCETON UNIVERSITY PRESS

Copyright © 1992 by Princeton University Press
Published by Princeton University Press, 41 William Street,
Princeton, New Jersey 08540
In the United Kingdom: Princeton University Press, Oxford

All Rights Reserved

Library of Congress Cataloging-in-Publication Data

Grover, Dorothy, 1936–
A prosentential theory of truth / Dorothy Grover.
p.   cm.
Includes bibliographical references and index.
ISBN 0-691-07399-6 (cl)
1. Truth. 2. Language and languages—Philosophy.
3. Proposition (Logic) I. Title.
BC171.G76   1992   121—dc20   91–36788

This book has been composed in Linotron Trump

Princeton University Press books are printed on acid-free paper
and meet the guidelines for permanence and durability of the
Committee on Production Guidelines for Book Longevity of the
Council on Library Resources

Printed in the United States of America

10 9 8 7 6 5 4 3 2 1

DESIGNED BY LAURY A. EGAN

IN MEMORY OF MY SISTER ELEANOR

Contents

Preface

This volume contains previously published papers on prosentences and the prosentential theory of truth. The Introductory Essay, which provides a prosentential perspective on some other theories of truth, is printed here for the first time.

Because the papers included in this volume were written over a period of some twenty years and appeared in different publications, their notation and style vary. Some light editing has been done with respect to style and format, but differences remain. Readers will note, for example, that although '$\forall p$' and '$\forall x$' are usually used for universal quantification, '(p)', '(x)', '$[p]$', and '$[x]$' are used in Chapter 11. The first pair are used for quantifiers that are given a domain-and-values interpretation while the second pair are used for quantifiers given a substitutional interpretation. Further notational variations occur in Chapter 11 because the notation is designed to reflect other distinctions.

Many friends and colleagues have provided essential advice along the way. Some of these are mentioned in footnotes. Among those due special mention are Nuel Belnap, from whom I learned much, early in my career, about how to pursue a research project. Also, my colleagues Charles Chastain and Kent Wilson gave me sage advice and encouragement when I needed it. Thanks also to Charlotte Jackson, who has guided me through the intricacies of various WordPerfect software programs.

Finally, special thanks to my family for their support over the years: Mum, Dad, Ray, Colin, and Pamela; and, more recently, to Roy and Michael for their patience.

Publication details and Acknowledgments

Reprinted by permission of
Kluwer Academic Publishers:

"Propositional Quantifiers," *Journal of Philosophical Logic* 1 (1972), 111–136 [Chapter 2 of this book]

"A Prosentential Theory of Truth," co-authored with Joseph Camp and Nuel Belnap, *Philosophical Studies* 27 (1975), 73–124 [Chapter 3 of this book]

"Prosentences and Propositional Quantification," *Philosophical Studies* 35 (1979), 289–297 [Chapter 5 of this book]

"Truth: Do We Need It?" *Philosophical Studies* 40 (1981), 69–103 [Chapter 7 of this book]

"On Two Deflationary Theories of Truth," in *Truth or Consequences*, ed. Michael Dunn and Anil Gupta, Dordrecht: Kluwer, 1990 [Chapter 9 of this book]

Reprinted by permission of
the *Journal of Philosophy*:

"Inheritors and Paradox," *Journal of Philosophy* 74 (1977), 590–604 [Chapter 4 of this book]

Reprinted by permission of
Asa Kasher, editor of *Philosophia*:

"Truth," first published in *Philosophia* 10:3–4 (1981), 225–252 [Chapter 6 of this book]

Rights held by author:

"Berry's Paradox," *Analysis* 43 (1983), 170–176 [Chapter 8 of this book]

"Propositional Quantification and Quotation Contexts," and "Quantifying in and out of Quotes," the latter co-authored with Nuel Belnap, both in *Truth, Syntax, and Modality*, ed. Hugues Leblanc, Dordrecht: Reidel, 1973, 101–110 and 17–47, respectively (these papers establish technical results assumed in the prosentential theory papers) [Chapters 10 and 11 of this book]

A Prosentential Theory of Truth

1

Introductory Essay*

At the beginning of the century, it was common to write about the nature of truth. Correspondence theorists advocated an analysis of truth in terms of a correspondence relation between linguistic entities, or beliefs, and extralinguistic entities. Pragmatists have been described as reducing truth to "what works" or to "what scientists are destined to agree upon"; and coherence theorists offered analyses in terms of consistency and comprehensiveness. Frequently different schools of philosophical thought are associated with these theories, e.g., realists are often identified as correspondence theorists, while instrumentalists and anti-realists are assumed to endorse a pragmatic account of truth. In §1, I present a brief survey of some versions of these theories of the nature of truth, thereby providing the background against which the prosentential theory of truth was presented.

In §2 I review the papers on the prosentential theory included in this volume. A principal claim of the prosentential theory of truth is that truth talk—all the truth talk we need—can be explained without appeal to any kind of analysis of the nature of truth. I claim the truth predicate helps facilitate certain kinds of discourse and that this role can be explained in terms of the concept of a "prosentence." Joseph Camp, Nuel Belnap, and I developed this idea in part by drawing analogies with bound variables in formal languages and pronouns in English and in part by exploring the philosophical implications of this prosentential characterization. For example, with respect to the implications, I show that the prosentential theory offers a simple account of "paradoxical" expressions like the

* I thank Kent Wilson, Charles Chastain, Max Cresswell, Nuel Belnap, Michael Devitt, and referees for Princeton University Press for helpful comments on earlier drafts. Thanks also to the Humanities Institute at the University of Illinois, Chicago, for the year of research in 1989–90. Comments I received on portions of this introductory essay that I presented in a seminar to members of the Institute were particularly helpful.

Liar sentence ('This is false') according to which they are not contradictory. The prosentential theory can also explain, without appeal to a substantive truth property, cases where philosophers have
mistakenly claimed an explanatory role for truth.

In §3 I consider the implications of the prosentential theory for
the so-called correspondence, pragmatic, and coherence theories of
truth. In denying that we need an analysis of the nature of truth,
the prosentential theory denies a basic assumption of these three
theories as they have been traditionally construed. I show that the
prosentential theory offers a new slant on some issues over which
these theories contend. I show that among the diverse theories that
have been classified as theories of truth, there are theories that have
something to say about the nature of truth (Russell's correspondence theories), theories that have something to say about meaning
(again, correspondence theories), theories that have something to
say about the truth predicate (Tarski and the prosentential theory),
theories that have something to say about what-is-true (some pragmatic and coherence theories), and theories that have something to
say about epistemological issues concerning what-is-true (again,
some pragmatic and coherence theories). These last two cases need
further explanation because we are going to read 'true' in 'what-is-
true' prosententially.

It emerges that a prosentential theorist has the option of endorsing significant aspects of the traditional theories. For example, even
though the nature-of-truth issue is eliminated on the prosentential
scheme, she has the option of endorsing the idea that language-
world connections may have an explanatory role. Also forthcoming
is an explanation of how a philosopher (like Quine) can endorse a
so-called deflationary account of the truth predicate while at the
same time endorsing views that resemble those we associate with
coherence theorists.

1. On "the Nature of Truth"

Correspondence theorists seek an analysis of truth that will capture
the idea that "true sentences agree with reality" (or the idea that "it
is the world that makes sentences true"). A *correspondence theory
of truth* typically presents truth as a relational property: Truth is a
correspondence relation that connects bearers of truth and falsity
(e.g., sentence types or tokens, propositions, or belief states) with
extralinguistic entities (e.g., facts) with which the bearers corre-

spond. Though the intuitions behind this theory appealed to many, the problem of providing an adequate account of the correspondence relation, and of identifying the two kinds of entities between which the correspondence relation is alleged to obtain, has proved recalcitrant.

Russell (1906–07), for example, struggled with several versions of the correspondence theory. First there was the idea that beliefs or sentences are true if there are *facts* in the world that make them true. The simplest version of this theory is the *existence theory*—so-called by Prior (1967). The existence theory treats sentences a bit like names, except that the objects with which they are related are facts, not objects. For example, 'The cat is on the mat' is true, it is said, if the world contains the fact that the cat is on the mat. A major problem for this theory is posed by false beliefs (or sentences), as both Plato (in the *Theaetetus*) and Russell realized. For example, Russell, in "On the Nature of Truth," says, "When [beliefs] do correspond, the beliefs are true, and are beliefs in facts; when they do not, the beliefs are erroneous, and are beliefs in nothing." The problematic question is, How is false belief possible? Indeed, falsity poses a variety of challenges for correspondence theorists.[1]

Modifications of the existence theory were introduced that yielded slightly more satisfactory versions of a correspondence theory. At various stages Russell first tried adding to his ontology objective falsehoods and then negative facts. The idea was to have something with which false sentences would correspond. But the problems do not go away without much more explanation. For suppose a situation where there is a dog on the mat and the cat is up the tree: With what does 'The cat is on the mat' correspond? The dog's being on the mat? The cat's being up the tree? Or does it correspond with the objective falsehood, the cat's being on the mat, or with the negative fact, the cat's not being on the mat? What are facts, objective falsehoods, or negative facts? I have not (yet) seen an account of any of these that leads to a satisfactory analysis of "the nature of truth."[2]

[1] Current theories of representation seem to face a similar problem in that it proves difficult to account for misrepresentation. (See Cummins 1989 on the problems that misrepresentation poses for current theories of representation.) I hope sometime to compare and contrast the problems correspondence theories have faced with those representational theories are facing. The Russell quote is from the cited essay in *Proceedings of the Aristotelian Society* 7 (1906–1907), p. 49.

[2] I suppose a modern-day proponent of some such correspondence theory could borrow from possible world semantics for an account of objective falsehoods. Con-

Both Russell and Plato seemed to think the answer might lie in the grammar of the sentences used in expressing beliefs. For then a sentence can be both about something—the subject of the sentence (the cat)—yet false (not on the mat). Russell himself recognized that saying only this much does not yield an account of the correspondence relation. What is the correspondence relation?

A "picture theory" of truth (or meaning) may be one way to make sense of the correspondence relation. For one is supposed to just *see* that a linguistic entity pictures the object with which it corresponds. Unfortunately people do not just see what a picture is a picture of; furthermore, what would a "false picture" (e.g., the false sentence 'the cat is on the mat' in the case where the dog is on the mat and the cat is up a tree) be a picture of? We need an account of 'picture of.'

Some recent proposals have tried to wrestle a correspondence theory out of Tarski's truth definition. I know of three such attempts. However, because two of these accept Tarski's (1936) definition (or something like it) as providing all there is to know about truth, they promote only a "deflationary" account of truth. For this reason, I will review those two versions in §3.

Other philosophers have thought there is more to the concept of truth than is captured by a Tarski-style truth definition. For example, Dummett (1978) complains that a Tarskian definition fails to give an account of the point of the predicate. He says, "What has to be added to a truth-definition for the sentences of a language, if the notion of truth is to be explained, is a description of the linguistic activity of making assertions." (p. 20) Davidson (1990) claims that, in addition to "the formal properties of the concept," we need "to indicate how a theory of truth can be applied to particular speakers or groups of speakers." (p. 314) Although I agree that we need an account of assertion and linguistic activity generally, I doubt that such an account has much to do with "the truth concept" itself. One thing I think we need beyond what Tarski has given us is an

---

sider, for example, the following proposal: Let each sentence "correspond" to a set of possible worlds. Then a sentence is "true" if the real world is included in the set with which it corresponds, and a sentence is "false" if the real world is not included in the set with which it corresponds. Facts would then be those sets of possible worlds that contain the real world; "objective falsehoods" would be defined as the set of possible worlds that do not include the real world. In this case a false sentence would "correspond" to an objective falsehood. Two problems: It is no longer the world (alone) that makes sentences true or false, and the correspondence relation is unexplained.

understanding of the utility of the truth predicate. This should help us understand how so-called theories of truth have been many and various. This supplementation is different from that which others have described.[3]

Though Tarski claimed to capture the intuitions of the correspondence theory, most who call themselves correspondence theorists also think we need more on the truth concept than a Tarskian definition provides. For example, Sellars (1962) developed a version of the picture theory as supplementation to Tarski.

Perhaps the most ambitious, most provocative, way of wrestling a correspondence theory out of Tarski has been suggested by Hartry Field (1972). Field is one among those who have claimed Tarski has failed to capture much that is important about truth. A problem with Tarski's definition, according to Field, is that it defines truth for only one language at a time. He says that if we are to have an account of truth that applies to all languages, we must add, at the level of the base clauses, physicalistically acceptable reductions of 'refers' and 'applies'. This, Field claims, would yield a definition that incorporates the kinds of causal language-world relations that correspondence theorists think we need.

Field's most recent argument for an explanatory role is based on a complex case. He speculates that correspondence truth is required to explain a certain kind of systematic reliability that an individual person may have concerning a certain topic or group of topics. An example he appeals to is that of an expert's reliability on social movements, including the Kronstadt rebellion. Field says: "We will need an explanation of the striking correlation between her belief-states and the events involving the Kronstadt sailors. It seems likely the explanation would have to involve something like causal networks of information. . . ." Let us grant Field's point, that some kind of causal network is needed to explain T-reliability. What does this have to do with truth? Field continues:

> A familiar proposal for giving a correspondence theory of truth (perhaps most explicit in Field 1972) is to explain the truth conditions of sentences in terms of reference or reference-like relations for the basic parts of the sentence, and then to give explanations of the reference-like relations for the parts; and it is often assumed that something like causal networks of information of the sort just alluded to will play a role in the

---

[3] There are other discussions of Tarski that I cannot cover here; for example, Etchemendy 1988 and Davidson 1990.

theories of reference for the parts; ... a central feature of the proposal is to build into the theoretical explication of correspondence truth just the sort of thing needed to *explain* the striking T-reliability and converse T-reliability that agents have (about some matters), under the interpretations that we find useful in explaining their success. (Field 1986, p. 104)

Field's point is that the language-world connections he proposes incorporating, in his version of the correspondence theory, are needed to explain T-reliability.

I have argued elsewhere that Field has failed to establish his point because he has not really given truth itself an explanatory role. The primary problem is that in Field's scheme the causal language-world connections are *the same* for true *and* false sentences, because the language-world connections of causal-historical theories of reference (the connections he suggests utilizing in unpacking 'refers' and 'applies') are the same for true and false sentences; indeed, they are also the same for questions and commands. On Field's scheme, a difference between true and false sentences arises in a clause that says something about only extralinguistic reality. This "difference" is captured by T-sentences. Because no causal relations are uniquely associated with truth, truth as a substantive language-world relation does not have its own explanatory role.[4]

What Field's suggestion would perhaps show—if Field's reductions of 'refers' and 'applies' were successful—is that the language-world connections of *reference* have an explanatory role.[5] But even then, the most such connections might contribute is something toward an explanation of the conditions under which people become articulate, or perhaps an explanation of the content of a person's beliefs.[6] They can hardly explain "the striking T-reliability and converse T-reliability that agents have (about some matters)"; other kinds of causal connections are needed for that. Of course one can call any kind of explanatory relation a correspondence truth relation; however, Field does suggest ties with traditional correspondence theories, and traditional theories have *different* language-world connections for true and false sentences. That is what one would expect if truth, as a language-world relation, is to have an

---

[4] I have argued these points in greater detail in Grover 1990b.

[5] There are many who think Field's extension of Tarski faces difficulties, e.g., Davidson (1977), Stalnaker (1984), Leeds (1978), McDowell (1978), and Putnam (1981). Others, e.g., Devitt (1984), think it is on the right track.

[6] In fact, Field seems mostly concerned with arriving at a theory of "content."

explanatory role. So Field's claim that his correspondence theory gives truth an explanatory role is questionable.[7]

I am inclined to think that those sympathetic to Field's concerns should separate an explanatory role for reference from the issue of truth. After all, in Field's case, the only reason for tacking truth onto some kind of reference theory seems to be to give truth an explanatory role. Given that reference connections provide the substance of the explanation Field envisages, there is really no reason for claiming that truth itself provides the explanation, unless the motivation is to save the correspondence theory.

By the end of his paper (1986), Field himself entertains the possibility of separating the issues, stating, "Indeed, explanations of those phenomena (e.g., the 'success phenomena' . . . or the fact that an agent is highly T-reliable and converse T-reliable under certain specific interpretations) is clearly important, whether or not one thinks that it will lead to a correspondence theory of truth." (p. 105) Michael Devitt (1984) also appeals to Field's suggestions as to the structure of a correspondence theory of truth. In his attempt to establish an explanatory role for truth, Devitt presents a case where he thinks we need to ascribe wide content to speakers. Though I find this a helpful discussion in general, Devitt's concern is really with establishing an explanatory role for reference connections—as it was for Field.

Perhaps there are other contemporary philosophers who have worked out the details of a correspondence theory, but I am not aware of them. Indeed, in discussions of scientific and moral realism and in epistemology, there are many references to "truth" where a correspondence theory is assumed, but the writers do not describe the details of the correspondence theory (the relation and the relata) they have in mind. There are also references to "realist truth" by those who presumably think correspondence truth is constitutive of realism. But again, I am not sure what these philosophers have in mind as a correspondence theory.[8]

Why did philosophers think it important to develop theories of "the nature of truth"? We have seen that Field argues we need such

---

[7] I should mention that Field leaves room for alternative ways of eliminating 'refers' and 'applies' from Tarski's base clauses. He allows that some other kinds of causal chains might be utilized. I do not know that anyone has successfully worked out the details.

[8] I doubt realism should be tied to the correspondence theory anyway. I have been persuaded by Michael Devitt (1984 and forthcoming); however, I am not as convinced as he is about the value of the ongoing discussions of realism.

a theory because he thinks truth has an explanatory role. In our terms, we might think of Russell as another who at least sometimes assumed that truth has an explanatory role. For example, Russell sometimes raised questions about truth in the context of discussions of knowledge.[9] In his view (and Plato's also), an account of knowledge called for an account of the difference between true and false belief. I presume Russell thought an account of the nature of truth would lead to an account of this difference. Russell's investigation of language and meaning also led him to take up the issue of "the nature of truth."

Although there is some reason to think that Russell in some way assumed truth had what we call an explanatory role, it is not clear that any of the pragmatic or coherence theorists made such an assumption. Though it is often assumed the pragmatic theory is a theory of the nature of truth—the theorists themselves sometimes spoke this way—it is doubtful that they really had an interest in "the nature of truth" as such, nor is it likely they were (even implicitly) interested in an explanatory role for truth. Indeed, some of their remarks sound revisionary, the idea being that truth concepts should be abandoned in favor of other more pragmatic concepts. Nevertheless, the things pragmatic and coherence theorists say about truth, and about what is true, have frequently been interpreted as focused on the nature of truth. For the moment, I will go along with that characterization. What, then, was their theory (if they had one) of the nature of truth?

There are two problems for those who may try to determine what a fully developed *pragmatic theory of the nature of truth* may look like. First, the pragmatists said a number of apparently quite *different* things about what is true (compare the slogans 'Truth is what works' and 'Truth means verification'); second, none of their suggestions seems to have been developed in a systematic way. At least three apparently distinct themes are found in what the pragmatists have written that have been construed as statements about the nature of truth. Peirce (1878) began with the assumption that there is convergence in science; and he concluded that truth is that upon which the experts will agree in the long run. Dewey (1931), on the other hand, has suggested that truth is instrumental—truth is what works. Dewey also argued that truth "means" verification.

The difficulties such theories face are well-known. If we define truth in terms of what scientists agree upon in the long run, there

---

[9] For example, Russell 1921.

would seem to be no grounds for thinking we now have true beliefs. If we were to agree with Peirce's assumption that there is convergence in science, then perhaps we would know that some of our beliefs are "approximately" true. But first we must establish that science converges. And that, I take it, may be impossible to do.[10] On the other hand, if we analyze truth in terms of what present experts now agree upon (or in terms of verification), then truth would seem to be mutable. Similarly, it would seem that truth would be mutable were it defined in instrumental terms; for a given hypothesis may work in one context but not in another. For those who are unhappy with the idea that truth is mutable, this approach also faces difficulties.

The basic idea for a traditionally construed *coherence theory of truth* (e.g., Blanshard 1939) is that a sentence is true if it "coheres" with a theory, or with a system of beliefs, that is consistent and comprehensive. The truth of sentences is therefore not determined on an individual basis. In this sense the coherence theory is like some versions of the pragmatic theory and unlike the correspondence theory, according to which sentences correspond on an individual basis with facts or objects in the world. Indeed, depending on what account one might give of how beliefs are acquired and what account one might give of 'consistent and comprehensive,' if one were to keep the background metaphysics fixed, a fully developed coherence theory of truth could look much like a fully developed pragmatic theory of truth.

Like the correspondence and pragmatic theories, the coherence theory faces challenging issues. For example, many are concerned that the coherence theory does not guarantee the existence of a unique, consistent, and comprehensive system of beliefs. Mutability of truth may also be a problem.

While the disputes among proponents of the traditional theories were going on, first Frege and then Ramsey noted that in ordinary everyday examples predicating 'true' of a sentence seems to add nothing to the claim that would be made with the sentence alone. For example, Frege (1915) says: "The thought expressed in these words ['that it is true that sea water is salt'] coincides with the sense of the sentence 'that sea water is salt'. So the sense of the word 'true' is such that it does not make any essential contribution to the thought. . . . the word 'true' has a sense that contributes nothing to the sense of the whole sentence in which it occurs as predicate"

---

[10] See Fine 1984, for example.

(p. 251); and from Ramsey (1927) we have "[I]t is evident that 'It is true that Caesar was murdered' means no more than that Caesar was murdered, and 'It is false that Caesar was murdered' means no more than that Caesar was not murdered."

The suggestion they are making is that the truth predicate is content-redundant.[11] Indeed, Ramsey concludes there is no separate problem of truth. Does truth not have a nature? Is the truth predicate redundant? Ramsey is often described as subscribing to a redundancy theory of truth. If this is taken to mean that Ramsey thinks we could drop 'true' without loss, this is not his position. For Ramsey also says that 'It is true' and 'It is false' are "phrases which we sometimes use for emphasis or for stylistic reasons. . . ."[12] He then points out that we cannot eliminate 'true' from something like 'He is always right,' given the resources of ordinary language. So, though Ramsey seems to deny the nature-of-truth theorists' assumption that truth has a nature, he does not claim the truth predicate is redundant. I note this because the prosentential theory of truth enters the picture at this point.

The *prosentential theory of truth* can be viewed as developing and explaining Ramsey's (1927) and Strawson's (1950a) suggestive insights concerning the content-redundancy and utility of the truth predicate. For the prosentential theory shows how the truth predicate can be content-redundant yet not redundant; it explains the truth predicate's usefulness when we want emphasis. The prosentential theory also explains how the truth predicate works in combination with indirect reference to provide a way of generalizing.

Briefly, a principal claim of the prosentential theory is that 'That is true' and 'It is true' are "prosentences." Pro*sentences* function much as pro*nouns* do, except that prosentences occupy the positions in sentences that declarative sentences occupy, while pro-

---

[11] The claim as regards content redundancy is that " 'Snow is white' is true," and "It is true that snow is white," etc., say no more nor less than that snow is white. How one generalizes on this claim (e.g., including cases where indexicals, etc., occur in the antecedent) will depend on one's account of language. Because I do not have a theory of meaning or use worked out, I use phrases like 'same content' and 'say the same thing' without further explanation. I am inclined to think an adequate account of language and meaning needs to take account of conceptual, pragmatic, and inferential roles, as well as some kinds of speaker-world relations. Brandom's approach to these issues (deriving in part from Sellars) may offer a promising start. See Brandom 1988a.

[12] Strawson (1950a) develops this feature of the truth predicate. See also Ayer 1946 for another early version of those theories that have been classified as redundancy theories.

nouns occupy the positions names occupy. Just as pronouns of laziness can acquire their referents from antecedent expressions, as 'he' and 'her' do in the sentence

Bob is happiest with Mary, and I think *he* will marry *her*.[13]

so also prosentences of laziness can derive their propositional content from antecedent sentences.[14] The idea is that 'that is true' in

BETTY: My sister finds humid weather debilitating.
JANET: If *that is true*, she should move to a drier climate.

acquires its propositional content from Betty's statement.[15] The idea is that, in this context we think of 'that is true' as standing in for "my sister finds humid weather debilitating." So, just as pronouns can be used to establish connections between parts of a discourse, e.g., to establish co-referentiality, so also prosentences are useful for establishing connections with what others have to say, e.g., in reflecting on the comments of others and expressing agreement or disagreement. Pronouns can also be used for generalizing with respect to nominal positions; similarly, prosentences (and more complex prosentential constructions) can be used for generalizing with respect to sentence positions. Accordingly, the prosentential theory of truth is a theory that has something to say about the grammatical role and utility of the truth predicate.

There are important similarities between the prosentential theory and another contemporary theory, the *disquotational theory of truth*:[16] The disquotational theory both assumes content redundancy and defends the utility of the truth predicate. There are some differences in that disquotational theorists seem to focus on a syntactical metalinguistic predicate while the initial focus of the prosentential theory is on some ordinary language uses of the predicate. This is perhaps one reason why disquotational theorists place

---

[13] The literature on pronouns shows that anaphoric connections can be much more complex than this example suggests.

[14] This is only a very rough sketch of the grammatical and semantical features of prosentences. The connections between antecedents and anaphoric expressions generally, can be very complex. Readers who are unfamiliar with the details of the prosentential theory should take a look at Chapter 3 before proceeding. Others may wish to read over the early sections of Chapter 4 for a quick review of the theory.

[15] This mention of "propositional content" is also used without further explanation. See footnote 11 for an explanation of my hesitancy.

[16] Those who have endorsed one form or another of a disquotational theory include Quine (1970), Leeds (1978), Horwich (1982 and 1990), Soames (1984), and Williams (1986).

greater emphasis on T-sentences (i.e., on sentences of the form 'x is true if and only if p,' where 'p' provides a translation of x). A more significant difference concerns the content redundancy of the truth predicate: Only the prosentential theory offers an account of how the truth predicate keeps discourse at the level of the object language—i.e., only the prosentential theory offers an explanation of the fact that truth talk is typically about extralinguistic matters. I return to these and other comparisons later in this introductory essay. They are also discussed in greater detail in Chapter 9.

We have, then, a contrast between (i) theories that have been described as "substantive" or "robust" theories of truth, e.g., traditional versions of the correspondence theory, and (ii) theories that have been described as "deflationary" theories of truth, e.g., Ramsey's theory. I believe this terminology is supposed to capture the idea that traditional versions of the correspondence theory treated truth as a complex relational property, while Ramsey's theory and its derivatives deny that truth is a complex property. (I have used the phrase 'the nature of truth' as I assume many in the correspondence tradition used it; that is, as carrying the presupposition that truth is a substantive property.)

How might this division between substantive and deflationary theories be extended to contemporary theories? For the present, and somewhat tentatively, I will reserve *substantive* for those theories of truth that claim truth is a property with an explanatory role. Those theories that deny or imply that truth is not a property with an explanatory role would then be *deflationary* theories. Deflationary truth theorists typically claim a pragmatic or logical role for the truth predicate. That is, even though deflationary theorists claim the truth predicate is content-redundant, they do not usually (ever?) claim the truth predicate is redundant in every respect. Examples of deflationary theories of truth include the prosentential theory and the disquotational theory. Horwich's (1990) *minimalist theory of truth* would also be classified as deflationary; for though he claims that truth is a property of propositions (on the grounds that the truth predicate has an extension), he denies that truth has an explanatory role. Davidson's (1990) view that truth is a simple property with an explanatory role is a substantive theory.[17]

In §2 I introduce readers to the papers that I have included in this

---

[17] I think this way of making the distinction conflicts with Field's classification. He seems to require additionally that deflationary theories reject the idea that any language-world relations may have an explanatory role.

volume. My discussion of the traditional theories resumes in §3, where I illustrate my point that the prosentential theory offers a way of disentangling important issues from discussions of the "nature of truth." In the process, I say something about the neutrality of the prosentential theory and show why I think a prosentential theorist can endorse significant aspects of the traditional theories of truth, and how a prosentential reading of the truth predicate often provides a means to this end.

2. The Prosentential Theory—Review and Reflections

Because the papers in this volume were written over a period of some twenty years, I have returned more than once to issues that have puzzled me. It is primarily because the ensuing changes of mind may cause problems for readers that I am including this review. I will try to identify those places and attempt to explain why I changed my mind. I hope that this section will also direct readers to the topics they will find most interesting.

Readers should note that, with the exception of the last two chapters of this book, I have arranged the chapters according to the chronological order in which they were written. My reason for the exception is that the last two chapters contain technical material: Though readers may be interested to know that certain technical results are available, I doubt many will want the book to begin with those details.

I first began thinking about the possibility that English might contain prosentences when, as a graduate student, I was working on some problems concerning formal languages with quantifiers that bound propositional or sentence variables. In question were variables that occupied sentential positions, for which sentences would be instantiated. Though I usually call these variables "propositional" variables and call their quantifiers "propositional" quantifiers, I do not usually presuppose a domain of propositions, but rather a substitution range of sentences. The variables and quantifiers could just as easily be referred to as "sentential" variables and "sentential" quantifiers.[18]

Prompted by remarks of Wilfrid Sellars, two of my fellow gradu-

---

[18] Variables that are instantiated with names of sentences are also sometimes referred to as either propositional or sentential variables, but the grammar of such variables is different; nor do I treat sentences as names.

ate students[19] badgered me with questions about my propositional quantifiers, wanting to know what kinds of readings I would provide of formulas containing them. To answer this question, I began thinking about the grammar of propositional quantifiers. The resulting paper, included as Chapter 2 of this volume, led to the prosentential theory.

The reason my friends' questions seemed to me interesting and important was that, as far as I could see at the time, there did not seem to be expressions in English that would provide readings of bound propositional variables in the way that pronouns provide reasonably good readings of formulas that contain bound individual variables.[20] Certainly we cannot simply use a pronoun like 'it', alone, to provide a reading of the bound variable in something like

Snow is white $\rightarrow \exists p(p)$

because

If snow is white, then something is such that *it*.

is not well formed. It seemed that if I were to arrive at readings in English of such formulas, I would need sentential expressions that would function anaphorically somewhat in the way pronouns do. This was the path by which I arrived at *prosentences*. It is also, of course, the path by which I arrived at the principal claim of Chapter 2, that prosentences would provide the required readings—in what would perhaps be an extension of English—of formulas containing bound propositional variables. Deciding that prosentences would be needed was the easy part; determining how prosentences and prosentential constructions, generally, might function in English was the hard part.

Because I was initially doubtful that English had any expressions that could be classified as prosentences,[21] I added 'thatt' to English. I stipulated that 'thatt' would be generally available for anaphoric work in the way pronouns are available, but with the difference that 'thatt' would occupy sentential positions. The goal was to give 'thatt' the features needed to provide, in English + 'thatt', a way of generalizing with respect to sentence positions. So it was only to-

---

[19] John and Lauren Blank.

[20] Even though the match between pronouns and individual variables is not always clear—in the surface structure, at least—we seem to rely on whatever match there is, in making intuitive sense of bound individual variables.

[21] It seemed at the time that the closest might be expressions like "yes" and "such and such," but prosentences perform many jobs that these do not perform.

ward the end of this first exploration of prosentences that the question of a prosentential account of the role of the truth predicate began to enter the picture. It was then that Joe Camp pointed out that 'That is true' seemed to do the work in English that I had described 'thatt' as doing. The task of determining in what sense English did indeed contain prosentential expressions, and the philosophical ramifications of this fact, came later.

I describe these events to keep readers from being confused by some of the claims I make in Chapter 2. For example, in §1 I claim that "there appear to be no faithful and perspicuous readings in English [of formulas containing bound propositional variables]." Confident as I now am (which is as confident as one can be in such matters) that a prosentential account of the truth predicate is on the right track, this early speculation no longer reflects my view. We *can* provide readings in English of bound propositional variables without additional resources like 'thatt'—'It is true' and its cognates can be used for that purpose.

Chapter 3, co-authored with Joe Camp and Nuel Belnap, introduces the reader to the prosentential theory. Here we explain what it means to say that 'That is true' and 'It is true' function as prosentences, and in general what it means to say that the truth predicate has a prosentential role. All of this prepares the ground for our conjecture that all ordinary truth talk (that we need) can be explained in terms of a prosentential role of 'true' and 'false.'[22] In our view prosentences, pronouns, and possibly other kinds of proforms provide the various kinds of anaphoric connections that we seem to need for communication—ways of expressing agreement and disagreement, ways of establishing that we are talking about the same thing, and ways of generalizing. In English, the truth predicate and its cognates provide some of these anaphoric connections. (In formal languages, we have tended to rely on bound variables to do some, not all, of this work.[23]) Because we were inclined to think that we need, for purposes of communication, anaphoric connec-

---

[22] Because any generalization about English is likely to be false, this claim is almost certainly too sweeping to be true—unless much is made of some of the built-in vagueness. It seemed better, at the time, to opt for a (fairly) clear thesis over an extremely vague one. There were probably better ways of handling the issue. I hope readers have not, as a result, been encouraged to underestimate the complexities of natural language.

[23] I now make this comparison somewhat tentatively. Kent Wilson has drawn my attention to the fact that pragmatics play a significant part in anaphora while propositional quantification is a syntactic phenomenon with a semantics overlay.

tions of some kind, we claimed in Chapter 3 that the truth predicate is not redundant in English. It is content-redundant, however.

There is one aspect of Chapter 3 that I am now inclined to think about differently. This concerns the significance of the subject-predicate structure of prosentential constructions in English. In developing my account of prosentences, I had my eye on pronouns. But that analogy can take one only so far, because prosentential constructions, as found in English, e.g., 'That is true' as distinct from 'thatt', have a structure that introduces features pronouns do not have: Verbs can be modified and subjects can be manipulated in various ways. We drew attention to the first difference in Chapter 3, §2.6, but not to the second. We highlighted the utility of modifiable verbs in prosentential constructions. Just as we can modify verbs in other sentences, we can modify verbs in prosentences. For example, the modified prosentence 'That was true' can be used when we want to express only qualified agreement with what someone else has said. I, for one, had blinders on when it came to the range of options made available by the subject term position in English prosentences—even though, at the time, I suspected there was much that I was missing.

I think a reason for this blindness was the path by which I arrived at the prosentential account of the truth predicate: from propositional variables and pronouns to 'thatt'—all without syntactic structure. While working on various versions of the Liar sentence, however, I began to recognize how we do indeed utilize alternative subject terms in making the connections we need to make in discourse. In those situations where 'That is true' will not suffice for the anaphoric connections we want, definite descriptions, quotation names, and demonstratives can be used in place of 'that'. Let me illustrate this point. Suppose, in a dispute, Kiri expresses her opinion by means of

(1) John's last claim is true.

Let us suppose a situation where Kiri does not want to repeat what John has said because that would take too long, and it would bore everyone anyway. In this situation, where John, along with many others, have said different things, she cannot simply use 'That is true' because that would introduce ambiguity; she therefore uses 'John's last claim' to locate the antecedent, John's statement, with which she wants to express agreement. Of course, locating an antecedent can be a complex business, whether we are faced with a prosentence or a pronoun; in the process listeners may need to take account of shared knowledge concerning associated features of the discourse. Consider, for example, the figuring we would need to do, in a given context, in the case of something like "Your employee's recent comments on political graft are true."

I claim the details of the locating work done by the subject term (and anything else involved) are not part of what may be expressed by a prosentential construction. In the case above, neither the intended referent nor any other possible referent of Kiri's 'John's last claim' features in the content of what she says. I think of the locating work accomplished by noun phrases such as 'John's last claim' as "busy homework" done off to the side, for I am supposing a case where Kiri is not really talking about John and what he said. She expresses an opinion about whatever (extralinguistic thing) it was that John expressed an opinion about. For comparison, consider

> Mary loves chocolate ice cream, but she doesn't eat it because she is not supposed to have caffeine.

Just as the second clause in this sentence is not about the antecedent of 'she', the name 'Mary', but about Mary herself, so also 'John's last claim is true' is not about its antecedent, John's statement, but about snow or whatever subject was in dispute. In Chapter 4 I call sentences like (1), used in this "lazy" anaphoric way, *inheritors*—prosentences like 'That is true' and pronouns like 'she' are both included as inheritors. Interpreted as an inheritor, all the participant asserts in uttering (1) is what John asserted.

In Chapter 3, §2.4, we analyze sentences like (1) as always involving quantification, e.g., 'For each proposition, if it is John's last claim, then it is true.'[24] In those cases where the speaker does not know what John has said, such an analysis can be appropriate, but it does not do justice to the situation I have just described—where both the speaker and audience know what John said, and the speaker is not really interested in saying anything about John. This means that I am *not* now inclined to endorse the clause I have italicized in the following from Chapter 3, §2.4:

> When an English* speaker says, 'That is true' in response to 'Snow is white', as in the repetition case above, *his 'That' is not an independently referring pronoun*, denoting the statement that snow is white. (emphasis added)

---

[24] For more on the difficulties of our first stab at getting the facts right, and the suggestions reviewed here, see Chapters 4 and 8; Brandom (1988b) also addresses this issue in §6 of his article.

English* is an imaginary piece of English in which we suppose the truth predicate neither isolable nor modifiable. I now think 'that' in 'That is true' may sometimes be construed as an independently referring pronoun that picks out the antecedent of the prosentence. In figuring out what is said, we must distinguish between the grammatical subject term 'that' and the logical subject of 'That is true'. The grammatical subject term is 'that' and it locates the antecedent; the logical subject derives from the logical subject of the antecedent, and there can be complications. On this analysis, 'true' and 'false' are a sign that prosentential anaphora is being employed—the sign that, e.g., 'That is true' and 'John's last claim is true' are inheritors that inherit their content from antecedent sentences.

Both 'thatt' and English* were used in Chapter 3 partly as heuristic devices to impress on the reader what it is to read the truth predicate prosententially. Discussion with readers since then has led me to believe that 'thatt' in Chapter 3 has generated confusion rather than understanding—a syntactically complex prosentence would have done the job better. So I now drop 'thatt' from my explanations of prosentences (e.g., in presentations or classroom situations). However, English* was also used to "give support" to the claim that "*all* our truth talk can be viewed as involving only prosentential uses of 'that is true'." (Chapter 3, §2.4) It is important to note that "support" is all that we can ask of English*. Kent Wilson's (1990) insightful critical evaluation of the prosentential theory shows there is a long way to go before we can give anything like a full defense of a prosentential analysis of the truth predicate *as it occurs in English*. He shows the syntactic details are especially challenging. The task of showing conclusively that we *need* the resources of something like a prosentential truth predicate (and pronouns) is equally daunting.

One should also note that, even if our all "truth talk" (talk of what's true, etc.) can be so explained, there remain many other uses of 'true' of which we have no account, as when, for example, we speak of a "true likeness." I doubt such cases present a challenge unique to the prosentential theory; however, I have to admit I have not given this issue much thought. My approach to this question would probably begin with the suggestions contained in Frege's (1918) comment in "The Thought": "One finds truth affirmed of pictures, ideas, statements and thoughts. It is striking that visible and audible things occur here alongside things which cannot be perceived with the senses. . . . Obviously one would not call a picture true unless there were an intention behind it. . . . If I do not know that a picture is meant to represent Cologne Cathedral then I do not know with what to compare the picture to decide on its truth." (p. 509)

Chapters 4 and 8 address paradoxes of truth and reference. The first is on the Liar sentence, 'This is false'. The second discusses Berry's paradox of reference, 'the least integer not described in less than nineteen syllables'. I argue that inheritor readings of both the Liar sentence and Berry's description eliminate all sign of the apparent inconsistency in these expressions.

My analysis draws attention to three facts about inheritors: (1) Inheritors are dependent on their antecedents for their content; inheritors are parasitic. (2) Inheritors can be modified with 'not'. (3) Inheritors are universally available in that they can have as their antecedents words and phrases of any grammatical category, whether or not they are appropriate, as suppliers of semantic content. Together, these three facts lead to some weird cases, for example, cases where the antecedent does not supply content, perhaps because the antecedent is itself an inheritor without content; cases where only part of the antecedent supplies content—the antecedent may be a disjunction that contains an inheritor that does not have an antecedent—and, most importantly, cases where a modified inheritor is its own antecedent.

The problem with the Liar sentence is that it is an inheritor, and it is its own antecedent. This means the Liar sentence, an inheritor, is not connected to the kind of sentence that can "supply" content. So the Liar sentence fails to have content. In addition, the Liar sentence is a modified inheritor, modified by 'false'. I show why this makes the Liar sentence appear to harbor an inconsistency, which, in fact, it does not because the Liar sentence lacks content. The situation is more complex, but similar, for the Berry expression and strengthened versions of the Liar.

In making these points, I show how a prosentential reading of the truth predicate can be used to motivate many important aspects of Kripke's (1975) version of Tarski's truth definition. That such a match exists is not surprising because Kripke's construction assumes no more than one would assume of a prosentential truth predicate. I suspect connections can also be made with more recent modifications of Tarski. That may help our understanding if these constructions offer ways of keeping track of the strange things that can happen with sentential inheritors. While on the topic of formal treatments, I should mention that the issues discussed in §8 and

§11 of Chapter 4 need more attention than I gave them there. I show only how I convinced myself that the prosentential account of the generalized and strengthened versions of the Liar sentence are free of inconsistency. A thorough formal treatment is required.

Finally, in §10, I explain why I think "adding" a substantive property-ascribing role to a prosentential truth predicate would introduce inconsistency. Whereas a modified inheritor, alone, simply lacks content, if 'false' were also property-ascribing, inconsistency would result. This fact provides a good reason for not adding (if at all possible) a substantive property-ascribing role to the utility role of the truth predicate.

My interest in properties (or the concept of a *property*) was prompted by the fact that a prosentential truth predicate seems to lead to an extension for 'true'; for if anyone can successfully define an extension for the truth predicate, a prosentential theorist can. This is true because a prosentence like 'It is true' can be used in the following kind of way: The sentence 'Sea water is salt' belongs in the extension of the truth predicate if and only if it is true, the sentence 'Roses are red' belongs in the extension of the truth predicate if and only if it is true, etc. It is obvious we can get an extension for formal languages—just read Tarski's truth predicate prosententially. The hesitancy I expressed with 'seems' arises from the fact that natural languages, which contain indexicals and other context-sensitive features, pose a greater challenge. But let us suppose we have an extension; does an extension suffice for a truth property?[25] When do we have a property?[26] I sought help with these questions from the literature, but I found little on properties—perhaps I looked in the wrong places.[27]

These are the issues I struggled with in Chapters 6 and 7. I pondered the fact that at the drop of a hat we could introduce all kinds of properties with predicate expressions to match, if an extension sufficed for a property. For example: I can stipulate the letter *a* be-

---

[25] Many seem to assume that if one has an extension one has a property, e.g., John Pollock's (1977) comment on Chapter 4. Pollock assumes without argument that we have a truth property (of propositions) if there is an extension.

[26] It is also easy to imagine we have the option of associating with the truth predicate a mapping from possible worlds into a set of sets of sentence tokens (types, utterances, or propositions). One could keep the language (tokens or utterances) fixed and let the worlds change, or keep extralinguistic reality fixed and allow the language(s) to vary from world to world; or one could utilize both possibilities. I do not know whether there is a coherent option among these, but even supposing there were, would it yield an interesting property?

[27] I now realize Field (1972) had useful things to say on this issue.

longs to the extension of 'blah' just in case snow is white, and that the letter b belongs to the extension of 'blah' just in case there is life on Mars; and c belongs to the extension of 'blah' just in case light travels in straight lines.

Though 'blah' has an extension, there seemed initially no reason to think of blahness as a property that would be of any interest to us. But then it occurred to me that one could imagine situations where 'blah' could be useful; we could use 'blah' to keep track of information, as a sort of coding device. Perhaps the truth predicate is useful in this way also. I defend this possibility in Chapter 6, arguing that it could be useful in certain discussions of meaning and in logic where we tend to talk about "object" languages. Such a truth property might facilitate connections with the subject matter of the object language.

But then I changed my mind, returning to the issues in Chapter 7. For though there remains much that I do not understand about predication and properties, I quickly became convinced that an extension does not suffice to establish that we have an *interesting* property.

My main reason for skepticism regarding a purported substantive truth property is that we do not seem to *need* it. Granted, in logic and some discussions of meaning the truth predicate is useful because we are working in a metalanguage; however, a prosentential truth predicate suffices for the tasks I envisioned. I show that a reason for moving to a syntactical metalinguistic predicate is that we sometimes need a way of making explicit the syntactic features of given sentences that are implicitly used. Inheritors like " 'Snow is white or snow is not white' is true" facilitate that goal, for inheritors provide a way of explicitly displaying a sentence whose content we want to consider or possibly affirm. For example, the inheritor " 'Snow is white or snow is not white' is true" can be used successfully to display, for example, the disjunctive form of the sentence 'Snow is white or snow is not white' at the same time that it is used to affirm that snow is white or snow is not white.

So the problem with the "property" I entertained in Chapter 6 was that it did not seem to *explain* anything. Readers will in any event have noted that the "property" I entertained as deriving from an extension (defined with a prosentential truth predicate) has little in common with the substantive properties that correspondence theorists seem to have in mind—a property that is supposed to have an explanatory role. I return to this issue in §3 of this chapter.

If we were to trivialize properties so that an extension alone suffices for a property, then my point would be that an extension alone does not show that we have an interesting or needed property. Our language does not need to contain predicates for all such properties.

One further point on Chapter 7. Though I continue to agree with the overall outcome of the paper, there is an argument against a truth property, in §2, that I no longer like. I claimed that a property should partition its domain of application. At the time, I thought a property could not have an explanatory role if there were indeterminate cases. This assumption led me to suppose that truth is not a property because we cannot consistently ascribe either truth or falsity to the Liar sentence. But the assumption was not a good one, because we do indeed rely on vague predicates and indeterminate properties.[28]

I mentioned above that the prosentential theory of truth is not the only theory that urges the (mere) utility of the truth predicate and that the disquotational theory defends both the content redundancy and utility of the truth predicate. Thus Quine (1970) says: "Where the truth predicate has its utility is in just those places where, though still concerned with reality, we are impelled by certain technical complications to mention sentences. . . . The truth predicate is a reminder that, despite a technical ascent to talk of sentences, our eye is on the world. This cancellatory force of the truth predicate is explicit in Tarski's paradigm:

'Snow is white' is true if and only if snow is white.

. . . By calling a sentence ['Snow is white'] true, we call snow white." (pp. 11–12) Quine goes on to argue the point that we need the truth predicate for generalization with respect to sentence positions.

In Chapter 9 I compare the disquotational theory with the prosentential theory, principally arguing that there is a way of looking at the two theories which includes the disquotational theory as a special case in the prosentential theory.[29] I note some of the major differences of approach. First, disquotational theorists focus only on those cases where the truth predicate is predicated of a quoted sentence or used for generalization. I think disquotational theorists have had their eye on philosophical discourse, where the truth pred-

---

[28] An important influence on my thinking has been Mark Wilson's (1982), "Predicate Meets Property."

[29] Because little has been said about the disquotational theory, there are probably many different ways of filling out the details. My suggestions are likely to be incompatible with many of these possibilities.

icate is paradigmatically featured in a metalanguage. Second, disquotational theorists have made no attempt to explain these, or other, uses. They seem satisfied with only an account of the logic of the truth predicate, as offered by Tarski or by Kripke.

The prosentential theory, on the other hand, was initially motivated by uses of the truth predicate in ordinary English, where the truth predicate is rarely, if ever, predicated of a quoted sentence. More importantly, in addition to claiming the truth predicate has utility, it explains what this means: how the truth predicate is used to express agreement or disagreement,[30] and its usefulness when we want to generalize. Our characterization of truth predicate constructions as prosentential anaphoric expressions accomplishes all of that.

Some philosophers may be inclined to think the most important difference between these two deflationary theories shows up in the formal representations of truth predicate generalizations. Disquotational theorists are inclined to employ individual quantifiers ranging over a domain of sentences, with the truth predicate "canceling" ascent. (Quine's use of sentence schemas in generalizations are an exception.) By contrast, the prosentential theory appeals to formulas that contain propositional quantifiers in its formal analyses.[31] On my way of comparing the two theories, this is not an important difference, but only a difference in approach. Certainly, it can be shown that this difference is not significant in extensional languages, for in Tarski-style constructions sentences of the form 'For any x $(\ldots x \ldots Tx \ldots)$' are provable just in case sentences of the form 'For any p $(\ldots 'p' \ldots p \ldots)$' are provable. One reason I like employing propositional variables in my analyses is that they "emphasize" the point that prosentences, indeed, inheritors generally, can be used (indeed, typically are used) when discourse is about extralinguistic matters. Though the truth predicate may often appear in philosophical discussions as a syntactical metalinguistic predicate, it is not semantically metalinguistic—according to most deflationary theories.[32]

While we are on the topic of propositional quantifiers, it is appropriate to say more about my use of propositional quantifiers in Chapter 9, and in this introductory essay. In both places I assume a substitutional interpretation of the quantifiers. Some of the advan-

---

[30] Strawson (1950a) draws attention to these features.

[31] Neither of us gets very close to matching the surface syntax of natural language uses of the truth predicate in generalizations.

[32] Horwich's theory may be an exception.

tages of such an interpretation are explored in Chapters 10 and 11. At the time these papers were written, many philosophers thought quantification in and out of quotation contexts was a no-no. Both Tarski and Quine had denied the possibility on the grounds that " 'p' " can only name the letter 'p', and quantification cannot penetrate the quotes around 'p'. There is also the difficulty that a version of the Liar sentence can be formulated in a language that has propositional quantification, quotation, and negation. For if 'M' names '$\forall p('p' = M \rightarrow \sim p)$', then the latter says of itself that it is false.[33]

I appeal to a substitutional interpretation of the quantifiers in addressing both these issues. This means that I assume associated with each bound propositional variable a *substitution range* consisting of a well-defined set of closed sentences. The value of a quantified formula is then a function of the value assigned the instances generated from this substitution range. '$\forall p(p \lor \sim p)$', for example, is equivalent to the possibly infinite conjunction of its instances. Therefore, if the sentence 'Seawater is salt' is in the substitution range of 'p', then 'Either seawater is salt or seawater is not salt' is an instance of '$\forall p(p \lor \sim p)$'. I also assume that a substitutional interpretation can be combined with a domain and values interpretation of the individual variables (if any) contained in the language. So nothing need be lost in moving to a substitutional interpretation of any propositional quantifiers that one may add to a first-order language.[34]

Utilizing such a substitutional interpretation of the quantifiers, I show both that Tarski and Quine were wrong about quantification and quotation, and that the Liar sentence can be avoided with suitable restrictions.[35] In Chapter 10 I employ a hierarchy of languages to avoid the Liar sentence. At the time I wrote the article, I described this move as required to avoid inconsistency. But now, thinking of substitutionally interpreted propositional quantifiers as inheritors, I would describe the situation as a matter of finding ways of avoiding the problems of ungroundedness that universally

---

[33] I assume in this context that 'it is not the case that' and 'is false' are intersubstitutable. This suffices for the generation of "paradox."

Even before the prosentential theory, this formula was compared to the Liar sentence; yet it is only since the prosentential theory that we have been in a position to say something about the parallels between the role of the truth predicate in English and the role of bound propositional variables in formal languages.

[34] Something may be gained by associating a domain of "propositions" with the propositional variables—as well as a substitution range. I leave that question open until more is known about the rest of language.

[35] Kripke (1976) also defends substitutional interpretations and quantification in and out of quotation contexts.

available inheritors generate.[36] Though Chapters 10 and 11 initially appeared in print after Chapter 2 (which introduces prosentences) appeared in print, readers should note that they were actually written before Chapter 2.

The primary goal of Chapter 11 (Belnap and Grover, 1973) was to show that quantification in and out of quotes is a useful resource for logicians who design and talk about formal languages. On the way, we also have some things to say about truth and meaning. We show that Tarski (1931) need not have rejected the prospect of defining the extension of 'true' with

(2) $\forall p('p'$ belongs to T if and only if $p)$

because quantification in and out of quotation can be legitimate and often sensible. For an appropriately defined substitution range, a definition such as (2) satisfies Convention T. (See Chapter 11, §3.4.1, for a definition of Convention T.) This result shows Davidson was wrong about a couple of things he said early about truth and meaning. He assumed satisfaction of Convention T guarantees a definition of truth that will highlight compositional features of language; however, a definition along the lines of (2) satisfies Convention T, without analysis of compositional features. The second point is that this shows the satisfaction relation is not an interesting language-world relation for truth, because we can dispense with it in defining an extension for the truth predicate. So it is not a relation that provides Davidson with justification for defending Tarski's theory as a correspondence theory. I will say more about these issues in §3. 'Satisfies', like 'true', provides a way of generalizing when quantification in and out of quotes (or some equivalent) is not available— or not believed to be available.

It is time to take a look at the implications the prosentential theory has for the correspondence, pragmatic, and coherence theories of truth.

3. Implications for Some Other Theories of Truth

To many readers, the prosentential theory must seem a far cry from a theory that addresses the really important issues with which "truth" has traditionally been connected, perhaps via explanatory

---

[36] The work of Kripke (1975), Gupta (1982), and others, open up the possibility of better ways of avoiding the problems of ungrounded inheritors. See also David Wray's (1987) work on the formal structure of the languages I present in Chapter 10 (Grover, 1973).

role. Truth has been connected with issues like language-world connections, realism, belief, meaning, and justification.[37] Indeed, whether or not we agree with the proponents of the correspondence, pragmatic, and coherence theories, they expressed intuitions we should probably not ignore. So I will take another look at what some proponents of these theories have said, but this time I will often read the truth predicate they use as a prosentential truth predicate. This exercise will show that the prosentential theory offers a way of making clearer the questions that are raised when we use the truth predicate.

My review will also cast light on another issue concerning the traditionally construed theories. If we were to go along with the assumption that correspondence, pragmatic, and coherence theorists all offered analyses of the nature of truth, we would thereby be presented with several different truth properties—that is, several different substantive theories of truth. There are the language-world relational properties of the correspondence theory, then the various kinds of mostly epistemic or consequential properties of the pragmatic and coherence theories. It has puzzled me why there have been such disparate analyses of "truth." I believe some philosophers have thought the various theorists were answering different questions. For example, although it is generally agreed that correspondence theorists offer a theory of the nature of truth, some have thought the pragmatic and coherence theories of truth offer only criteria of "truth."[38] I agree that different questions were at issue, but I do not think that is the way the pie slices, for a prosentential reading of the truth predicate suggests a greater variety of questions, most of which do not presuppose that truth has a substantive nature.

It will also emerge that a prosentential theorist has the option of either affirming or denying many significant "aspects" of the traditional theories; the prosentential theory is a neutral theory in this sense.[39] In sum, it emerges that the prosentential theory offers more

[37] Despite what a number of writers seem to assume, deflationary truth theories, like the prosentential theory, do not even imply skeptical positions with respect to these issues.

[38] Some may argue that correspondence theorists, pragmatists, and coherence theorists are motivated by different examples. Thus, the correspondence theory is motivated by observation sentences. A version of the coherence theory may be motivated by molecular sentences, while pragmatic considerations determine the choice of the true scientific theory.

[39] The prosentential theory is neutral with respect to these issues in exactly the sense that a theory of pronouns would be.

than a useful truth predicate and neutrality: It offers a way of disentangling importantly distinct issues from the ever elusive nature-of-truth dispute.

3.1 CORRESPONDENCE THEORIES

To the extent that the prosentential theory (and similar theories) offer compelling explanations of the usefulness of the truth predicate by means of an account that does not involve a property-ascribing role, to that extent the prosentential theory poses a challenge, on grounds of parsimony, to theorists of the nature of truth. As a result, the issue as to whether truth has an explanatory role has become one primary focus of recent discussion of correspondence analyses of truth. Do we need more than a deflationary account of truth?

In §1 I argued that Field's and Devitt's recent efforts at establishing an explanatory role for truth was problematic because, among other things, reference as a language-world relation (if anything) was really what provided truth and falsity with (the same) explanatory role. Because their attempts at establishing explanatory roles for truth and falsity themselves have not so far been successful (or so I believe), Field and Devitt have not succeeded in persuading me that deflationary analyses of truth, like that of the prosentential theory, are inadequate.

There have been other attempts at establishing an explanatory role for truth. But, again, I have not been persuaded by them. I will mention a few.

Field's first suggestion as to an explanatory role came in his discussion of Tarski's theory, in 1972, where he claims the correspondence account of truth explains that we learn about what is going on in the world from those whom we believe speak the truth. In response, we claimed (Chapter 3, §4.5) that there is no need to assume truth is a language-world relation in the case Field describes. A prosentential reading of the truth predicate suffices. He grants our point in a later paper (Field 1986).

Other attempts at establishing an explanatory role for truth are unsuccessful for the same kind of reason. A case in point is Putnam's (1978a, pp. 20–22) argument that correspondence truth explains the success of science. It seems that Field (1972), Putnam, and others initially assumed that if one could show the truth predicate is used in an explanation of something important then one had demonstrated the existence of an explanatory role of truth. But that is obviously a poor argument. It must first be shown that the explanation in question calls for something more than just a prosentential (or some other deflationary) reading of the truth predicate.[40]

What of the need to capture the difference between true and false belief, which I mentioned earlier? We can state the difference between true and false beliefs without assuming a substantive truth property. Thus, Plato's beliefs are true, just in case

For any p, if Plato believes that p then p.

while Russell's beliefs are false just in case

For any p, if Russell believes that p then $\sim p$.

For a given sentence 'A', '$\sim$A' stands for the contradiction of 'A'.

On the other hand, it might be argued that the truth predicate may seem to have an explanatory role in situations where philosophers say of an utterance that it is "neither true nor false." The classic example of a sentence of which this is said is 'The king of France is wise'. Do we use 'It is neither true nor false' to explain what is wrong with 'The king of France is wise'? A prosentential theorist does not have that option. She must seek an explanation from a theory of language of what can go wrong in discourse, and in particular, what can go wrong when a term fails to denote. But what of the response, 'That is neither true nor false'? I have suggested that this phrase might be used in a gesture of rejection. (See Chapter 7, §7, and Chapter 9, §5.2.) This is only an ad hoc explanation, of course, because the prosentential account of the truth predicate does not compel that explanation. But that does not matter, because the prosentential theorist does not need to respond with 'neither true nor false'. There are other things one can say if one wants to get on with the conversation.

Yet others have thought that they need to predicate 'true' and 'false' of sentences in other languages, and that a prosentential truth predicate would not allow them to do this. This issue is touched on in Chapter 3, §3.2. We point out that a prosentential truth predicate might be particularly useful in those cases where we do not have a good translation available in our own language of a foreign language sentence. Sometimes we incorporate the foreign sentence in our own language and then use it, as in

If schnee ist weiss, as he says, then . . .

---

[40] See Devitt 1984 for a systematic discussion of such cases.

But we cannot always say what we want to say in that way. Perhaps we want (as in logic) to draw attention to the structure of the sentence involved. Then, even in those cases where a translation is available, we might want to utilize the resource of the prosentential truth predicate, making our point in the following way:

If 'Schnee ist weiss' is true, as he says, then . . .

We can think of the truth predicate as useful in providing us with an alternative kind of "translation." Obviously, 'true' cannot be eliminated in those cases where the foreign sentence "translated" does not have a translation in the normal sense.

Obviously, the jury is still out on the explanatory role issue.[41] Until I understand language and linguistic activity better, I must leave open the question whether we need a substantive truth predicate. In the meantime, I remain skeptical that we need anything more than something like a prosentential truth predicate. Aside from considerations of parsimony, the threat of inconsistency discourages me from adding a possibly needless substantive property-ascribing role to a prosentential predicate.

This does not mean, however, that all aspects of the correspondence theory need be denied. There are aspects that the prosentential theory captures in a deflationary way and yet other aspects that the prosentential theorist could affirm, should she want to.

The correspondence theory of truth is often presented as *the* theory that gives voice to the intuition that the world makes sentences or beliefs true. We have seen that correspondence theorists seek to capture this idea through a correspondence relation and appropriate relata. However, deflationists, e.g., Prior (1967) and Quine (1987), have claimed no such substantive relation is needed because T-sentences capture all we need of the intuition. Indeed, in Quine's view (I think Tarski's, also), such equivalences are, as far as truth goes, all that is worth saving from the correspondence theory. Thus Quine (1987) says, taking the standard T-sentence " 'Snow is white' is true if and only if snow is white" as his example: "[It] is the significant residue of the correspondence theory of truth. To attribute truth to the sentence is to attribute whiteness to snow. Attribution of truth to 'Snow is white' just cancels the quotation marks and says snow is white. Truth is disquotation." (p. 213) Sometimes this

---

[41] I have not discussed Davidson's (e.g., 1990) arguments for an explanatory role for truth. I suspect a prosentential predicate in locutions like 'what is true' would suffice in his explanations.

point is made in another way. T-sentences preserve the realist inclination of correspondence theorists; for so long as T-sentences hold, the truth of a sentence depends *only* on the way the world is.

Obviously the prosentential theory captures the deflationary rendering of the so-called "realist" intuition of the correspondence theory, because all T-sentences—insofar as it is clear that they are T-sentences[42]—are affirmed on the prosentential theory. It is the world that makes 'Snow is white' true, i.e., it is the world that makes snow white.[43] Thus the prosentential theory provides a deflationary analogue of this "realist" aspect of the correspondence theory.

Note that some have classified Tarski's (1936) theory as a correspondence theory, because it implies all T-sentences—on the grounds that T-sentences capture the realist intuition. This way of classifying theories as correspondence theories is a bit misleading, however, because the correspondence theory would not then be distinguishable from other theories and virtually all truth theories endorse T-sentences.[44] Also, traditional correspondence theorists have thought there is more to truth; those who require only affirmation of all T-sentences deny this significant assumption. For these reasons, I will generally not refer to Tarski's theory as a correspondence theory.

Tarski's theory has also been claimed to be a correspondence theory by virtue of the satisfaction relation. Because the satisfaction relation obtains between objects (or sequences of objects) and sentences, it allegedly provides the language-world relation that correspondence theorists have sought. Davidson (1969) was one proponent of this notion. Putnam (1978b, pp. 29–30) has also entertained the idea. There are problems with this second attempt to relate Tarski's definition and the correspondence theory. I mentioned one problem in §2: 'Satisfies' would not have been needed for truth if Tarski had allowed quantification in and out of quotation contexts. If the satisfaction relation is not required in a truth definition, the correspondence relation would become superfluous.

Then there is the problem that apparently led Davidson (1990) to

---

[42] I am cautious here because of the difficulties that both context-sensitive features and ungrounded prosentences introduce.

[43] Whether or not this is in fact a realist position is presumably going to be determined by what one thinks the world is like.

[44] Theorists who pay special attention to "paradoxical" sentences may be exceptions. For example, not everyone will want to affirm a T-sentence for a sentence like the Liar. As I mentioned before, indexicals also pose a problem.

reject the idea: All true sentences would "correspond" to all sequences of objects. Davidson says, "The oddity of the idea is evident from the counter-intuitive and contrived nature of the entities to which sentences 'correspond' and from the fact that all true sentences would correspond to the same entities" (p. 302, n. 36). A correspondence relation that fails to distinguish between true sentences is unlikely to capture the interest of those seeking an explanatory role for truth. Nor is the correspondence relation explained. I do not see anything that a prosentential theorist need contemplate capturing in this version of the correspondence theory.

Nuel Belnap has drawn my attention to yet another argument against construing satisfaction as a language-world relation of the kind wanted by correspondence theorists. It was arbitrary that Tarski defined truth as satisfaction by *all* sequences. Because the only thing he was (or anyone is) interested in was (is) truth for *closed* sentences, he could equally well have defined truth as satisfaction by *some* sequences, or indeed, by some privileged sequence picked out by the axiom of choice (say). It would have made no difference at all, either technically or conceptually, for the truth of *closed* sentences.

None of this means that a prosentential theorist should ignore 'satisfies'; 'satisfies' has formal or logical properties, much as 'true' and 'false' do,[45] along with whatever pragmatic properties may follow. A prosentential theorist has the option of resorting to such a logical predicate in contexts where it might have utility, e.g., in discussions of the compositional features of language.[46]

The correspondence theory seems also to have been considered *the* theory of truth that one should endorse if one thinks language-world relations have an explanatory role. If one is sympathetic to the suggestions prosentential theorists have made as to the utility of the truth predicate, there are the reasons I have given before (parsimony and threatening inconsistency) for not assigning the truth predicate a language-world relational property-ascribing role as well.

It should be noted that denying that *truth* is a language-world relational property, as a prosentential theorist does, does not mean that one must also deny language-world relations an explanatory role. Perhaps some kind of language-world relation will explain, for

[45] See Chapter 3 (Grover, Camp, and Belnap 1975), §4.9, for our reasons for classifying the truth predicate as providing "logical" expressibility.

[46] See, for example, Chapter 11 (Grover and Belnap, 1973), §3.3.2.

example, Field's T-reliability, or perhaps some (possibly different) language-world relations will explain the content of belief or the content of sentences; and perhaps the causal chains of reference will be featured somewhere in all of this. A prosentential theorist has the option of exploring (or ignoring) any of these possibilities because language-world connections are separated from the role of the truth predicate and from truth. A case in point of a deflationist who does just this, is Quine. He argues that stimulus-response connections have an explanatory role.[47]

In summary, then, a prosentential theorist denies that truth has an explanatory role—a basic assumption of correspondence theories. But all is not lost. The option of endorsing two important aspects of traditional correspondence theories remains: should she want to, a prosentential theorist can endorse the "realist" idea that the world makes a sentence true; a prosentential theorist also has the option of endorsing the idea that language-world relations (of some kind) may have an explanatory role.[48]

3.2 THE PRAGMATIC AND COHERENCE THEORIES

In similar fashion, I will now review the pragmatic and coherence theories from the point of view of the prosentential account of the truth predicate.

I am inclined to think that the nature-of-truth mold does not do justice to the intuitions of the pragmatists because that mold is not really compatible with "the pragmatic method."[49] Figuring out how best to arrive at a theory of truth or a theory of anything else (like a theory of justification) from their comments has also probably been hindered by the tradition of emphasizing the pragmatic slogans, at the expense of more significant features of the pragmatists' analysis of truth talk. This last is Robert Brandom's point, defended in an

---

[47] Despite these facts, philosophers have occasionally assumed that it is constitutive of the disquotational theory (if not the prosentential theory) that language-word relations be denied. The fact that some proponents of the disquotational theory (e.g., Leeds and Quine) and of the prosentential theory (Brandom 1984) are deflationists with respect to truth *and reference*, does not justify this characterization of deflationary theories generally. (I recommend Brandom 1984 to those readers who want to consider the possibility of extending the anaphoric approach of the prosentential theory to 'refers'.)

[48] Interested readers should note that Paul Horwich (1990) draws attention to aspects of the traditional theories that his kind of deflationist can affirm.

[49] See Rorty 1982 for more on this.

article he wrote in 1988 (Brandom 1988b).[50] Brandom argues persuasively that the pragmatists were primarily concerned with (what we might describe as) performative and normative aspects of making truth claims. He describes their project in the following way: "The pragmatists start with the idea that in calling something true one is *doing* something, rather than, or in addition to, *saying* something. Instead of asking what property it is that we are describing a belief or claim as having when we say that it is true, they ask about the practical significance of the act we are performing in attributing that property. . . . the recommendation is for a *performative* analysis of truth talk. In Fregean terms it is the suggestion that 'true' is force-indicating, rather than a sense-expressing, locution." (p. 77) Brandom's analysis is responsive to the pragmatic method; Brandom also shows how the pragmatists' approach to truth talk connects with the (later) approaches to language of Strawson, Wittgenstein, and Austin. But what are we to make of the passages from which the slogans we associate with the pragmatists derive? Brandom goes on to argue that, with respect to truth, the pragmatists are phenomenalists:[51] "For the classical pragmatist, the facts about what is true supervene on the facts about taking-true, that is, on the actual action-guiding roles of beliefs. In order to appreciate the significance of the pragmatists' phenomenalist strategy, one must first consider the development of the basic idea that truth locutions are force-indicating . . ." (p. 82) If one assumes some kind of pragmatic truth property, this passage would suggest the pragmatists thought of the truth property as a property we could analyze away in terms of takings-true. However, I am not sure the passage should be read with this assumption. For one reason, in other places Brandom seems to favor construing the slogans as part and parcel of the pragmatists' revisionary stance. Whatsoever, I think there is yet another way of construing the slogans. It is possible, but I am not sure, that my suggestion will be compatible with Brandom's overall approach.

I am going to suppose a pragmatist who denies that truth has a nature; I shall also suppose her to be equipped with a prosentential truth predicate. I then suppose a prosentential reading of the truth predicate, as it occurs in passages from which some of our slogans

---

[50] Brandom's analysis of the pragmatists' approach to truth is in part inspired by Rorty (1986).

[51] Brandom's goal is to show that the prosentential theory, together with his anaphoric account of 'refers' (Brandom 1984), offers a way of saving the pragmatists' "phenomenalist" approach from the difficulties simple performative analyses (e.g., of such words as 'good') usually face.

derive. This yields a different interpretation of the passages (and slogans) in question. The readings prove interesting because they show that talk that the tradition has interpreted as offering a substantive theory of truth may perhaps be better construed as talk about the way the world is; they also show how deflationary philosophers like Quine, and other philosophers (perhaps Davidson, Dummett, and later Putnam) have the option, should they want it, of endorsing aspects of views we have traditionally associated with the pragmatists, without assuming a truth property.

If there is no substantive property, what remains of "truth" to attract our attention? There is the logical and grammatical role of the truth predicate, as well as the pragmatics of what it is to take something as true. Seemingly, that is not all there is, however, for there are questions that can be asked with the help of the truth predicate, for example, 'What makes a sentence true?' 'What relation (if any) holds between a sentence and the world when the sentence is true?' 'Do we know whether any of our beliefs are true?' Among such questions is one that will serve to introduce my approach to the pragmatic theory: What is true?

On a prosentential reading, 'What is true?' has instances like 'Do electrons have mass?' 'Does light travel in straight lines?' and 'Do you eat Thai food?' Included among the answers to 'What is true?' will be responses like 'Electrons have mass,' 'Light travels in straight lines,' and 'I do not eat Thai food.' On this reading we have an almost ordinary question, with ordinary kinds of answers, because the prosentential reading keeps the discourse focused on extralinguistic concerns—at the level of the object language, so to speak. 'What is true?' is a question about extralinguistic reality. (In contrast, a correspondence theorist may possibly have answered, 'Bob's belief that electrons have mass' or "The sentence 'Electrons have mass'.")

When a *philosopher* asks, 'What is true?' he or she may not be looking for answers to instances of the question, but for a general answer to a general question. For myself, I would probably be a bit baffled by the general question and may respond unhelpfully with something like 'The world is the way it is.' (For any p, p if and only if p.) The things pragmatists have had to say about what is true may suggest they would answer the general question in yet a different way. Consider Peirce's (1878, §4) claim: "Now, as we have seen . . . the ideas of truth and falsehood, in their full development, appertain exclusively to the scientific method of settling opinion. . . . The opinion which is fated to be ultimately agreed by all who investigate, is what we mean by the truth. . . ." (p. 133) On a prosentential reading of the truth predicate, Peirce's claim would come to roughly the following:

For any p, p if and only if at the end of inquiry investigators are fated to agree that p.

I have chosen to use propositional quantifiers with a substitutional interpretation in paraphrasing this passage from Peirce (and passages from Dewey and Bradley, later) rather than individual variables and a truth predicate. I hope the resulting formula will help those readers wedded to a property-ascribing predicate see the form of a prosentential reading of the truth predicate unambiguously. The instances of the quantified formula look like "Electrons have mass if and only if investigators are fated to agree at the end of inquiry that electrons have mass." The what-is-true general question turns out to be a question about the way the world is. Note also that this reading may be viewed as presenting an anti-realist position, because the way the world is (what-is-true) seems to depend on us: Whether or not electrons have mass "depends" on what investigators are fated to agree on.[52] This possibility of describing the pragmatic theory as anti-realist is preserved without an appeal to a substantive truth property.

Dewey (1931) said different things about truth. For example, in describing the pragmatic attitude, he said it consists in

> looking away from first things, principles, 'categories', supposed necessities, and . . . looking towards last things, fruits, consequences, facts. . . . In the natural sciences there is a tendency to identify truth in any particular case with a verification. . . . Even the most scientific and harmonious physical theory is merely an hypothesis until its implications, deduced by mathematical reasoning or by any other kind of inference, are verified by observed facts. It is therefore in submitting conceptions to the control of experience, in the process of verifying them, that one finds examples of what is called truth. Therefore any philosopher who applies the empirical method without the least prejudice in favor of the pragmatic doctrine, can be led to conclude that truth "means" verification, or if one prefers, that verification, either actual or possible, is the definition of truth. (p. 23)

---

[52] Obviously one needs to consider the rest of what Peirce has to say before we can classify him as anti-realist. For example, we need to know what he means by 'fated'. Indeed, there is evidence Peirce considered himself a realist.

This passage suggests that with a prosentential truth predicate at his disposal Dewey could have responded to the question "What's true?" with an answer paraphrasable with the help of propositional quantifiers, as follows:

> For any p, p if and only if it has been verified or can possibly be verified that p.

Instances include

> Light travels in straight lines if and only if it has been verified or can possibly be verified that light travels in straight lines.

In another place Dewey (1920) has other, seemingly different, thoughts about truth:

> *If* ideas, meanings, conceptions, notions, theories, systems, are instrumental to an active reorganization of the given environment, . . . then the test of their validity and value lies in accomplishing this work. If they succeed in their office, they are reliable, sound, valid, good, true. . . . Confirmation, corroboration, verification lie in works, consequences. . . . That which guides us truly is true. . . . The adverb 'truly' is more fundamental than either the adjective, true, or the noun, truth. An adverb expresses a mode of acting. . . . The hypothesis that works is the *true* one; and *truth* is an abstract noun applied to the collection of cases, actual, foreseen, and desired, that receive confirmation in their works and consequences. (pp. 156–57)

This passage supports Brandom's suggestion that "taking-true" is an essential element of the pragmatists' approach to truth. It also gives support to the commonly accepted idea that there is a strand of the pragmatic theory of truth which "identifies" truth with what works. However, this last proposal can also be expressed with a prosentential truth predicate along the following lines:

> For any p, p if and only if we promote our desired ends by assuming that p.

Among its instances is

> Light travels in straight lines if and only if the assumption that light travels in straight lines promotes our desired ends.

Because I have had to keep the instances simple, I have substituted individual sentences for 'p' in forming instances. This may suggest that sentences are true individually, but that is not what Dewey intended. Dewey argued against any suggestion that assumptions can be verified on an individual basis, or that they "work" individually. For this reason it should be noted that conjunctions of sentences can be substituted for 'p', e.g., a conjunction of the assumptions of a theory could be substituted.

A prosentential theorist can also express a deflationary version of Putnam's (1981) claim regarding truth that "truth is an *idealization* of rational acceptability. We speak as if there were such things as epistemically ideal conditions, and we call a statement 'true' if it would be justified under such conditions." (p. 51) A prosentential reading of Putnam's truth predicate is captured in

> For any p, p if and only if under epistemically ideal conditions it would be rational to accept that p.[53]

What all of this shows is that one can endorse aspects of the slogan-like theses of the pragmatists as to what-is-true, or how the world is, without assuming that truth has a nature. Nothing much is lost along the way, except unnecessary worries about a substantive truth property. It is even the case that most of the old problems remain. For example, one can still question whether there should be a difference between justification and truth, e.g., "Isn't it possible that we are justified in believing that electrons have mass, even though it may turn out that electrons do not have mass?" And the skeptic can use a prosentential truth predicate in facing Peirce: "On your view, it is possible we have no knowledge. It is possible that all of our beliefs may be false, because in the long run investigators may then deny all that we now believe." There is no need to assume a truth property to make these charges.

Note that more cautious prosentential theorists have the option of endorsing prosentential construals of weaker versions of the pragmatic slogans, e.g., the claim that we are justified in believing that something is true if it can be verified.

> For any p, we are justified in believing that p if we have verified that p.

This brief survey shows that the truth predicate seems to be used in asking important questions that happen to have nothing to do with any kind of substantive truth property. This means that a theory we have traditionally labeled as a theory of truth, perhaps un-

---

[53] I believe that one can also parallel Putnam's distinction between the internalist and externalist perspectives with the help of a prosentential predicate and without appealing to a substantive theory of truth.

wittingly because the truth predicate is used in the questions asked, may really be a theory of something else. Indeed, up to this point, I have distinguished three different kinds of theories.

First, there are *theories of the truth predicate*. These include theories like the prosentential theory and the disquotational theory that focus on the utility of the truth predicate, as well as Brandom's version of the pragmatic theory. The formal theory of Tarski and those formal theories that have followed Tarski's, which focus on the logic of the truth predicate are also included. I include under this head theories that address the syntactical, pragmatic (useful), and logical features of the truth predicate. Then there are the *theories of a substantive truth property*. Included is the correspondence theory and traditional versions of the pragmatic and coherence theories. These are also by implication theories of the truth predicate, because they give the truth predicate a property-ascribing role.

I have also shown that there is another way of classifying the pragmatic theory—as it is represented in the slogans. We can extract a *theory of what-is-true*. (Read 'true' prosententially.) On the prosentential reading, a theory of what-is-true is a theory about the way the world is. Scientific theories, as well as theories that might be expressed by my prosentential renderings of the pragmatic slogans, are included.[54] Again, some philosophers may prefer to extract from the slogans of the pragmatists a theory that lays out the *conditions of true belief*, i.e., a theory of justification. The tradition has tended to refer to the first three kinds of theories as theories of truth. I have no quarrel with that, so long as people are not misled into assuming these must all be substantive theories.

While Blanshard is sold on the idea that truth has a substantive nature that we must analyze, Bradley talks of offering only "criteria of truth." This is one reason why I will examine quotations from

---

[54] I do not know for sure, but I doubt anyone would want to extract from the correspondence theory a theory of what-is-true, i.e., a theory of the way the world is. Consider, for example, the claim that a sentence is true if and only if it corresponds to reality. A prosentential reading yields

> For any p, p if and only if the sentence 'p' corresponds to reality.

which has the following as an instance:

> Electrons have mass if and only if the sentence 'Electrons have mass' corresponds to reality.

The correspondence theory may not be a realist theory on this construal because whether or not electrons have mass would depend on how language relates or corresponds to the world.

Bradley rather than from Blanshard. Bradley defends coherence and comprehensiveness on the grounds that they provide criteria of truth. Need we assume that the criteria offered are criteria of a substantive truth property?

Bradley's theory is presented in the context of his attack on the foundational views of knowledge and justification of philosophers like Russell. In denying that there are infallible judgments of perception or memory, Bradley opts for a holistic view in which judgments (or beliefs) are compared with other judgments (or beliefs). So, as with the pragmatists, judgments are not judged true on an individual basis but in the context of a whole structure of judgments. Bradley (1909, p. 210) says:

> My object is to have a world as comprehensive and coherent as possible, and, in order to attain this object, I have not only to reflect but perpetually to have recourse to the materials of sense. I must go to this source both to verify the matter which is old and also to increase it by what is new. And in this way I must depend on the judgments of perception. Now it is agreed that, if I am to have an orderly world, I cannot possibly accept all "facts." Some of these must be relegated, as they are, to the world of error, whether we succeed or fail in modifying and correcting them. *And the view I advocate takes them all as in principle fallible.* On the other hand, that view denies that there is any necessity for absolute facts of sense. *Facts for it are true, we may say, just so far as they work, just so far as they contribute to the order of experience. If by taking certain judgments of perception as true, I can get more system into my world, then these "facts" are true, and if by taking certain "facts" as errors I can order my experience better, then so far these "facts" are errors.* (My emphasis.)

From among the points Bradley makes here, I will focus on those I have italicized. Following the same procedures that I used with the slogans of the pragmatists, I will demonstrate that we do not need to assume a truth property to capture much of what Bradley has to say: He could have supposed that he was providing criteria of what-is-true.

A prosentential reading of the first italicized sentence can be paraphrased in the following way:

> The view I advocate affirms that for each p, it is possible that I believe that p, yet $\sim p$.

Here, Bradley denies the basic assumption of the foundationalists, that there are infallible judgments. He then offers his own view as to when we are justified in assuming something is true. The following provides one way of interpreting the second italicized passage:

> For any p, insofar as hypothesizing that p leads to more system in my world, to that degree it can be assumed that p; and in so far as hypothesizing that $\sim p$ leads to more system in my world, to that degree it can be assumed that $\sim p$.

In offering this paraphrase I am taking Bradley at his word, when he said that he offers only a criterion of truth. The prosentential reading interprets Bradley as saying something about a criterion of what-is-true (read 'true' prosententially). If readers want to interpret the passage as saying something about what-is-true, the words 'it can be assumed that' should be deleted. Bradley denies we can reach "absolute" truth. On his account, judgments are true insofar as they contribute to a coherent comprehensive system; and because in Bradley's view there are at least two reasons why we can never have a fully comprehensive system, we can never acquire absolute certainty. He makes the point this way: " 'Then no judgment of perception will be more than probable?' Certainly that is my contention. 'Facts' are justified because and as far as, while taking them as real, I am better able to deal with the incoming new 'facts' and in general to make my world wider and more harmonious. The higher and wider my structure, and the more that any particular fact or set of facts is implied by the structure, the more certain are the structure and the facts. And, if we could reach an all-embracing ordered whole, then our certainty would be absolute. But, since we cannot do this, we have to remain content with relative probability." (p. 211) We can make this point in roughly the following way:

> Because we can never reach an all-embracing ordered whole (a coherent and comprehensive system), we can never be (absolutely) certain for any p, that p.

I suspect a prosentential truth predicate would suffice for many, if not all, of Bradley's purposes. If so, we have the option of thinking of Bradley as providing criteria of what-is-true rather than criteria of "the nature of truth."

Philosophers have objected to the coherence theory on the ground that truth is explained in terms of consistency (and comprehensiveness). There is a problem, they say, because consistency must be explained in terms of truth. The objection would be a disturbing one, only if the coherence theory were a substantive theory. For someone who supposes only a prosentential truth predicate, there is no problem.[55] The consistency requirement can be taken care of in the following way:

'S' is consistent if and only if $\sim\exists p(S \to (p \;\&\; \sim p))$

I believe Quine is one philosopher who has addressed the issues (what-is-true and justification) that I have assigned to pragmatic and coherence theorists. (Indeed, Quine serves as an example of a deflationist who endorses aspects of all the traditional theories.) Quine's naturalism leads him to seek from science the answers to 'What is true?' For example, he says that if any theory can tell us what is true, scientific theory can. Thus Quine (1981) says: "Our scientific theory can indeed go wrong, and precisely in the familiar way: through failure of predicted observation. But what if happily and unbeknownst, we have achieved a theory that is conformable to every possible observation, past and future? In what sense could the world then be said to deviate from what the theory claims? Clearly in none, even if we can somehow make sense of the phrase 'every possible observation.' " (p. 22) The truth predicate is not used explicitly in stating this view, but it is there implicitly in 'wrong', 'failure', and 'deviate'. Let us suppose our scientific theory is 'S'. Then, one reading of Quine's position would be

> Suppose 'S' is conformable with any p such that it were possible in principle, in the past or future, to observe that p [i.e., Suppose $(p)((\text{in principle it can be observed that } p) \;\&\; (\sim\exists q((S \;\&\; p) \to (q \;\&\; \sim q))))$] then S.

I have ignored the caveat and turned the rhetorical questions into statements. If one wants, the propositional variables could be replaced by individual variables (ranging over a domain of the sentences I assume included in the substitution range of the propositional variables) and a disquotational truth predicate.

We would need to look at what Quine has to say about the methodology of science to more carefully compare his views as to what-is-true with my prosentential versions of the pragmatic and coherence theories. Suffice it to say, Quine's emphasis on prediction suggests he endorses a deflationary version of one aspect of the pragmatic theory; and his holism and fallibilism suggest he endorses a

---

[55] I think Blanshard (1939) makes a mistake in assuming that coherence as a criterion of truth must be accompanied by a substantive coherence theory. See Williams 1980 for further discussion of this issue.

deflationary version of an aspect of Bradley's theory. Of course, Quine has more to say about what-is-true. There is his sectarian view.[56] Discussion of these issues is left for another occasion.

Like many others, Ralph Walker (1989) assumes coherence theorists are substantive truth theorists. Yet he has included Quine among those whom he classifies as (impure) coherence theorists. This is a mistake because Quine is a disquotational theorist who does not subscribe to any kind of substantive coherence theory. I hope the above discussion will show that it is indeed possible for someone like Quine to endorse aspects of the coherence and pragmatic theories, and (as noted in §3.1) aspects of the correspondence theory, without subscribing to the idea that truth has a nature.[57]

One last point: Some readers will have noted that my formulations of the pragmatic and coherence theories can easily be rephrased so that an extension for truth would seem to be defined. In illustration of this point, let us reconsider Dewey's proposal that what-is-true is what is verifiable. I could have formulated this proposal as

For any p, 'p' is true if and only if 'p' has been verified or can be verified.

Does this show that the prosentential version of the pragmatic theory is committed to a truth property? Answer: We need more than an extension for a property—unless we trivialize the notion of property.[58] This question returns us to the issues of Chapters 6 and 7 (Grover 1981a and b).

4. Final Reflections

The prosentential theory of truth provides an account of the role of the truth predicate. In bringing 'true' and 'false' under the umbrella of anaphoric devices, it offers an explanation of our use of the truth predicate in expressing agreement, etc., and for generalizing with

---

[56] See Quine 1981, 1986, and 1990.

[57] It is the distinction a prosentential truth predicate makes available between theories of "the nature of truth" and theories of what-is-true that makes the difference. I believe Davidson's (1990) discussion of the theories of truth would be a bit clearer if this distinction were made. See especially his comments on Quine on p. 298.

[58] Of course it is not that easy to define an extension in a real-life situation. Will pragmatists or coherence theorists select theories for membership in the extension, or sentence types, or sentence tokens, or something else?

respect to sentence positions. Because there is the problem of the "reintroduction" of inconsistency (in Liar-like sentences), the prosentential theory leaves little or no room for an explanatory property-ascribing role for the truth predicate. This makes the prosentential theory apparently incompatible with the correspondence, pragmatic, and coherence theories as they have traditionally been presented. However, as it has not yet been shown conclusively that truth has an explanatory role, this incompatibility seems to pose no problem for the prosentential theory. What the prosentential theory does, is provide an enlightening perspective from which to view the other theories that have been classified as theories of truth.

Indeed, I have shown a prosentential theorist has the option of affirming or denying some other key aspects of the correspondence, pragmatic, and coherence theories. With respect to the pragmatic and coherence theories, a prosentential truth predicate seems to suffice for the things the alleged proponents of the traditional theories have had to say about what-is-true and justification. Prosentential theorists also have the option of either affirming or denying key aspects of the correspondence theory. The possibility that language-world relations have an explanatory role is not ruled out. Nor, seemingly, is the option of being a realist—though this depends on what one thinks a realist is. The neutrality of the prosentential predicate is further illustrated by the fact that these aspects of the traditional theories seem to lose nothing of their contentiousness on the prosentential re-construal.

Where does all this leave us? At the beginning of the century, the debates concerning truth centered on "the nature of truth," with correspondence theorists, pragmatists, and coherence theorists seemingly offering conflicting and disparate analyses of a substantive property. A puzzling aspect of all this was that each theory seemed to appeal to intuitions that most of us have. But then, if we begin questioning the basic assumption of this way of representing the theories—as offering analyses of a substantive truth property—as Ramsey did (perhaps Tarski also, and later, prosentential theorists)—and if we take a closer look at the pragmatic aspects of the truth predicate, another way of looking at the debates emerges. We see that the correspondence theory may be the only genuine contender as a substantive theory. Beyond that, a number of quite different issues may have been in contention: the role of the truth predicate, the way the world is (what-is-true), and justification. Theories of truth have been many things to many people. It is important that we know which questions are being answered.

2

Propositional Quantifiers*

A Preview

Propositional quantifiers—are we doing something "bad" like quantifying "over propositions"? Must we have sentences "doubling as names"? Does Carnap's semantic definition of truth lack an essential predicate? It is to questions such as these that we address ourselves.

Quine (1940) has drawn attention to the "pronominal" character of bound individual variables: Such a characterization is justified by the facts that individual variables are terms (with predicates they form sentences), that the substituends of individual variables are names or definite descriptions of some kind, and that by means of individual variables linguistic cross-references are made. Quine (1970) argues that we can give an account of propositional quantification only if we construe sentences as names—names of "fictitious" objects such as truth values, or names of propositions. It appears from this he assumes that bound *propositional* variables also have a pronominal character. I accept Quine's pronominal characterization of individual variables, but I shall argue against his account of propositional quantification: Propositional variables are not pronominal.

In this paper I give an alternative account of propositional quantification based on a close consideration of the problem of reading such quantifiers in English. According to my account, I am not forced to construe sentences as names. The principal thesis I develop and defend is that *propositional variables have a prosentential character*. My "prosentential" characterization recognizes the facts that propositional variables are sentential, that propositional

* Special thanks are due to Nuel D. Belnap, Jr., who has given me much valuable assistance with the preparation of this paper. I also thank Alan Ross Anderson, Joseph Camp, Jr., Steven Davis, and Wilfrid Sellars for suggestions and corrections. The preparation of this paper was partly supported by a NSF grant.

variables take sentences as substituends, and that propositional variables, like individual variables, make linguistic cross-references.

1. Introduction

Let p take sentences as substituends; then how should the formula $\exists pp$ or the formula $\forall p$(If John knows that p then p) be read in English?

The usual reason for providing readings in English is to make clear which concepts we're interested in, and by making connections with familiar notions, to start the reader's intuitions moving in the right direction before beginning on the formal development. Neither of these motives is behind the questions to be raised here: We all know that quantifiers were introduced to make general statements in the formal language and that $\exists$ is standardly read as 'for some' or 'there is a,' and that $\forall$ is read as 'for all'. But grave objections have been raised as to the *grammatical* proprieties involved in reading formulas with bound propositional variables; it is these I first address.

I am concerned initially with sentences in languages containing quantifiers binding variables occupying the argument places of connectives. That is, the variable positions are sentential and the quantifiers binding them are connectives. My principal claim is that readings that do justice to such bound propositional variables must be given in an *extension* of English. This thesis has two parts: I first argue that *for many sentences in the formal language I consider, there appear to be no faithful and perspicuous readings in English, and then that readings can be given in a sensible and philosophically innocuous extension of English.*

The extension of English I recommend arises by adding a few words very like some we already have. I call the new words 'prosentences'; prosentences help make explicit the role, or grammar, of bound propositional variables.

As I also have something to say about the use of propositional variables in the semi-technical language philosophers use, I distinguish between English and "philosophers' English." By *philosophers' English* I mean the technical language philosophers use. I can compare such a language to the language chemists use in communicating with each other where they introduce, for example, special symbols referring to different substances. Philosophers' English includes English words and constructions; some technical devices, e.g., quotation marks of various kinds; and—crucially—variables. What criteria should I use in determining whether a sentence in philosophers' English is grammatical? I shan't try to set up criteria for all constructions in philosophers' English, but I will make some recommendations as far as propositional variables are concerned. My principal claim about philosophers' English is that *propositional variables that take sentences as substituends can sensibly be used in philosophers' English.*

In §2 I discuss languages in which the propositional variables take sentences as substituends. And because it has sometimes been argued that propositional variables must take either names of propositions, "that-clauses" ('that' followed by a sentence, e.g., 'that snow is white'), or names of sentences as substituends, in §3 I discuss languages in which propositional term variables can take "propositional terms" (it is convenient, although a little inappropriate, to use 'propositional term' to refer to names of propositions, that-clauses, and names of sentences) as substituends. A summary of the results of my discussion is given in §4.

There are (at least) two ways of specifying what the functors in a formal language mean: on the one hand by giving a formal semantics or interpretation of the language, and on the other by giving a number of readings in English. In general a formal interpretation is provided by some abstract system into which the sentences of the language are mapped. Such an interpretation can help our understanding for a variety of reasons. For example, it may be that we have, or can obtain, more information about the system providing the interpretation than about the formal language being interpreted; also, a cluster of formal languages are more easily compared if they are mapped into similar abstract systems.

Partly to highlight the contrast between formal semantics and English readings, and partly because the meanings given the functors by a formal interpretation should agree with the meanings given the functors by readings in English, I begin in §§2 and 3 with a description of an interpretation that might be given the quantifiers.

2. A Language in Which Sentences Are the Substituends of Propositional Variables

In §2.1 I describe the language and its formal semantics. In §2.2 I show that its propositional quantifiers can be given readings in an extension of English; and in §2.3 I show how propositional variables can be correctly used in philosophers' English. In §2.4 I examine some things Suppes and Quine say about propositional quantification. The main point is that *an account can be given of propositional quantification which does not construe sentences as names.*

2.1. DESCRIPTION OF THE LANGUAGE

The language may have some *sentence parameters*. In the discussion we assume that there are at least two: 'Snow is white' and 'Grass is green'. It has a denumerable list of *propositional variables;* I let 'r' and 's' be the first two, and 'p' is used metalinguistically as ranging over the whole set. The language has some *sentence connectives*. In the discussion I use an uncommitted 'if . . . then . . .' ($\rightarrow$) connective, and others such as 'John believes that . . .' The connectives of particular interest are the universal ($\forall$) and existential ($\exists$) quantifiers. Sentences are defined in the usual way, with A and B ranging over them. $A(p)$ is a sentence possibly containing p, and given $A(p)$, $A(B)$ results from substituting B for free occurrences of p in $A(p)$ (after alphabetic changes have been made in the bound variables of $A(p)$ so that variables free in B do not become bound in $A(p)$). $A(p)$ is said to be a *substitution instance* of $\exists pA(p)$ and of $\forall pA(p)$.

The quantifiers are connectives that take a variable (open sentence) p, and a sentence $A(p)$ to produce, in the case of the existential quantifier, the sentence $\exists pA(p)$, and in the case of the universal quantifier, the sentence $\forall pA(p)$.

On the intended interpretation, the sentences are mapped into the elements of a lattice, and the functors of the language are interpreted as either operations or relations defined on the lattice. Following Curry (1963) and Belnap (1967), we may think of the elements of the lattice as propositions, the operations as operations on propositions, and the relations as relations between propositions.

Either a substitution interpretation or a domain and values interpretation of the quantifiers could be used for such a language. We illustrate.

A mapping I is a *substitution interpretation* if each variable is provided with a substitution range, and I maps the sentence parameters and variables into a (complete) lattice L; (1) $I(\exists pA(p)) = \bigvee \{I(A(B)): B$ is in the substitution range of $p\}$; (2) $I(\forall pA(p)) = \bigwedge \{I(A(B)): B$ is in the substitution range of $p\}$. (For $X \subseteq L$, $\bigvee X$ is the lattice least upper bound of X, and dually for $\bigwedge$.)

A mapping I is a *domain and values interpretation* if it satisfies the following: (1) I maps the sentence parameters and variables into a lattice L; (2) $I(\exists p A(p)) = \bigvee \{I'(A(p))\colon I'$ agrees with I with respect to the sentence parameters and variables, except perhaps at $p\}$; and (3) $I(\forall p A(p)) = \bigwedge \{I'(A(p))\colon I'$ agrees with I with respect to the sentence parameters and variables, except perhaps at $p\}$.

In defining the substitution interpretation, we restrict the set of substituends of p by talking of the 'substitution range of p'. The reason is that in general the definition might be circular.

2.2 READINGS IN ENGLISH

For many sentences in a language such as the language just described, there appear to be no sentences in English that serve as faithful and perspicuous readings. I have often heard it argued that exceptions are sentences in languages containing connectives such as 'John believes that . . .'. For example it is suggested that

(1) $\forall r((\text{John believes that } r) \rightarrow (\text{Bill believes that } r))$

can be read as either

If John believes something, then Bill does too.

or as

Bill believes everything that John believes.

A problem with these readings is that they do not follow the form of (1), e.g., the predicate 'John believes . . .' replaces a connective 'John believes that . . .' For such sentences as

(2) $\exists r(r \rightarrow (\text{snow is white}))$

the closest in English are sentences like

(3) There is something such that if it is true then snow is white.

or

(4) Something implies that snow is white.

A problem with (3) is that it introduces a predicate '. . . is true' not featuring in (2). Variations of (3) using such predicates as 'it is the case that . . .' and '. . . holds' are equally unsatisfactory. A problem with (4) is that the arrow is no longer being read as a connective: Instead of 'if . . . then . . .', there is '. . . implies that . . .', which must in its first argument place take a term, usually either a that-clause or the name of a sentence.

In suggesting readings in English of quantified formulas, it is essential to find something that does the job in English that the variable does in the formal language. There is no *single* kind of linguistic entity that is adequate for either quantifiers binding individual variables or quantifiers binding propositional variables. In the case of quantifiers binding individual variables, this point is seldom or never mentioned but is nonetheless true: The effect of the variable is obtained in English through the use of a *combination* of *common* nouns that indicate the kind of variable, and anaphoric uses of relative pronouns that do the cross-referencing required. (Anaphoric: referring to a preceding word or group of words. <the -pronoun *one* in 'I prefer a big bun to a little one'> <the -verb *do* in 'act as we do'>, according to *Webster's Third International Dictionary*.) Examples of the latter are 'it', 'who', and 'the first'. For example:

(5) $\exists x \forall y (x$ admires y and y knows $x)$

can be read as

(6) There is some individual such that for each individual the first admires the second and the second knows the first.

or, in more colloquial English:

(7) Some individual admires all individuals and all individuals know that individual.

(6) is a sentence derived from (5) as follows: The first occurrence of each bound variable is replaced by a common noun and the remaining occurrences of each bound variable are replaced uniformly by relative pronouns: 'the first' and 'the second'. (See Quine 1940, p. 71, for a discussion of the pronominal character of the individual variable.) As (7) demonstrates, a more colloquial reading can be obtained by breaking away from the systematically obtained reading (6). But clearly, if there is some systematic way of obtaining a reading, we can be sure that there is a reading (even though it may be rather ugly) for all sentences and not just for some of them.

As in the case of quantified formulas in a formal language, I can speak of the *substitution instances* of such sentences as (6). Simply detach the 'there is some individual', etc., and replace, consistently throughout, all pronominal words and phrases by appropriate proper nouns, definite descriptions, etc. An example of a substitution instance of (6) is

Fred admires Bill and Bill knows Fred.

Using both the formal and English notions of substitution instance, an English reading of a quantified formula is said to be *adequate* if the substitution instances of the reading are readings of the substitution instances of the original quantified formula. Given our current definition of 'substitution instance', (3) and (4) are not adequate readings. For example, a substitution instance of (3) is

If that snow is white is true then snow is white.

whereas a reading of a substitution instance of (2) is

If snow is white, then snow is white.

To summarize, pronominal phrases and words are used, in reading individual quantifiers, to achieve two things: (1) They are used anaphorically to make in English the cross-references made in the formal language by the variables; and (2) through reference to them, an appropriate set of English substitution instances can be determined, answering to the formal substitution instances. Thus they perform in English two crucial functions performed in the formal language by the variable.

I now return to propositional quantifiers. As I mentioned earlier, readings in English do not appear to be available. The reason no readings come to mind is that the translation that worked for quantifiers binding individual variables does not appear to work for quantifiers binding propositional variables. To carry out such a translation, I need some words or phrases that "stand in" for sentences in the way pronouns "stand in" for proper nouns or definite descriptions. That is, I need some "prosentences" to obtain appropriate readings. But what are prosentences? And what would English look like if it had some prosentences?

Roughly, the relationship between a sentence and a prosentence is supposed to resemble that between a proper noun and a pronoun, a picture that leads to the following definition: A word or phrase is said to be a *prosentence* in a language if in that language its use is given by (a)–(c) below. ('Thatt'—speaking of anaphoric uses of 'that'—is used as a prosentence in the examples given below.)

(a) A prosentence occupies a position in a sentence that a sentence could occupy, just as a pronoun occupies a position in a sentence that a proper noun or noun phrase could occupy. This means a prosentence can be an argument of any connective. For example, with the connective 'John believes that . . .', we have

John believes that *thatt.*

A prosentence beginning with a capital letter and followed by a period is a case of this; for example,

Thatt.

(b) A pronoun is like a proper noun in that it can be used to refer to an individual. For example, in

BILL: Fred is overworked.
JANE: *He* would manage if *he* worked more efficiently.

both Bill and Jane refer to Fred. Similarly, prosentences can be used in many ways that sentences can be used. A simple example is one where a prosentence is used to make an assertion, as in

BILL: Snow is white.
JANE: *Thatt.*

Another example: A sentence can be used to state the antecedent of a conditional, and so can a prosentence, as in

BILL: Snow is white.
JANE: If *thatt,* then it reflects the sun's rays.

Insofar as it is clear that the prosentence in each of the last two examples has a cross-reference to the sentence Bill uttered, we can say that in each example the prosentence 'thatt' stands in for the sentence 'Snow is white'.

(c) A principal function of prosentences is their anaphoric use, which prosentences have in common with pronouns. For example, in

John finished the book and then *he* went to the picnic.

'he' is used anaphorically. As with pronouns, in the trivial cases, an anaphoric use of a prosentence may merely save repetition. For example, instead of

Either snow is white or it is not the case that snow is white.

we could use a prosentence:

(8) Either snow is white or it is not the case that *thatt.*

A more complicated example emerges if we give a "systematically obtained" reading of (1).

(9) For each proposition, if John believes that *thatt*, then Bill believes that *thatt*.

As in the case with pronouns, the cross-referencing done by a prosentence is to something that has recently been featured in the context of that particular use of the prosentence. Previous examples demonstrate this feature of prosentences. In (8) the cross-reference is to 'Snow is white' and the prosentence is standing in for 'Snow is white'. In (9) the cross-reference is to 'each proposition'.

It is worth pointing out that prosentences have something else in common with pronouns: They can be used ambiguously. For instance, just as we do not know who 'he' is being used to refer to in

Bill and John went to the picnic and *he* went for a swim.

so also it is not clear what is expressed by means of 'thatt' in

If snow is white and grass is green, then *thatt*.

Is 'thatt' standing in for 'snow is white', 'grass is green', or 'snow is white and grass is green'? It could be any of them. We can adopt conventions to dispose of some of the ambiguities. For example, a prosentence (when there is only one) is tied, grammatically, to the first complete sentence, or the first linguistic entity standing for an arbitrary sentence, e.g., 'each proposition' in (9), occurring in the sentence in which the prosentence occurs; and if there isn't one, as in the dialogues above, then it makes a cross-reference to the sentence coming immediately prior to the sentence containing the prosentence in question.

To show how prosentences can be used to provide readings of propositional quantifiers, I add some to English, and in this way I obtain the *extension* of English mentioned in §1. I use 'thatt', 'the-first', 'the-second', etc., as prosentences. The double 't' and the hyphen are used to remove any ambiguity that may arise because of other (standard) uses of these words and phrases. I give some examples. A systematically obtained reading of (2) in our extension of English is

(10) For some proposition, if *thatt*, then snow is white.

or, if we don't like 'proposition',

(11) For something if *thatt*, then snow is white.

For

(12) $\forall r(r)$

we have either

(13) For each proposition, *thatt*.

or

(14) For everything, *thatt*.

For

(15) $\forall r \, \exists s(r \rightarrow s)$

we have

(16) For each proposition, there is some proposition, such that if *the-first* then *the-second*.

or

(17) For everything there is something such that if *the-first* then *the-second*.

These last readings are reminiscent of the Stoic's (Kneale 1962, p. 163)

(18) If the first, then the second; but the first; therefore the second.

I now extend our notion of *substitution instances in English* to cover sentences in our extension of English: (i) Detach 'there is some individual' and 'for some proposition' etc.; (ii) replace, consistently throughout, all pronominal words and phrases by appropriate proper nouns, definite descriptions, etc.; and (iii) replace, consistently throughout, all prosentences by sentences.

Then (10), (11), (14), etc., above, are all adequate in that they yield substitution instances that are readings of substitution instances of the original formulas. For example, two substitution instances of both (12) and (13) are

Snow is white.
Grass is green.

I return to individual quantifiers for a moment. Given a sentence $\exists x A(x)$, which can be pictured as

$\exists x(\ldots x \ldots x \ldots)$

readings were obtained by replacing the first occurrence of '*x*' by a common noun, and the remaining occurrences by pronouns. So we moved to

> For some (common noun) (. . . (pronoun) (pronoun) . . .)

If we wished to be fussy, we should in the case of propositional quantifiers move from

> $\exists p(\ldots p \ldots p \ldots)$

to

> For some (common sentence) (. . . (prosentence) . . . (prosentence) . . .)

But as the introduction of "common sentences" would make our account unnecessarily complicated, I stop with prosentences. Although subsequent discussion may call for them, the points I wish presently to make can be made without inventing common sentences.

I have claimed—at least implicitly—that if English is to have some prosentences, then I must add some prosentences. But is such an extension necessary? Perhaps there are already some prosentences in English. Some phrases certainly do "stand in" for sentences. Consider 'such and such', in

> If such and such and so and so, then such and such.

Is 'such and such' a prosentence? It is not, because it does not do all the anaphoric work required of prosentences. Consider

> If snow is white, then such and such.

'Such and such' does not express in the sentence above what 'snow is white' expresses. A prosentence in that position in the sentence would stand in for 'snow is white'.

J. Camp has suggested (in conversation) that it might plausibly be argued that 'it is true' is acting as a prosentence in (3). A check through the definition of 'prosentence' reveals that 'it is true' satisfies all the conditions. It does occupy a sentential position in sentence (3); it is standing in for an (unspecified) sentence; and by means of 'it', 'it is true' has an anaphoric use in the sentence. If we take this approach, then in accord with our extended notion of substitution instance, given above, (3) is a reading of (2). Does 'it is true' *always* act as a prosentence? I leave this question, and the question of what repercussions such an approach would have for the redundancy theory of truth, for another occasion.

2.3. PROPOSITIONAL VARIABLES IN PHILOSOPHERS' ENGLISH

I mentioned earlier that philosophers' English is the language that philosophers use. It includes, for example, quotation marks, corners, and dot quotes. There is no doubt we should value any technical device developed by philosophers to make exposition clearer than it would otherwise be. But there is always the question of whether the technical devices are as precise and as useful as their philosophical deployment demands. I am interested in how propositional variables can be used in philosophers' English. Heidelberger (1968) has made certain claims concerning the grammar of propositional variables which I believe to be mistaken. On his view some sentences that are ruled out as ill-formed in philosophers' English should be counted as well-formed. My interest is in sentences like

(19) There is an r such that if r then snow is white.

which, I claim, provides a "partial reading" (i.e., a reading in philosophers' English) of (2).

In (19) the variable of the formal language is retained, and readings in English are given of the connectives. In arguing that sentences in philosophers' English like (19) are well-formed, I assume— this is a substantive assumption—that the grammar of variables used in philosophers' English is determined by the grammar of these variables in the formal language from which they are borrowed. Therefore, a sentence like (19) could be ill-formed for one of two reasons: Either (1) the grammar of the variable in the formal language is assigned an inconsistent role in the language; or (2) the grammar of English sentences cannot accommodate without inconsistency a linguistic entity with the grammar of the variable. On these two points I make the following comments:

In the last section I gave a detailed account of the grammar of those propositional variables that take sentences as substituends in terms of words and phrases that have to be used to obtain the effect of the variable in English sentences. That I was able to give such an account is evidence that the role of propositional variables in formal languages is free from inconsistency. That is, there is nothing wrong with our well-formed formula definitions. Furthermore, in virtue of the fact that I could provide readings of formulas containing propositional variables, by using prosentences, where prosentences are very like pieces of standard English—namely, pro-nouns—I have also shown that *the grammar of propositional variables is not incompatible with the spirit of English grammar.* Therefore, we are free to use propositional variables—as I construe them—in philosophers' English.

For philosophers' English I now establish a criterion for determining which sentences containing propositional variables are well-formed. On the assumption that the grammar of propositional variables in philosophers' English is determined by the grammar of propositional variables in formal languages, and given that a propositional variable in a formal language can occur in the argument place of any connective (including quantifier connectives), then I require in philosophers' English (where $\exists$ is being read as 'for some' and $\forall$ is being read as 'for all') that a propositional variable either follow 'for some' or 'for all', or occupy a position in the sentence that a sentence could occupy.

A check reveals that, given an appropriate definition of 'substitution instance' for philosophers' English, well-formed readings in philosophers' English, e.g., (19), of quantified formulas in the formal language, e.g., (2), are adequate. Therefore, my criterion of well-formedness for philosophers' English is consistent with what has gone before.

I am now in a position to comment on what others have said of propositional variables in what I have called philosophers' English. In the following I argue that Heidelberger (and as we see later also, Suppes) are wrong when they say that propositional variables must take either names of propositions, that-clauses, or names of sentences as substituends.

Of sentences containing propositional variables, Heidelberger (1968, p. 214) has this to say:

In "Facts and Propositions" Ramsey considered the statement

He is always right.

for which he suggested the paraphrase:

$\forall p$If he asserts p then p.

It is not clear whether Ramsey intended the last occurrence of 'p' to fall within or outside the scope of the universal quantifier; either way, however, the paraphrase is unsuccessful. If it falls within the scope of the quantifier, then it is simply an isolated variable to which no predicate is adjoined.

The assumptions behind this claim are made explicit later in the article when Heidelberger discusses Carnap's (1946, pp. 50ff.) semantical definition of 'is true', which follows:

A sentence S is true $=$ $_{df}$ There is a (proposition) p such that $Des(S,p)$ and p.

Heidelberger gives a reading of the designating functor and the result is (roughly)

A sentence S is true $=$ $_{df}$ There is a proposition p such that S designates that p and p.

Heidelberger does not include 'that' before the next to last occurrence of p. I do because that was Carnap's suggestion (p. 52) for rendering the sentence in English (or in our terms, in philosophers' English). Of this definition Heidelberger says (p. 216): "Carnap tells us that 'p' in his formula is a propositional variable; therefore any constant with which we might replace this variable would be the name of a proposition. But if 'S' is replaced by a name in Carnap's definition of 'true', the locution that results will be unmistakenly ill-formed."

It can be seen from these passages that the sentences in question are held to be ill-formed because it is believed that in philosophers' English propositional variables might be noun-like and as such take propositional terms as substituends. Because the grammar of propositional variables in philosophers' English is the same as the grammar of propositional variables in formal languages, this requires that propositional quantifiers in formal languages be functors that take an open term (a propositional term variable) and an open sentence to produce a sentence; and also, that propositional variables take closed terms (e.g., 'that snow is white') as substituends. But this is not the kind of language Carnap uses. He has propositional variables taking sentences as substituends, as we do.

According to my criteria, the following version of Carnap's definition is well formed:

There is an r such that S designates that r and r.

What of the word 'proposition' Carnap has in parentheses? I suggest that the function of such words is to tell the reader what kind of variable is being used, as in

There is an r (where 'r' is a propositional variable) such that S designates that r and r.

This should not seem strange as we have the same kind of situation in the case of quantifiers binding individual variables. Consider

$\forall x(x$ is tall $\rightarrow$ John is short).

which is often read as

(20) For each individual x, if x is tall then John is short.

The grammar of (20) seems best "explained" by

For each x (where 'x' is an individual variable), if x is tall then John is short.

The parenthetical remark is, as above, metalinguistic.

So much for Carnap's definition. What of the Ramsey (1927) paraphrase mentioned by Heidelberger, of 'He is always right'? As it stands, it is not well formed but easily fixed:

$\forall p($if he asserts that p then $p)$

which can be read as

For each (proposition) p, if he asserts that p then p.

Philosophers sometimes argue as if sentences (in philosophers' English) containing several occurrences of a variable are well-formed only if there is some single word or phrase that, when substituted for all occurrences of the variable in the sentence, yields a well-formed English sentence. Such a criterion must fail to be useful if (and I have argued it is the case) there is no single kind of linguistic entity in English that has the grammar of a variable—either an individual or propositional variable. Partly for this reason, and partly because it seemed to be the natural thing to do, I required that the grammar of variables in philosophers' English be determined by the grammar of the same variables in formal languages. An immediate consequence of my approach is that we can read '$\exists p$' as 'there is a (proposition) p' without introducing the problems Sellars (1963) sought to avoid, because 'there is a (proposition) p' does not require that p be a singular term variable, and also, 'p is a proposition' is, on our account, ill-formed.

In the next subsection, I show some of the ways in which my analysis of the grammar of bound propositional variables casts light on philosophical problems concerning quantification. It is worth noting that the results of our investigations are in the spirit of those developed by Sellars (1963), who also argues for the utility of providing perspicuous readings of formulas containing quantifiers.

2.4. PROPOSITIONAL QUANTIFICATION WITHOUT CONSTRUING SENTENCES AS NAMES

In this section I take a closer look at what prosentences do for us, and I offer a criticism of the work of Suppes and Quine. These two claim that a satisfactory account of propositional quantification (where the propositional variables take sentences as substituends) can be given only by construing sentences as names. Suppes (1957, pp. 123ff.) puts it this way: "The standard view of logic is:

(I) When a variable is replaced by a term which itself does not contain variables, then the substituted term must name some entity."

Then later, when discussing an example in which the sentence '1 = 1' is substituted for a propositional variable, he says: "Since the variable 'p' is replaced by the sentence '1 = 1', according to (I), this sentence must be the name of some entity. Thus the need for propositions when variables are used for which we substitute sentences and not names of sentences."

Quine (1970) classifies propositional quantification as 'simulated quantification'. He makes the following (inconsistent) assumptions: Quantified variables occupy positions that call for noun substantives, sentences are not names, and propositional variables can be bound by quantifiers. For example, (p. 74) "Sentences are not names. Their positions are not positions for quantified variables." Quine grants we can formally bind such variables and give truth definitions of the resulting formulas, but, he argues, to give an account of such quantification we must have sentences doubling as names: names of propositions (p. 12) or names of 'fictitious objects' that may be identified as truth values (p. 75).

According to Suppes, the introduction of propositional quantifiers requires that sentences be construed as names of propositions. This follows from (I), but must we agree with (I)? I claim (I) is false for the following reasons: In giving an account of propositional quantification, I was able, using prosentences, to "reduce" sentences in the formal language to sentences in an extension of English. Prosentences and common nouns were used to do the job in English that bound propositional variables do in formal languages. Common nouns (or better, common sentences) indicate the kind of variable used, and prosentences accomplish the complicated cross-referencing required. From this I concluded that propositional variables function like prosentences, not like pronouns. Furthermore, in moving from a formula containing a quantifier to its substitution instances, a tidy move was made from prosentential-like variables to sentences—there was no move from pronominal-like variables to terms, nor an untidy move from pronominal-like variables to sentences. For these reasons propositional quantification does not force us to construe sentences as names; sentences are sentences. Given the prosentential character of propositional variables, Suppes's and Quine's accounts of propositional variables fail to correctly assess what is going on in the formal languages I have considered.

I now move to the question of whether propositional variables "range over" domains of propositions, sentences, or truth values. I suggest two reasons for "range over" talk. The first is based on natural language considerations. Do I need to introduce names of propositions in giving an account of the relation between propositional quantification and natural language? I have argued that I do not: Because propositional variables are prosentential and occupy sentential positions, we need prosentences and sentences only—no names. The second reason is based on the kind of formal semantics provided. Do I have, on a domain and values interpretation, a domain of propositions? No. It is true the variables are mapped into the elements of a lattice, but so also are the sentences of first-order logics. Even in the classical case, it is customary to map the sentences into the elements 1 and 0 of the Boolean two-element lattice; in the case of nonstandard logics, the lattices are fancier. Therefore, I need introduce talk of propositions and formulas "ranging over" propositions in giving an account of propositional quantification, only if necessary in a domain and values interpretation of first-order logic.

I have, in §2, highlighted some of the differences between propositional quantifiers and individual quantifiers. Should I, with Quine, classify propositional quantification as "simulated" quantification? I argue that—despite the grammatical and domain differences—propositional quantifiers do the job required of quantifiers: to make general statements. Therefore it is wrong to call such quantification simulated.

It is worth noting one advantage of using propositional quantifiers. Quine (1970, p. 11) argues:

Where a truth predicate has its utility is in just those places where, though still concerned with reality, we are impelled by certain technical complications to mention sentences. . . .

What then are those places where, though still concerned with unlinguistic reality we are moved to proceed indirectly and talk of sentences? The important places of this kind are places where we are seeking generality.

And following this through, Quine continues, "So, to gain the desired generality, we go up one step and talk about sentences: 'Every sentence of the form "p or not p" is true.'" Now if propositional quantifiers are used, the required generality is obtained without either mentioning sentences or using the predicate '. . . is true', as follows:

$\forall r(r \lor \sim r)$.

3. A Language in Which Propositional Terms Are the Substituends of Propositional Term Variables

In this section I present and discuss formal languages that might be developed if propositional variables take propositional terms, i.e., names of propositions, that-clauses, or names of sentences, as substituends.

In §3.1 I describe the language, and in §3.2 I show how formulas in such a language can be read in English. In §3.3 I discuss some advantages and disadvantages of different versions of this kind of language.

3.1. DESCRIPTION OF THE LANGUAGE

The language may have some *sentence parameters*. I use 'P' metalinguistically as ranging over these. In the discussion I assume that there are at least two: 'Snow is white' and 'Grass is green'. The language may have some term parameters (possibly, propositional terms). In the discussion the that-clauses 'that snow is white' and 'that grass is green' are used; and 'k' with or without subscripts ranges over the whole set. There is a denumerable list of propositional term variables. In the discussion I use 'u' as a propositional term variable and 'x' ranges metalinguistically over the set. The language also contains some unary predicates. For example, 'John believes . . .' and 'Bill asserts . . .'; G ranges metalinguistically over the whole set. The predicates are used to form sentences from term parameters. In addition, the language has some sentence connectives.

In the discussion use is made of an uncommitted 'if . . . then . . .'
(→) connective. As before I have both a universal quantifier and an
existential quantifier, but this time they bind propositional *term*
variables.

The quantifiers are functors that take a propositional term variable, x, and an open sentence $A(x)$ to produce a sentence, $\forall x A(x)$, in
the case of the universal quantifier, and in the case of the existential
quantifier, the sentence $\exists x A(x)$.

As before, the sentences of the language are mapped into the elements of a lattice, the elements of which may be thought of as propositions that the sentences express.

The language is said to have a *substitution interpretation* of the
quantifiers if each variable is provided with a substitution range and
the interpretation provided is a mapping I satisfying:

(a) I maps the atomic sentences into a lattice L (where the sentence parameters and the sentences formed from a predicate
and a term parameter are the *atomic sentences*).
(b) $I(\exists x A(x)) = \vee \{I(A(k)): k$ is in the substitution range of $x\}$
(c) $I(\forall x A(x)) = \wedge \{I(A(k)): k$ is in the substitution range of $x\}$

In the case of a *domain and values* interpretation, we might first
introduce the notion of an "assignment" upon which is based the
mapping of the sentences of the language into the lattice that provides an interpretation.

An *assignment* α is defined as an ordered triple $<D, L, \mu>$, where
D is a domain of propositions (which may or may not have some
structure), L is a lattice (which may be thought of as providing some
structuring of the propositions), and μ is an assignment function for
D and L such that (i) for each parameter, k, $\mu(k) \in D$; (ii) for each
propositional term variable, x, $\mu(x) \in D$; (iii) for each sentence parameter, P, $\mu(P) \in L$, and (iv) for each predicate, G, $\mu(G)$ is a function
from D into L.

A mapping is said to be an *interpretation based on an assignment*
α if it is a mapping of the sentences of the language into L satisfying: (1) $I(P) = \mu(P)$, for each term parameter P; (2) for a sentence Gk,
$I(Gk) = (\mu(G))\mu k$; (3) for a sentence Gx, $I(Gx) = (\mu(G))\mu x$; (4) for a
sentence $\exists x A(x)$, $I(\exists x A(x)) = \vee \{I'A(x)): I'$ is based on an assignment
μ', where μ' is like μ except perhaps at $x\}$; (5) for a sentence $\forall x A(x)$,
$I(\forall x A(x)) = \wedge \{I'A(x)): I'$ is based on an assignment μ', where μ' is
like μ except perhaps at $x\}$.

The interpretation just defined illustrates some of the features a
domain and values interpretation of the quantifiers might have.

3.2. Readings

The problem of finding readings for these quantifiers is no greater than it is for quantifiers binding individual variables because the variables are pronoun-like, and so the standard pronouns can be used. For example:

(21) $\forall u$(John believes $u \to$ Bill believes u)

can be read as

(22) For each proposition, if John believes it then Bill believes it.

or as

(23) Bill believes everything that John believes.

I leave open the question whether (1) or (21) provides a better analysis of (23).

3.3. A Discussion of "Propositional Term" Languages

In this section I discuss problems that arise from a desire to have interconnections between sentences and propositional terms. According to §3.1, we might have a batch of sentences $A_1, \ldots A_i, \ldots,$ and also a batch of propositional terms $k_1, \ldots, k_i, \ldots,$ but it would seem that such a language is interesting only if there is some interconnection between the A_i and the k_i—an interconnection not required by §3.1. In particular we might wish to have a pairing between the sentence A_i and the propositional term k_i, a pairing that might be described by saying that k_i denotes the proposition expressed by A_i, or, if the propositional terms are names of sentences (rather than names of propositions), k_i is said to be a name of the sentence A_i.

I assume, to begin with, a language without any interconnections between sentences and propositional terms. For such languages I still want to use illustrations like 'that snow is white'; but to indicate that this propositional term is to be treated as atomic, and not as constructed from, and hence paired with, the sentence 'Snow is white' I write it with hyphens: 'that-snow-is-white'. (Example: John knows that-snow-is-white.)

Suppose now I wish to add to this language some features allowing interconnections between propositional terms and sentences. One possibility is to introduce into the language a predicate, T, which, when applied to a term parameter, produces a sentence and is interpreted as '. . . is the case', or as '. . . is true'. Then the term parameter, k, will be said to denote the proposition expressed by Tk. In the formal semantics, I can make use of the interconnection between Tk and k. For example, for some predicate G, the value of a sentence Gk on the interpretation can be defined in terms of the value of the sentence Tk. I might want to do this in the case where G is the predicate 'John knows . . .' and k is 'that-snow-is-white'. A possible theorem is

(John knows that-snow-is-white) → (that-snow-is-white is true)

If a truth predicate is wanted anyhow for other purposes, then the introduction of a truth predicate T is an acceptable move. But if a truth predicate is not wanted for independent reasons, then there is some disadvantage in relating sentences and term parameters in this way. The problem is that the closest that can be obtained in the language to such sentences as

If, if *grass-is-green* then *snow-is-white*, then if John believes *that-grass-is-green* then John believes *that-snow-is-white*.

where I utilize the fact that 'grass-is-green' expresses the proposition denoted by 'that-grass-is-green', etc., is

If, if *that-grass-is-green is true* then *that-snow-is-white is true*, then if John believes *that-grass-is-green* then John believes *that-snow-is-white*.

because only in sentences formed from propositional terms is this information made explicit.

Another way of pairing sentences and propositional terms is to have a functor that, when applied to a sentence, produces a propositional term. Such a functor can be read as 'that'; or, if I am thinking of propositional terms as names of sentences, then the functor can be interpreted as a quotation functor. In the former case, the functor, when applied to the sentence 'snow-is-white', produces the propositional term 'that snow-is-white'; in the latter case, the functor produces the propositional term " 'snow-is-white'." In such a language, there will probably be sentence parameters but no term parameters, i.e., only sentences are atomic. Let t be such a functor.

I can now pair the propositional term tA with the sentence A, and this fact makes it possible, on a given interpretation, to define the value of a sentence $G(tA)$—a sentence formed from a predicate and a now nonatomic propositional term—in terms of the value of the sentence A now explicitly "contained in" the propositional term tA. For example, we can have as a theorem

(John knows (that snow-is-white)) → (snow-is-white)

Unfortunately difficulties emerge when quantifiers are introduced. Given a sentence

$G(tP) \to P$

Universal Generalization yields

$\forall x(Gx \to P)$

and now I have lost the form of the sentence $G(tP) \to P$. In fact, as Heidelberger and Sellars have pointed out, we can never have

$\forall x(Gx \to x)$

because there is a predicate missing. If, as above, we introduce a truth predicate, say T, then we get something that is grammatically acceptable, namely

$\forall x(Gx \to Tx)$

but it does not have $G(tP) \to P$ as a substitution instance.

Assuming the substitution instances of a formula containing a quantifier are defined in the usual way, I claimed above, $\forall x(Gx \to Tx)$ did not have as a substitution instance $G(tP) \to P$. But I can, by treating the truth predicate T as a special case, modify the definition of 'substitution instance' so that $G(tP) \to P$ *is* a substitution instance of $\forall x(Gx \to Tx)$. For each closed sentence B, let us say that $A(B)$ is a *substitution instance* of the sentences $\exists x A(x)$ and $\forall x A(B)$ if $A(B)$ is obtained from $A(x)$ as follows: For each free occurrence of x in $A(x)$ occurring in the scope of the predicate T, Tx is replaced by B, and for each free occurrence of x in $A(x)$ that does not occur within the scope of T, x is replaced by tB. An advantage of this move is that, where the value on an interpretation of $\forall x(Gx \to Tx)$, say, is defined in terms of sentences such as $G(tP) \to P$, it can be done by talking of the values of the "substitution instances" of $\forall x(Gx \to Tx)$. In this case we may have as theorems

$(G(tP) \to P) \to \exists x(Gx \to Tx)$

and

$\forall x(Gx \to Tx) \to (G(tP) \to P)$

Rather than redefine the set of substitution instances of quantified formulas, I might, as the referee has pointed out, adopt a version of Tarski's principle. In my language I take this as meaning adding all instances of

$T(tP) \rightarrow P$

Then

$\forall x(Gx \rightarrow Tx) \rightarrow (G(tP) \rightarrow P)$

follows from

$\forall x(Gx \rightarrow Tx) \rightarrow (G(tP) \rightarrow T(tP))$

On either approach a truth predicate is introduced to obtain generality. This is in the spirit of some of Quine's (1970) remarks about the need for, and function of, the truth predicate in English. (I refer the reader back to the quotation from Quine 1970 at the end of §2.)

It is worth comparing these results with the language of §2, where propositional variables take sentences as substituends. A sensible epistemic functor is, for example, 'John knows that . . .' Then we have generality without a truth functor. For example:

$\forall r \forall s((r \rightarrow s) \rightarrow ((\text{John knows that } r) \rightarrow (\text{John knows that } s)))$

and

$\forall r((\text{John knows that } r) \rightarrow r)$

But if a truth functor is wanted—it seems that such a functor is redundant—it can be introduced and yields sentences like

$\forall r((\text{John knows that } r) \rightarrow (\text{that } r \text{ is true}))$

In this case the truth functor reads, 'that . . . is true'.

4. Summary

In discussing propositional quantifiers, I have considered two kinds of variables: variables occupying the argument places of connectives, and variables occupying the argument places of predicates.

I began with languages that contained the first kind of variable, i.e., variables taking sentences as substituends. My first point was that there appear to be no sentences in English that serve as adequate readings of formulas containing propositional quantifiers. Then I showed how a certain natural and illuminating extension of

English by prosentences did provide perspicuous readings. The point of introducing prosentences was to provide a way of making clear the grammar of propositional variables: Propositional variables have a prosentential character, not a pronominal character. Given this information, I was able to show, on the assumption that the grammar of propositional variables in philosopher's English should be determined by their grammar in formal languages (unless a separate account of their grammar is provided), that propositional variables can be used in a grammatically and philosophically acceptable way in philosophers' English. According to my criteria of well-formedness, Carnap's semantic definition of truth does not lack an "essential" predicate—despite arguments to the contrary. It also followed from my account of the prosentential character of bound propositional variables that in explaining propositional quantification sentences should not be construed as names.

One matter I have not discussed is whether such quantification should be called 'propositional', 'sentential', or something else. As my variables do not range over (they are not terms) either propositions or sentences, each name is inappropriate, given the usual picture of quantification. But I think the relevant question in this context is, Are we obtaining generality with respect to propositions, sentences, or something else?

Because people have argued that all bound variables must have a pronominal character, I presented and discussed in §3 languages in which the variables take propositional terms as substituends. In my case I included names of propositions, that-clauses, and names of sentences in the set of propositional terms. I made a few comparisons with the languages discussed in the second section. I showed among other things how a truth predicate could be used to obtain generality. In contrast, the languages of the second section, using propositional variables, obtain generality without the use of a truth predicate.

3

A Prosentential Theory
of Truth*

What is a theory of truth? Some take themselves to be giving an account of the property of being true, an explanation of what it is that makes X true when it is true (correspondence, coherence), while others address themselves to the problem of what sorts of things are most fundamentally to be said to be true (propositions, statements, sentences). Underlying these theories and others is a standard grammatical analysis of ordinary English sentences containing 'is true': 'X is true' is analyzed into a subject 'X' and a predicate 'is true', where the role of the predicate is to express the property *truth* that an utterer of the sentence ascribes to the referent of 'X'. Our purpose here is to offer a coherent alternative to this subject-predicate analysis. But why the need for an alternative to the obvious one we all love so well? Our principal reason is simply that a given grammatical analysis can sometimes mislead, or sometimes restrict, our philosophical intuitions. We claim that our alternative account—a prosentential theory of truth—eliminates some of the problems about truth; by no means all, but some of those it fails to eliminate it at least relocates in what we shall argue are advantageous ways. Moreover, we think our analysis provides independent insight into the role of truth locutions and also constitutes a natural framework for a wide range of insights various philosophers have had about truth—insights scattered around in such as Frege (1892), Ramsey (1927), Strawson (1950a), Quine (1970), and Prior (1971). Fi-

* This article was co-authored with Joseph Camp and Nuel D. Belnap, Jr. Research has been supported in part by Grant GS-28478 from the National Science Foundation, to whom we give thanks. We are indebted to Marvin Loflin for assistance in the earlier stages of the paper, especially in those areas touching on linguistics. Further help came from discussions at the University of Wisconsin-Milwaukee and the University of Illinois at Chicago, and from comments by A. Gungadean, R. Keim, and P. Teller.

nally, the alternative analysis suggests directions in which philosophizing about truth might move—directions not at all suggested by the standard account.

1. Ramsey

A natural way into our theory is provided by Ramsey's so-called "no-truth" or "redundancy" theory, so we shall begin there. Then, in succeeding parts of this paper, we shall (§2) explain and (§3) defend the prosentential theory and finally (§4) look at its consequences and applications.

1.1. RAMSEY: EXPOSITION

We are about to present a semantical analysis of truth talk which we label the *redundancy theory* and which might well be one Ramsey (1927) had in mind. We say 'might well' because Ramsey's explanation of his theory is so condensed it is hard to see exactly what he does have in mind. Anyhow, our explication of Ramsey's theory goes like this: If we allow ourselves to enrich English in a rather modest way—by the addition of machinery for propositional quantification—we can say *without* the help of a truth predicate anything we can say *with* it.

Ramsey's idea was that in many simple cases the truth predicate can be dropped with no loss of assertional content.

(1) That snow is white is true.

and

(1') Snow is white.

presumably come to the same thing. We use 'is true' sometimes 'for emphasis or for stylistic reasons', he says, but the truth predicate brings no new assertional content. 'True' plays many other roles in ordinary usage, however, and we need to look at all of them before we can sensibly evaluate the redundancy claim. If we call (1), (1') and its cousins cases of the *disappearing* kind because the truth predicate disappears without residue, perhaps we should call the next set of cases *repetition* cases. We do not know if Ramsey considered them, but it is pretty clear how truth-free translations should go.

(2) Mary says that snow is white, but if that's true then snow reflects the sun's rays.

becomes

(2') Mary says that snow is white, but if snow is white then snow reflects the sun's rays.

Or, as in conversation:

(3) MARY: Snow is white. JOHN: That's true.

Presumably Ramsey's paraphrase would be

(3') MARY: Snow is white. JOHN: Snow is white.

So far the apparatus of propositional quantification hasn't figured in, but it does when we consider *quantificational* cases like

(4) Everything John says is true.

(5) Everything John says about the house is true.

(6) The consequences of true propositions are true.

(7) Every proposition is either true or false.

Using propositional quantification and some standard connectives, these come out as

(4') $\forall p(\text{John says that } p \to p)$

(5') $\forall p(\text{John says of the house that } p \to p)$

(6') $\forall p \forall q(p \ \& \ (p \Rightarrow q) \to q)$, where $\Rightarrow$ is a consequence connective.

(7') $\forall p(p \lor \sim p)$

Our translation (4') construes (4) as saying in part something about John and not simply as asserting what John asserted. But there are cases where, when asked for an opinion, in order either to save time or a lot of repetition, we say,

(8) What John said is true.

That it was John who said it doesn't matter much; what we're doing is making clear our position. So we might use the conditional of Belnap (1973), translating (8) as

(8') $\forall p(\text{John said that } p/p)$

Closely allied to the quantificational cases are the *indirect reference* cases, such as

(9) Goldbach's conjecture is true.

If we have a substitutional interpretation of our propositional quantifiers and the apparatus of quantification in and out of quotes as in Chapter 11 (Belnap and Grover 1973), we might try

(9') $\forall p$(Goldbach conjectured that p & $\forall q$ (Goldbach conjectured that $q \rightarrow$ ($'p' = 'q'$)) & p)

But this is right only if exactly one sentence is thought of as expressing Goldbach's conjecture. If, more plausibly, more than one sentence expresses the conjecture, we need something like

(9") $\forall p$(Goldbach conjectured that p & $\forall q$ (Goldbach conjectured that $q \rightarrow$ ($p \Leftrightarrow q$)) & p)

where $p \Leftrightarrow q$ only if $'p'$ and $'q'$ express the same conjecture. (But what connective is this?) A fifth category of cases, cutting across the others, is constituted by the *modified* cases, i.e., those in which the verb in 'is true' is modified by tensing or in some other way. Consider examples of "modified disappearing" or "modified repetition" cases.

(10) It is not true that someone is coming down the road.

(11) It might be true that there are people on Mars.

(12) BILL: Women are treated equally in the profession.
      JOHN: I wish that were true.

(13) JOHN: Rome is the center of the known world.
      BILL: That's not true, but it used to be true.

In these cases Ramsey would probably get the effect of modification of the verb in 'is true' by analogous modification of the interior sentence, e.g.,

(10') No one is coming down the road.

(11') There might be people on Mars.

(12') BILL: Women are treated equally in the profession.
       JOHN: I wish that women were treated equally in the profession.

(13') JOHN: Rome is the center of the known world.
BILL: Rome is not the center of the known world, but Rome used to be the center of the known world.

It might be a good deal harder to transfer the verb modification from 'is true' to the interior verbs in cases where the interior sentences are significantly more complex than in (11)–(13), e.g., with lots of subordinate clauses and verbs. Laying aside this doubt, however, as well as others that we shall shortly raise, suppose Ramsey's translation program *can* be carried through. What has he told us about the semantical role of 'is true' in English? What he has *not* done is define a single semantical role for the truth predicate, but he probably did not intend to give that sort of semantics for 'true'. It is more likely that he would have surveyed the rather wide variety of translations represented by (1')–(13') and concluded that 'is true' is what Russell called an "incomplete symbol." It isn't easy to say exactly what Russell meant by that, but this is pretty close: Suppose you have a fragment of English and you are considering in a Russellian spirit the "logical form" of the sentences in that fragment by seeing how they most naturally translate into some formal or semiformal target language—say (again Russellian) a language with the machinery of first-order quantification with identity plus a bunch of ordinary English, but without definite or indefinite articles. It might happen—in the case of definite and indefinite descriptions, for instance—that the target-language translations of English sentences do not contain any *one* kind of expression that we can pick out as the translation of, e.g., definite descriptions. Sentences containing 'the present king of France' will get translated by target-language sentences with various structures, leaving us no plausible candidate for the first-order-quantificational expression that means the same as 'the present king of France'. In such cases we can say that the English expressions in question are "incomplete symbols"—provided we remember the relativization of this claim to a particular choice of target-language. Ramsey might plausibly claim that he has shown the truth-predicate to be an incomplete symbol in this sense, where the target-language we have in mind is the truth-predicate-free part of English plus propositional quantification: There is nothing that translates 'is true', but there are ways of capturing (complete) expressions containing 'is true' as a proper part. Of course, Ramsey doesn't say anything like this, but it's a line he might have developed. That's our reconstruction of Ramsey's redundancy theory. Speculative though it is as exegesis of Ramsey's views, it seems to us a sensible theory, or at least a good first approximation to a sensible theory. Our own theory is in many respects a variation on Ramsey's theme but—so we shall urge—a variation that is also an improvement. Before presenting it, however, we should consider a number of objections that might be made against Ramsey.

1.2. RAMSEY: OBJECTIONS

We consider six rather different sorts of objections. The first two suggest that our data base is too small; i.e., that other cases cast doubt on the theory.

INDEXICALS

First a type of case where there is no obvious rule for systematic translation; namely, indexical repetition cases such as

(14) JOHN: I am greedy. MARY: That's true.

We cannot use simpleminded repetition here as we did in (3'), for clearly the translation should have Mary uttering, 'You are greedy' or perhaps 'John is greedy'; we do not want Mary saying, 'I am greedy'. However, although we are not even remotely in a position to advance a generally applicable translation schema for such examples, it seems to us plausible that there should be at least an approximation unto one; and in any event we shall indicate later (§3.1) how this objection can be placed in proper perspective by our own prosentential theory.

MODIFICATION

Now a type of case in which translation is simply impossible: modified quantificational and indirect reference cases such as

(15) Each thing Mark said might be true.

where there is no verb, such as that in (11), to which to transfer the 'might', and similarly

(16) Something Charlie said is either true or not true.

(17) All that Judith said was true, but none of it is true now.

Of course one might try for (15) something like

(15') $\forall p$(Mark said that $p \to$ it might be the case that p)

or

(15") $\forall p$(Mark said that $p \to$ that p might obtain)

but clearly being the case and obtaining are just variants of being true and, if allowed, would reduce the redundancy theory to triviality. In view of this problem, we think the "straight" Ramsey theory, which takes as its target English without truth but with propositional quantification, is false. But we can modify the theory along lines Ramsey might approve by adding to the target language not only propositional quantifiers but also a somewhat indeterminate array of connectives such as a possibility ('might') connective M; a past tense connective P, and a negation connective $\sim$ (which the reader presumably thought we already had anyhow). Then (15)–(17) could be translated by

(15''') $\forall p$(Mark said that $p \to Mp$)

(16') $\exists p$(Charlie said that p & (p v $\sim p$))

(17') $\forall p$(Judith said that $p \to$ (Pp & $\sim p$))

The general idea is to add a connective operating on sentences for each modification of 'is true' which we cannot otherwise handle, with the expectation that these connectives, like negation, would by and large be ones we would want for other purposes anyhow. It is this modified theory that we henceforth call the redundancy theory, the theory that truth is redundant given propositional quantification and some connectives answering to verb modifications. We rather believe that given this additional apparatus, translations in the spirit of Ramsey can generally be found, and we shall proceed on that basis. The next two objections question the accuracy of the translations.

ABOUTNESS

Someone might argue that 'That snow is white is true' is about the proposition that snow is white while its translation 'Snow is white' is about snow, and conclude that *therefore* the translation fails. We are not going to argue directly against this objection, involving as it does the Paradox of Analysis. What we *shall* do is offer what we believe to be a comprehensive theory rooted in the assumption that in at least the easy disappearing cases and repetition cases, the assertional content of the translation matches that of the sentence translated. We'll rely on the success of our theory as evidence for the reasonableness of this assumption.

PRAGMATICS

A more telling objection is that even if the translations preserve assertional content, they leave out other features of truth discourse, features that shouldn't be neglected.

The chief problem lies with the repetition cases. Is the translation of 'That's true' in

(3) MARY: Snow is white. JOHN: That's true.

as

(3') MARY: Snow is white. JOHN: Snow is white.

a good translation? Given the assumption that 'That's true' expresses what its antecedent expresses, the translation succeeds in this one respect. But remember the sage advice in Strawson (1950a) §4, that " 'true' and 'not true' have jobs of their own to do. . . . In using them, we are not *just* asserting that X is Y or that X is not Y. We are asserting this in a way in which we could not assert it unless certain conditions were fulfilled; we may also be granting, denying, confirming, etc." On some occasions John can grant that snow is white or agree that snow is white, by uttering the sentence 'Snow is white' (perhaps with emphasis), but there are occasions in which he would not do this as successfully as he would if he used the sentence 'That is true'. In using 'That is true', one acknowledges that there is an antecedent, and thereby one acknowledges the source of the idea. It is necessary that there be an antecedent for one to successfully grant or agree with something, and if one intends to express agreement, then the antecedent must normally be explicitly acknowledged. The stuttering suggested by the Ramsey translation (3') does not do this; put another way, by using 'That is true', John avoids the charge of plagiarism. Thus *pragmatically* the Ramsey translations fail. This is obvious also in those cases where the truth predicate is used as either an abbreviatory device or to save repetition. We endorse this objection and overcome it in our prosentential theory (see especially §2.4). The final two objections have to do with the legitimacy of propositional quantifiers such as those used in (4')–(9').

The first of these objections suggests that propositional quantification is mysterious and not at all in line with the rest of English. Or to put it another way, the objection is to calling Ramsey's theory a redundancy theory, because it doesn't show truth to be redundant in English itself, but only in some curious ad hoc extension of English. We postpone consideration of this objection until after our prosentential theory has been presented and then argue in §3.1 that its force is minimal.

GRAMMAR

The second objection claims that propositional quantification is just downright ungrammatical. Ramsey (1927, p. 45) anticipates the objection that variables have got to have predicates attached to them even if they occupy sentential positions, but unfortunately his reply isn't especially convincing: "We have in English to add 'is true' to give the sentence a verb, forgetting that 'p' already contains a (variable) verb. This may perhaps be made clearer by supposing for a moment that only one form of proposition is in question, say the relational form aRb; then 'He is always right' could be expressed by 'For all a, R, b, if he asserts aRb, then aRb', to which 'is true' would be an obviously superfluous addition. When all "forms" of proposition are included the analysis is more complicated but not essentially different. . . ." If there were just some few "forms" a substituend for 'p' might take, say 'aRb' and 'Fa', we could understand Ramsey as claiming that '$\forall p \ldots p \ldots$' is to abbreviate '$\forall a \forall R \forall b \ldots aRb \ldots$ and $\forall a \forall F \ldots Fa \ldots$', or something like that. But it is plain that the number of forms is in fact infinite, so talk of "variable verbs" cannot be made sense of along these lines. But even if Ramsey was confused about the logical machinery he wanted to use, we need not be. Propositional quantification can be made perfectly respectable both formally and informally, and it is a mistake to suppose that variables in the grammatical category of sentences—variables that take sentences as substituends—somehow need to have verbs stuck onto them to make grammatical sense. But it is a natural mistake, which might arise as follows:

Suppose we try reading (4'), which is in the Ramsey language with its propositional quantifiers, into unadorned English. If we follow the style of reading usually given formulas containing bound occurrences of individual variables, we will use pronouns to capture the bound variable, which gives

> For each proposition, if John said that it, then it.

As the quote from Ramsey already says, and as Heidelberger (1968) and others have pointed out, these sentences lack essential predicates. The obvious candidate, as Ramsey and the others suggested, is 'is true', giving

> (4″) For each proposition, if John said that it is true, then it is true.

All of which suggests that if the grammar of formulas containing bound propositional variables is to be in the spirit of English grammar, then the language with quantifiers should have a truth predicate (say 'T' read 'is true') so that instead of (4') we should have

> (4‴) $\forall p$(John said that $Tp \to Tp$)

But because 'T' is a predicate and 'Tp' a sentence, 'p' must be a *term* of the language, i.e., it must occupy nominal positions. This means that the quantifiers are binding *individual* variables (of a special sort) and not variables occupying *sentential* positions. So putting aside the disappearance of redundancy which follows upon the reintroduction of the truth predicate, the quantifiers turn out not to be as we described them in setting up the Ramsey language; Ramsey's variables bind variables occupying sentential positions. Some people would go one step further and claim that what is demonstrated here is the impossibility of giving a coherent account of anything but *individual* quantification.

But all this rests on a mistake; our own theory explains both the mistake and why it is natural. We follow Sellars (1960) and Prior (1971) in arguing that there is something essentially wrongheaded about the above analysis (see Chapter 2 [Grover 1972] for a more detailed account of our view on this matter): The fact is that although relative pronouns can be used to provide adequate readings of formulas containing bound occurrences of individual variables (occupying nominal positions), they do not cope with bound occurrences of propositional variables, because the latter occupy sentential positions. To obtain adequate readings, we need something that does the kind of cross-referencing achieved by variables and that also occupies a position a sentence could occupy. In the case of individual variables, the cross-referencing is done by pronouns, but they occupy nominal positions. So what is wanted is something like a pronoun but that occupies a sentential position. What is wanted is a *prosentence*. Roughly, just as a pronoun is sometimes said to stand in for a proper noun, and a proverb (e.g., 'do') for a verb, so prosentences stand in for sentences; that is, with respect to their own grammatical category, prosentences are to be generic in the sense that pronouns and proverbs are. An analysis of bound propositional variables in terms of prosentences rather than pronouns will in §4.3 show that these variables must not have predicates attached to them.

So much for the mistake; why is it natural? It is a natural mistake just because English—plain English—probably does not contain any generally available atomic (one-word) prosentences on a par with 'it' and its cousins. For this reason *easy* readings of sentences involving propositional quantifiers of the Ramsey variety are not available. But—and this is a principal thesis of this paper—English does have some prosentences, albeit nonatomic ones; we argue that 'That is true' and 'It is true' are prosentences, a fact that can be used to meet the "ungrammaticality" objection to Ramsey (as we shall spell out in §4). But the philosophical interest of prosentences goes far beyond the mere reading of propositional quantifiers; for instance, they will help us argue a version of the Ramsey redundancy thesis. Like Ramsey, we do not think the truth predicate need be construed as having a property-ascribing role in ordinary English. But unlike Ramsey, we think it is possible to say a bit more about what the usual semantical role of the truth predicate (i.e., 'is true') is. Specifically, we think 'is true' can be taken to be a fragment of a prosentence—either the prosentence 'It is true' or the prosentence 'That is true', *wherever* they occur. In the next section, we shall first explain what we take prosentences to be (§2.1); then we shall explain just what we mean by the claim that 'is true' is a fragment of a prosentence (§2.2–2.6).

2. Prosentential Theory: Exposition

Because our theory is that 'true' can be thought of always as part of a prosentence, we should try to get a little clearer about what prosentences are and how they work.

2.1. ANAPHORA AND PROSENTENCES

The key linguistic relation in this area is that of *anaphora*: For something to be a proform it must be able to be used anaphorically.

We shall not try to provide a full or rigorous account of the relation of anaphora; that is clearly a job for linguists, and none of them has yet developed an adequate theory even for the relatively simple cases where anaphoric expressions occupy nominal positions (see Partee 1970). What we'll do instead is discuss a number of examples, some of them taken from the literature, to show the variety of anaphoric expressions in our language, to illustrate their complexity, and to conjecture as to their point.

Anaphoric uses of pronouns have come in for the most discussion. Consider the following:

(18) Mary wanted to buy a car, but *she* could only afford a motorbike.

(19) If *she* can afford it, Jane will go.

(20) John visited us. *It* was a surprise.

(21) Mary said that the moon is made of green cheese, but I didn't believe *it*.

(22) Goldwater won in the West, but *it* didn't happen in the East.

In order to understand these sentences, we must be aware of the grammatical ties that obtain between, for example, 'she' and 'Mary' and between 'she' and 'Jane', because only then do we know that 'she' is used in the one case to refer to Mary and in the other to Jane. In such cases the pronoun is said to be used *anaphorically*. Pronouns can also be used to refer *independently* as in '*That* isn't my book' uttered along with a pointing gesture or the like. (The terminology derives from Parsons 1970; of course such pronouns are not independent of all context, but they refer independently of any antecedent.) Following the linguists, we call the word or phrase with which an anaphoric pronoun is linked, its *antecedent*; thus the antecedent of 'she' in (18) is 'Mary'. This terminology, though not of course the theory, ignores the possibility that an anaphoric pronoun may precede its antecedent as in (19). Whenever a pronoun is used anaphorically, the pronoun is said to be an *anaphor*. The relation between an anaphor and its antecedent is the relation of *anaphora*. It should be noted that although the relation of anaphora involves cross-referencing, an anaphor does not 'refer' to its antecedent in the sense in which proper nouns and independently referring pronouns are said to 'refer' to their referents; i.e., 'she' is not used to refer to 'Mary', but to Mary.

Geach (1967) called pronouns as used in (18) *pronouns of laziness*. We'll follow him in this even though the characterization this terminology suggests does not survive many examples. But the initial idea is that such pronouns 'stand in' for their antecedents and so may serve as abbreviatory devices, etc. This suggests that wherever a pronoun of laziness is employed we could just as well substitute its antecedent. In the case of (18), this yields

> (18′) Mary wanted to buy a car, but Mary could only afford a motorbike.

In some cases, and perhaps with (18′), substitution of the antecedent for the anaphor introduces ambiguities not present in the original. We suggest that one reason for using anaphoric pronouns is to make it clear that only one person or thing is being talked about throughout.

What's more, naive substitution of the antecedent sometimes isn't even possible, because in cases like (20) the grammatical categories of the anaphor and its antecedent differ: The antecedent of 'it' is the sentence 'John visited us'. To obtain the right word or phrase for substitution, we might move to either 'John's visit' or 'John's visiting us'. These we'll call *anaphoric substituends*. We include example (22) from Lakoff[1] partly to show that the anaphora relation can be complex. In order to find an appropriate anaphoric substituend for 'it' in (22), it seems we need to take into account not only grammatical considerations but also the sense of the whole sentence. Just reflect upon the contrast between the substituend for 'it' in (22) and in 'Goldwater won in the West, but it didn't surprise me'.

Anaphoric pronouns can also be used to make general statements. Borrowing from logicians, we'll call these *quantificational* uses of anaphoric pronouns. For example:

> (23) If any car overheats, don't buy *it*.

> (24) Each positive integer is such that if *it* is even, adding 1 to *it* yields an odd number.

We are far from clear as to precisely what should count as the antecedents of these pronouns, but we shall in all innocence pre-

---

[1] Lakoff 1970, p. 154.

sume them to be the quantificational phrases 'any car' and 'each positive integer'. Note that the relation between an anaphor and its antecedent in these cases differs radically from the relation in laziness cases: It won't do to substitute the antecedent (or a semantically equivalent transform) for the anaphor. Just consider

(23') If any car overheats, don't buy any car.

More profoundly, quantificational anaphoric pronouns don't pick up a *referent* from their antecedents the way pronouns of laziness do, in view of the fact that their antecedents usually can't be construed as referring expressions. They do, however, pick up both a family of anaphoric substituends and sometimes a family of objects, the former determining what is to count as an *instance* in the way that

(24') If 3 is even, adding 1 to 3 yields an odd number.

is an instance of (24). This subdivision into pronouns of laziness and quantificational pronouns is suggested by Partee (1970).

Some (not linguists, we suppose) might want to call 'her father' in

Mary loved her father

a pronoun on the grounds that it can be construed as having an antecedent, 'Mary', and an anaphoric substituend, 'Mary's father', but we rule it out as a pronoun *not* because it is compound but rather on the grounds that it lacks the generic quality of other pronouns; that is, within wide limits (gender, etc.), ordinary pronouns are completely generic or indeterminate with respect to what can be used as a substituend for them.

Anaphors do not always occupy nominal positions. There are, for example, proverbial uses of 'do'. 'Do' is used as a proverb of laziness:

Dance as we *do*.

Mary ran quickly, so Bill *did* too.

and as a quantificational proverb.

Whatever Mary *did*, Bill *did*.

Do whatever you can *do*.

'Such' and 'so' can be used anaphorically as proadjectives:

> The pointless lances of the preceding day were certainly no longer *such* (Scott).

> To make men happy and to keep them *so* (Pope).

It may not be possible to find clear cases where 'such' and 'so' are used as quantificational proadjectives. As a final example, consider the proadverb of laziness in

> She twitched violently, and while so twitching, expired.

As a generic term for 'pronoun', 'proverb', 'proadjective', etc., we'll use *proform* and explain prosentences as a species of this genus. Because anaphora is relational, one might speciate anaphoric proforms either according to the position they occupy (nominal, adjectival, etc.) or according to the grammatical category of their antecedent. Without implying that either principle of classification is likely to appear unrefined in a sophisticated grammar, we shall use the former, noting that linguists with whom we have conferred tend to employ the latter; e.g., the 'it' in (20) that we called a pronoun on the grounds that it occupies a nominal position, they would call a prosentence (if they had such a word) on the grounds that its antecedent is a sentence. As a consequence of our decision, a pronoun must occupy a nominal position, a proadjective must occupy an adjectival position, and a prosentence must occupy a (declarative) sentential position.

We have said that a prosentence is to be limited to (declarative) sentential positions; but what about its antecedents? Should its antecedents be limited to declarative sentences as well? (Recall from (20) that the antecedents of pronouns are by no means limited to nominal constructions.) We almost avoid deciding by labeling prosentences as such in either the *wide sense* or in the *narrow sense*, depending on whether they do or do not admit other than declarative-sentential antecedents; but we choose to use 'prosentence' as meaning 'prosentence in the *wide* sense' for at least the course of this paper. This means that in the laziness cases the antecedent need not be a declarative sentence, and in the quantificational cases that the antecedent might, for example, be a nominal quantificational phrase.

We draw these considerations together to come up with some rough criteria representing a good thing to mean by 'prosentence':

It can occupy the position of a declarative sentence.

It can be used anaphorically in either the lazy way or the quantificational way.

Consequently, in each such use it has an antecedent from which one may derive an anaphoric substituend (in the laziness cases) or a family of anaphoric substituends (in the quantificational cases)—in either case, the substituends are sentential, matching the position of the anaphor.

It is "generic" in the sense that, in one use or another, any declarative sentence might turn up as anaphoric substituend.

With this characterization, necessarily rough because of the primitive state of the theory of anaphora, we may ask, Does English have any prosentences? Or first, does English have any *atomic* (i.e., one-word) prosentences? Yes. Indeed J. Carson and R. Chisholm have pointed out to us that Brentano (1904) uses the very word 'prosentence' ('Furwort') to describe 'yes'. And if 'yes' is an atomic prosentence, so is the laziness use of 'so' in

I don't believe Rachel is sick, but if *so*, she should stay home.

although some troublemaker might prefer to say that there is ellipsis in this example and that in "the deep structure" 'so' is a proadjective. (Ditto for 'I think so' and 'I believe so'.) In any event, even if prosentences, and atomic ones, these are not *generally available* in the sense that they can be put in arbitrary sentential positions. One cannot say, 'I don't believe Rachel is sick, but if she has a fever, then so'. And one must say 'I know that that is so' (adjectival position), not 'I know that so' (sentential position as required for prosentences). We *have* heard 'I know so', but we've heard it in bars. From this kind of evidence we conclude that English as it stands does not have any generally available atomic prosentences. What would English be like if it did?

One method philosophers and logicians employ for presenting an analysis of some aspect of language in which they are interested is to show how the piece in question would look in some specially constructed (not necessarily formal) language. The point of introducing a special language may be to allow one to idealize the situation somewhat so that special features can be highlighted and the other features, judged to be irrelevant to the issue at hand, ignored. In such circumstances it is not (usually) going to be claimed that

English is *exactly* like the introduced language, but rather that bits of English can for certain purposes be thought of as working or fitting together in the way demonstrated. It might also be argued that, with respect to *just* that feature being analyzed, English might well have been constructed in this other way. We shall employ this method in getting clear on the concept of a prosentence in relation to English.

2.2. ENGLISH + 'THATT'

We ask you then (temporarily, and as a heuristic device) to pretend we have a generally available atomic prosentence, written 'thatt' (Prior [1971] proposes 'thether'; our 'thatt', deriving from Grover 1972 [Chapter 2 of this volume], where there is a fuller discussion of its point and purpose in relation to propositional quantification, is easier to say if you keep the final *t* silent.) That is, we ask you to consider a language English + 'thatt' in which 'thatt' is a generally available and atomic prosentence. We might use 'thatt' as a prosentence of laziness as in

JOHN: Snow is white. MARY: *Thatt.*

or in

BILL: There are people on Mars. SUSAN: If *thatt*, we should see signs of life very soon.

Here Bill's remark is the antecedent of Susan's utterance of 'thatt', and Susan's remark gets its content from this antecedent. But like other anaphoric proforms, 'thatt' is generic—when Susan utters it with 'There are people on Mars' as its antecedent, she gives it the sense of that sentence but, with another antecedent, 'thatt' would have another sense.

And quantificationally, 'thatt' could help us express such generalizations as 'Every proposition is either true or false' without recourse to a truth predicate—thus (using 'not' in the old-fashioned way as a connective):

For every proposition, either *thatt* or not *thatt.*

Or even

For every proposition, if John says that *thatt*, then *thatt.*

The analogy between quantificational uses of 'thatt' and bound propositional variables would parallel the familiar analogy between quantificational pronouns and bound individual variables. And we thereby solve the problem of reading Ramsey's propositional variables (without adding a truth predicate) not into English itself but at least into English + 'thatt'—with the further addition (as in the final form of the Ramsey language) of a variety of connectives answering to verb modifications. (We note that Prior [1971] takes the further step of introducing new expressions for the quantificational expressions as well as for the variables; instead of the still nominal quantificational phrase 'for every proposition' that we have [thus making 'thatt', we suppose, a prosentence in the wide sense], he has 'for everywhether' in analogy with 'everywhere', etc. We think the maneuver useful—see the remark in §2.2 of Chapter 2 [Grover 1972]—but suppress it in the interest of readability.)

A few things about our hypothetical generally available atomic prosentence are worth noting: First, 'thatt' is *never* a referring expression, whether used quantificationally or as a prosentence of laziness. When Mary says 'Thatt' in response to John's 'Snow is white', the prosentence behaves semantically like its antecedent. Because Mary is referring to snow just as John is, 'Thatt' functions sententially just as 'Snow is white' does. Second, in quantificational uses of pronouns, perhaps some sense can be given to questions like "What does 'it' *range over* in 'Whatever John wants, I want it too'?" Even here, though, there seems to be a rather quick assumption that any adequate semantics for quantificational pronouns in English would treat them as closely analogous to bound individual variables of formal domain-and-values quantification. But it is not at all easy to make intuitive sense of a question like "What does 'thatt' *range over* in 'Every proposition is such that either *thatt* or not *thatt*'?"— because 'thatt' always occupies a sentential position. The *instances* of this generalization are all things like 'Snow is white or not snow is white', 'Nixon is president or not Nixon is president', etc.; and although these instances are "about" things like snow and Nixon, surely *these* things cannot be what 'thatt' ranges over. Perhaps 'thatt' ranges over propositions, but how can that be so if the instances of the generalization aren't even about propositions? We won't pursue this further, but on the face of it, anyway, questions about what 'thatt' ranges over are misplaced, as are theories about ontological commitment that assume 'thatt' must "range over" something. Third, when Mary says 'Thatt' following John's 'Snow is white', she is repeating what he said in an obvious sense of 're-peat', but it would be a mistake to think her speech-act amounts to nothing more than just saying 'Snow is white' again. Mary isn't plagiarizing. Her choice of 'Thatt' as a way of asserting that snow is white has the interesting pragmatic property of *acknowledging* the presence of an antecedent. 'Thatt' would quite literally make no sense in the absence of an antecedent.

A last and crucial point: We believe that although English + 'thatt' is doubtless rather different from English *grammatically* (we shall emphasize this below), the addition of 'thatt' would not constitute a significant *conceptual* alteration of English. It is not like adding some new property-ascribing predicates or linguistic features that would allow us access to new domains of discourse or world views; rather, English + 'thatt' is conceptually the same as English. The difference is "merely" grammatical, and indeed as we have indirectly suggested in our account of anaphors, even the grammatical addition is in many respects (though not all) in the spirit of English grammar.

2.3. 'That Is True' and 'It Is True' as Prosentences

That takes care of 'thatt'. We return to a previous question and ask whether English itself contains any generally available prosentences—dropping now the requirement that they be atomic. And our answer is of course affirmative: 'That is true' and 'It is true' can be and should be thought of as anaphoric prosentences, just like 'thatt'. This claim contains several elements, the first and easiest of which involves checking the behavior of 'That is true' and 'It is true' against the criteria for prosentences.

The first requirement is satisfied because 'That is true' and 'It is true' clearly occupy sentential positions; furthermore, unlike 'so' and 'yes', they are generally available in that (roughly) they can occupy any such position.

For cases of the "repetition variety", the following holds: When 'That is true' or 'It is true' are used significantly, they are used in the context of some statement being made or considered. Further, as Austin (1950) and Strawson (1950a) recognized, 'That is true' and 'It is true' are usually thought to be intimately connected with the statement, or, as we prefer to put it, with the sentence used to express the statement. For instance:

> BILL: There are people on Mars. MARY: That is true.
> JOHN: Bill claims that there are people on Mars but I don't believe that it is true.

We claim 'There are people on Mars' can sensibly be regarded as the anaphoric antecedent of 'That is true' and 'it is true', and therefore as the sentence for which they are "standing in." Because this holds generally (i.e., for any declarative sentence and not just for the sentence 'There are people on Mars'), 'That is true' and 'It is true' are generic in the appropriate sense and can be thought of as prosentences of laziness. This account differs radically from the standard one, because on (what we have called) the subject-predicate account 'That' in 'That is true' is always treated separately as referring by itself to some bearer of truth, whether it be a sentence, proposition, or statement. On our account cross-referencing—without separate reference of 'that'—happens between the *whole* expression 'That is true' and its antecedent.

The only other feature of prosentences that needs checking is whether 'That is true' or 'It is true' can be used quantificationally. We have not found a case where 'That is true' is used quantificationally, but 'it is true' obviously can be so used, as in our earlier example

(4″) For each proposition, if John said that it is true, then it is true.

with instances like

(4*) If John said that Kate is a coward, then Kate is a coward.

Of course, there are many other examples.

Both 'That is true' and 'It is true' can be said to be prosentences for the following reasons: 'That is true' and 'It is true' occupy sentential positions: they are used anaphorically—both of them as prosentences of laziness and 'It is true' quantificationally—they are generic; and the notions of antecedent and anaphoric substituend are appropriate to them. (Following Prior [1971], we note that Wittgenstein [1953], though not of course using our terminology, was alert to the fact that certain sentences, including 'That is true', are used as prosentences; see Part I, 134–36.)

2.4. ENGLISH*

So some uses of 'It is true' and 'That is true' (to avoid duplication, henceforth we'll often just say 'That is true') are prosentential, but we are after bigger game than this. In the spirit of Ramsey, our claim is that all truth talk can be viewed as involving only prosentential uses of 'That is true'. In order to support this claim, we are going to have recourse to a second artificial language, but this time one that is a *fragment* of English instead of an extension like English + 'thatt'. English* is not to contain the truth predicate in any interesting sense, but English* *does* have the prosentences 'That is true' and 'It is true'; however, these are to be *treated as* atomic prosentences like 'thatt'. That is, the truth predicate will not be isolable: Sentences such as 'What Barbara said is true' do not belong to English*. And the verb 'is' in 'That is true' cannot be modified.

English* as so far (partially) defined will certainly not be able to accommodate all of English truth talk, in exact analogy to the deficiency of the Ramsey language with propositional quantifiers: Because English* does not permit us to tinker with the interior of prosentences, it needs some special connectives to get the effect of tensing, modalizing, and so on, in the modification cases—just like the Ramsey language. Because we want English* to be a proper fragment of English, we will not, however, allow ourselves to add some funny connective symbols; instead, we will draw from English itself such connectives as 'It was true that', 'It will be true that', 'It is possible that', 'It might be true that', 'It is necessary that', 'It is not true that', 'It is false that,' and so forth.

Upshot: In English* 'true' can only be used *either* in one of the prosentences 'That is true' or 'It is true' or in a connective employed in order to meet difficulties in connection with modification. With respect to the latter, we'll hyphenate (e.g., 'It-is-not-true-that') in order to reinforce our commitment to have the truth predicate non-isolable in English*.

Now we can sharply state a principal claim of our prosentential theory of truth: English can be translated without significant residue into its fragment English*. And a further claim is that such a translation is perspicuous and explanatory.

It should be pretty clear from our discussion of translation from English into the Ramsey language how English* paraphrases of truth locutions will go, but there are some nuances to be observed; so let us briefly gather together a sample of cases.

Some of the disappearing cases (§2.1) could be treated as in the translations into Ramsey by making the truth predicate disappear entirely, but the treatment of others can be *improved* in respect of explanatory power by invoking the prosentential features of English*. Consider

(25) It is true that snow is white, but it rarely looks white
     in Pittsburgh.

(26) That there have been cases when the IRA has been responsible for unwarrantedly brutal acts is true, but that none of their actions can be justified, is not true.

The usual reason for using a truth predicate in contexts like (25) and (26) is to explicitly grant a point, and then by means of a quick 'but,' go on to ask that not too much be made of the point. If the antecedent 'Snow is white' is obvious enough, one could just say

(27) That's true, but it rarely looks white in Pittsburgh.

instead of (25). We resort to the likes of (25) or (26) when the required antecedent is not at hand, or if it is at hand, because we think the audience needs to be reminded what it is. In English* we might get this effect by means of a complex speech act consisting of an explicit statement of the antecedent plus the I-grant-your-point bit, i.e., plus a prosentence. Thus

(25') Show is white. That is true, but it rarely looks white in Pittsburgh.

(26') There have been cases when the IRA has been responsible for unwarrantedly brutal acts. That is true, but it-is-not-true-that none of their actions can be justified.

Granting somebody's point is a very paradigm of prosentential talk. So we think it illuminates the pragmatics of (25) and (26) to think of them as English versions of the English* (25') and (26').

So much for the disappearing cases. The simple repetition cases are already in English* but we want to suggest that reflection upon English* deepens our understanding of these cases. When an English* speaker says, 'That is true' in response to 'Snow is white' as in the repetition case 3 above, his 'That' is not an independently referring pronoun, denoting the statement that snow is white, and his 'is true' is not a property-expressing predicate used to ascribe truth; it is a prosentence of laziness, anaphorizing to 'Snow is white' and thereby, on this occasion, meaning that snow is white. Of course this utterance of 'That is true' is not, as Ramsey may have supposed, literally replaceable by another utterance of 'Snow is white', because that would be plagiarism. 'That is true', like *all* anaphoric expressions, needs an antecedent, and its use acknowledges that an antecedent is there to be had.

Translation of quantificational cases is straightforward but not without interest. For example:

(4) Everything John says is true

gets read into English* as

(4") For each proposition, if John said that it is true, then
it is true.

It is understood that on the prosentential account the instances of
(4") in English* are *not* such as

If John said that that snow is white is true, then that snow
is white is true.

which construes the 'it' as the anaphor (a pronoun); rather, its instances are such sentences as

If John said that snow is white, then snow is white.

which takes 'it is true' as the anaphor (a prosentence) and 'snow is
white' as an anaphoric substituend.
   In order to get the effect of the indirect reference in

(9) Goldbach's conjecture is true.

in English*, we need to invoke a connective like 'that _____ is-the-
same-conjecture-as-that _____ ,' which we abbreviate by '⇔', and we
also need some device to keep straight the cross-referencing of our
quantificational prosentences, on pain of syntactical ambiguity.
Perhaps we should have an infinite stock of prosentences 'It is true',
'It is true$_1$', . . . paralleling the infinite stock of distinct propositional variables in the Ramsey language, plus a bunch of quantifying expressions with subscripts (for instance). Then we would say

(9") There is a proposition$_1$ such that Goldbach conjectured that it is true$_1$, and for every proposition$_2$ if
Goldbach conjectured that it is true$_2$ then it is true$_1$ ⇔
it is true$_2$, and it is true$_1$.

That's messy, but the idea is obvious enough.
   We remark that adding these additional prosentences extends English* but that nothing is going on here that is not already necessary
for reading ordinary first-order quantifications into English. That is,
unvoiced opinion to the contrary notwithstanding, we point out
that no one has ever provided a thorough translation of first-order
quantification into English *as it is*, as opposed to English with a
denumerable family of distinct pronouns and quantifiers.
   Last, we translate the various modification cases by utilizing the
various connectives provided for this purpose. For example:

That's not true (or: That's false).

goes into

It-is-not-true-that that is true (or: It-is-false-that that is true).

which, though awkward, has the merit of suggesting that the point of 'It's false' in English is not primarily to describe or characterize but rather to provide us with a way of asserting the contradictory of any given sentence, and with anaphoric overtones when we want them. This analysis, incidentally, ties in with Strawson's (1950a) observation that we tend to use 'not true' rather than 'false'; our explanation is that the former is closer to the prosentence 'That is true'.

If we consider an example of tensing such as

That was true.

we run into the difficulty that

It-was-true-that that is true.

is not grammatical English; the interior sentence must also be past tensed. The same does not hold for the future:

That will be true.

can grammatically go into

It-will-be-true-that that is true.

We think this rule of English not worth bothering about and continue to think of English* as a fragment of English. (Alternatively, we could complicate our description of English* by adding 'That was true' as a prosentence to be used only in certain contexts; namely, contexts requiring the past tense because of an already present past tense, so that the 'was' would have no semantic force whatsoever.)

The upshot is that ordinary English truth talk can be thought of as prosentential precisely as English* truth talk is prosentential. But in English we have different conventions for achieving the effects that we achieved in English* by combining prosentences with connectives. In English we are permitted to rewrite the interior of our prosentences in order to get the effect of tensing, modalizing, negating, and so on. Instead of the English* 'It-might-be-true-that that's true', we can say 'That *might be* true'. And instead of the

English* 'It-is-false-that that is true', we can say 'That is false'—in this case rewriting the 'true' part of 'That is true' instead of the 'is' part. Finally, English permits us to form elliptical and other "shorthand" locutions like 'Everything John says is true' instead of the full-blown "Everything (or 'Every proposition') is such that if John says that it is true then it is true." But aside from these grammatical differences, English truth talk is just like English* truth talk.

So English truth talk is semantically and pragmatically like English* truth talk. The two languages have different grammatical conventions, but in English, as in English*, the truth predicate does not play a property-ascribing role. Truth, to coin a phrase, isn't a real predicate.

2.5. 'TRUE' IN CONNECTIVES

The reader will have noticed a certain tension in our argument: On the one hand we characterize ourselves as offering a prosentential theory of truth, while on the other we keep honest by noting that English* 'true' is allowed not only in prosentences but also in connectives. In fact we think we can by and large both have and eat our cake by explaining these connective uses of 'true' without, however, explaining them away. There are two quite different contexts in which the connectives crop up: when the argument of the connective is a prosentence, and when it is not.

The first sort emerges from the modified quantificational cases like (15), or a modified indirect reference case, or a modified repetition case like

(13) JOHN: Rome is the center of the known world.
    BILL: That's not true, but it used to be true.

which we treat as a paradigm for all. (13) of course goes into English as

(13″) JOHN: Rome is the center of the known world.
    BILL: It-it-not-true-that that is true, but it-used-to-be-true-that that is (was) true.

Here we argue that the *extra* 'true' in the connectives is from a philosophical point of view redundant, as can be seen from the following consideration: English* would have been equally illuminating for these cases had we allowed (13) as it stands to be part of English*, with the proviso that its grammar, its "deep structure," is to be understood in terms of modified prosentences. That is, we might have allowed 'that is not true', 'it used to be true', and other cases of modified prosentences as already in English*, with the understanding that their "form" is, in sort of MIT lingo, PRO + MOD; just as MIT treats 'liked' as 'like + PAST'. (We remark in passing that there are complexities here, as nearly everywhere in linguistics; e.g., 'That was true' is sometimes to be understood *de dicto* as in 'The president is a Texan—that was true, but . . .' and sometimes to be understood *de re* as in 'The president is in California—that was true, but . . .'.) From the point of view of these cases, then, our only reason for putting connectives in English* was to allow ourselves to naively let deep structure appear on the surface.

Cases in which the argument of the connective is a proper sentence get a somewhat different treatment, and indeed these cases divide into two. In the first place there are the simple modified disappearing cases like

> It-is-not-true-that Rome is the center of the known world, but it-used-to-be-true-that Rome is (was) the center of the known world.

Here we think that the work of 'true' is to be semantically redundant while providing pragmatic punch by way of anaphoric overtones, as in our treatment above of the unmodified disappearing and repetition cases; consequently, though we make no effort to rid ourselves of 'true' in these connectives in these cases, we think the spirit remains prosentential. And although 'true' is irredundant in such cases, this should not be taken as implying that it functions ascriptively (see §4.9).

In the second place, we think—perhaps 'conjecture' would be more accurate—that there are cases falling under the rubric 'modified disappearing' in which there is no way to eliminate 'true' without semantic loss. Example: By the *contradictory* of a sentence we mean one that has exactly the opposite truth conditions; and we conjecture that there are in English sentences for which one cannot find an unambiguous contradictory without using a connective made from a predicate, such as 'it is not true that'. Whether or not one agrees that this is so depends heavily on the rest of one's views on English; e.g., depending on one's theory of indicative or subjunctive conditionals, it will or will not be easy to find contradictories for 'If the switch is up, then the light is on' or 'If Mary were to leave him, then Paul would expire'. Or the contradictories of various sentences on this page. Let us assume, however, that our conjecture is correct; we then have the task of explaining why the same 'true' that crops up in prosentences is also required to form connectives that, while at least apparently not performing any prosentential or quasi-prosentential role, seem to be essential in forming the contradictory (for example) of certain recalcitrant sentences. The best we can do as of this writing is to tell a story: In the beginning there were prosentences, and the people in those days used them in a lazy way, even in a modified lazy way, and some amongst them in redundant connectives in a modified disappearing way when they wished to endow their speech with prosentential overtones. Soon it came to pass that they saw the utility of these conventions and transferred them to cases in which their use was not redundant; and so it is unto this very day.

2.6. ENGLISH AND ENGLISH*

If (as we claim) English* can do everything English can, and more perspicuously at that, why is English English and not English*? Precisely, why are the prosentences of English *not* atomic as in English + 'thatt' but rather grammatically decomposable into a subject and predicate, and why in English is 'true' allowed outside of connectives and prosentences?

Our short answer is that English loves the noun-plus-verb-phrase (or N + VP, as MIT says) construction, and that vast numbers of its grammatical features cater to this love. For example, modal, tense, and other changes in an English sentence are typically made by some modification of the verb; e.g., the change from 'There are people on Mars' to 'There might be people on Mars'. An advantage of decomposable prosentences is that their verbs, like those of other sentences, are accessible to modification, so that changes can be made in prosentences in the standard manner:

> That might be true.

In contrast (as we have already indicated), if prosentences are not decomposable, then connectives must be included in English to do the jobs (e.g., modalization) usually done in English by verb modification:

> 'It-might-be-true-that that is true', or 'Maybe that is true'.

A special case of this arises when a prosentence is used to ask a question as in

> MARY: Snow is white. ANN: Is that true?

The change from the prosentence 'That is true' to 'Is that true' exactly mirrors the change from 'Snow is white' to 'Is snow white' which is, roughly, another way of asking the same question. Had there been available only atomic prosentences, then 'Is that true?' would have had to be rendered as the composition of a prosentence plus a functor that takes as input a declarative sentence and yields as output a yes-no question. So, given the way we do things in English, the subject-predicate structure of 'That is true' provides great flexibility.

Similarly, because there is a separable truth predicate, we can, when we wish to agree with all that someone else has said, use an already available nominalization (e.g., 'what John said') and then restore the sentential character of what is said by means of the innocuous truth predicate, giving

What John said is true.

which after all is much less clumsy than the English*

For each proposition if John said that it is true then it is true.

Such use of the truth predicate to take us from a nominalization to a sentence without semantic addition is further discussed in Belnap (1974).

So we are delighted to be speakers of English rather than English*, treasuring exceedingly the easy grammatical availability of 'true'; but let us not be blinded by "mere" grammar.

3. Prosentential Theory: Objections

It seems to us that the prosentential theory is of some philosophical interest and we shall try to explain where this interest lies. But first we need to consider some complaints our theory will doubtless have to face.

3.1. NONOBJECTIONS

Though we are supposed to be dealing with objections, it seems worthwhile to lead off by briefly considering how our theory avoids certain objections that we raised against the Ramsey theory.

INDEXICALS

Because our translation of the repetition cases leaves them as they were, there is simply no basis for a comparable objection. But the problem is relocated into the semantics of the fragment English* of English: When John says, 'I am greedy' and Mary replies, 'That is true', as in the indexical repetition case (14), Mary's remark does not—as we've already noted—mean that *she* is greedy. The semantics for English* will need rules governing this use of prosentences, rules specifying how 'That is true' can make the same assertion as 'You are greedy' when its antecedent is 'I am greedy'. The simple-minded formula "Prosentences of laziness assert what their antecedents assert" has to be refined, because in one sense Mary is asserting what John asserted, while in another sense she isn't. And we note the *advantage* of this relocation: The problem is one for the semantics of proforms *generally* and is in no way specific to prosentences or truth talk; e.g., there is the same or a similar problem with respect to the anaphoric 'he' in

> JOHN: My son has a wart on his nose. BILL: He is the image of his father.

or 'it' in

> LUCILLE: You dance well. FRED: It's news to me.

MODIFICATION

We have already supplied English* with some connectives to handle the verb modification problem, so again there is no basis for an objection unless it is felt that some of our connectives are strained or un-English, or that we leave unanswered just which connectives are needed. We certainly agree with the spirit of the last part of the objection but doubt that it affects our proposal to see truth talk in a new light. For example, if it is objected that "the same conjecture" connective ($\Leftrightarrow$) of (9") awaits explanation, we hasten to agree but add that those who set themselves the task of analyzing language must also account for such usage. Our claim is that truth doesn't complicate the issue: We believe that we can incorporate within the prosentential theory any account of such expressions which is thoroughly adequate for the rest of English without the truth predicate.

ABOUTNESS

Our response to this objection was given in §1.2 above.

PRAGMATICS

We take it that the prosentential account gets the pragmatics right as the Ramsey translations do not, especially with respect to what we have dubbed 'plagiarism'.

WHAT PRICE REDUNDANCY?

Not for a minute have we tried to show that 'true' is redundant; in fact we have continually urged the importance of the anaphoric role of *prosentences* involving 'true'. On the other hand, we have argued the redundancy of a *separable* truth predicate, but because English* is a proper fragment of English, it cannot be objected, as it was to Ramsey, that we have *added* something to English in order to make the separable truth predicate redundant. We'll return to the question of redundancy in §4.9.

GRAMMAR

Because English* is a fragment of English, no objection comparable to the alleged ungrammaticality of propositional quantifiers can get off the ground, though of course we think that objection is anyhow unsound.

3.2. Quotation

To turn now to real objections, probably the most obvious line of attack on our theory is that it ignores cases where we predicate truth of named sentences, e.g., quoted sentences. *Surely* truth is being ascribed in a perfectly straightforward way in a statement like

(28) 'Snow is white' is true.

We could take a Ramseyish stance here and insist that (28) means that snow is white. But again it seems to us that this obscures certain rather important pragmatic features of the case. These features are more obvious when a foreign language sentence is under consideration, so imagine that a German representative has said, 'Schnee ist weiss' in the course of some debate, and during a later discussion of the debate we say,

(29) If 'Schnee ist weiss' is true, then . . .

Why (29) instead of

If it's true that snow is white, then . . .

or

If snow is white, then . . .

There are several possible reasons. By quoting the German sentence, we make it quite clear that it is the German representative's claim that we're entertaining. Or if no elegant translation is available, quoting might enable us to preserve the original character of the remark. And similarly, if no elegant translation is available, or even if there is one but we're not sure what it is, by quoting we can consider what was said without worrying about a translation. Or ignorant of German grammar, we might resort to saying, " 'Schnee ist weiss' *must* be true; after all, Fritz has said so", because we know how to modalize the verb in 'is true' but we don't know how to modalize the verb in 'Schnee ist weiss'.

These pragmatic aspects of the use of quotation cum truth predicate suggest, as a first approximation, an account along the following lines: Suppose English* has a display-former 'Consider: _____'. One displays or exhibits a sentence by writing, say, 'Consider: Snow is white'. We think English*-speakers could get the pragmatic effects of quoting and saying 'is true' by performing the complex speech-act of uttering

(30) Consider: Snow is white. That is true.

Why not think of " 'Snow is white' is true", in English, as working just like (30) in English*? Maybe one reason not to think of it this way is that quotation is generally taken as involving *reference* to sentences or other expressions; quotes are name-forming functors. Our suggestion departs from this tradition. Of course we're talking here about quotation as used in ordinary English, not quotation as used in some formal or quasi-formal language. Maybe quotation in ordinary English should *not* be thought of as a matter of referring to expressions. We don't want to push this any harder now. It's food for thought, anyway.

A final morsel: Though we can understand and have accounted for (28) and (29), we doubt that sentences such as these are ever used in ordinary English, an absence possibly explained by their point-lessness in the context of the flexibility of our language. With respect to (28), a philosopher's insistence that the German sentence be quoted probably derives from a false belief that speakers of English can only mention but never use German sentences as part of their discourse. But as a matter of descriptive fact, this is not an accurate account of fluent English: We do not have such restrictions on the usage of sentences belonging to other languages, although, of course, if it is not expected that the audience will understand the sentence in question, then a translation should usually be provided. So in our German representative case, if we want either to preserve the character of the remarks, or if we haven't an easy translation, then what we do is say,

If schnee ist weiss, then . . .

or, if we want to be more careful about acknowledging an antecedent, we say

If it's true that schnee ist weiss, then . . .

thus providing a problem for semanticists.

3.3. Tunnel Vision

Do we like the prosentence account of truth because we suffer from tunnel vision? The charge goes like this: The suggestion that 'That is true' and 'It is true' function prosententially looks fine so long as you pay no attention to other, grammatically similar locutions. But if you *do* look at a somewhat broader slice of English, you'll notice usages like the following:

(31) JOHN: There are seven-legged dogs.
     MARY: That's surprising, but it's true.

(32) JOHN: The being of knowing is the knowing of being.
     MARY: That's profound, and it's true.

Take (31), for instance. Surely it is obvious that the first conjunct of Mary's reply, 'That's surprising', is in no way prosentential. It is a *characterization*, an ascription of the property *being surprising* to what John said. The same goes for 'That's profound' in (31). The proper analysis of 'That's profound' would treat the pronoun as referring demonstratively to John's statement, while 'is profound' expresses a property Mary intends to ascribe to that statement. Now wouldn't it be simpler to treat 'It is true' the same way? Why construe 'It is true' as a prosentence when the proper construal of other analogous locutions involves pronouns like 'it' and 'that' referring to statements or propositions, and properties being ascribed to such things? If one motivation for the prosentence account of truth is to avoid having our truth talk commit us to the existence of propositions as "bearers of truth," surely that motivation is undercut by the fact that we need to analyze 'that' in 'That is surprising' as referring to a proposition (or something proposition-like, such as a statement in the what-is-said sense of statement). Our talk is full of demonstrative pronominal reference to things other people say. Why complicate matters by treating 'That's true' and 'It is true' differently? Several things need to be said in reply to this charge. First of all, it simply isn't true that the pronouns in 'That's surprising' and 'That's profound' refer to statements in the what-is-stated, or "propositional content" sense of statement. What kind of thing is surprising? Facts, presumably, or events or states of affairs. The fact that John visited us was surprising, John's visit was surprising. Statements or assertions can be surprising, but only in the act, as opposed to the object, sense of statement, or assertion—statings or assertings. One can say, 'That there are seven-legged dogs is surprising', but only because this can mean that the fact that there are seven-legged dogs is surprising. And one can say, 'What he is saying is surprising', but only because this can mean that the fact he is reporting is a surprising one, or else that the fact that he is saying what he is saying is surprising. In (30) what is said to be surprising is the fact that there are seven-legged dogs. But the fact that there are seven-legged dogs is not what is said to be true (on the assumption that 'it' in 'it's true' refers to something being described as 'true'). The fact that there are seven-legged dogs, the state of affairs of *there being seven-legged dogs*, cannot be "true".

And propositions are not profound. Certain kinds of *acts* can be profound—insights or thoughts, for instance. Sta*tings* that formulate profound thoughts or insights can be profound, so in the *act* sense of statement there are profound statements. But statements in the *act* sense are not what are supposed to be true. The upshot of all this is that even if we construe both pronouns in 'That's surprising, but it's true' (for instance) as referring, they must refer to different things. One can make it appear that they refer to the same thing by noting that each can be replaced by some expression like 'that there are seven-legged dogs', but this is so precisely because the expression in question is ambiguous between 'the fact that there are seven-legged dogs' and 'the proposition that there are seven-legged dogs'. So a theory that treats both 'That' and 'it' in 'That's surprising, but it's true' as referring demonstratively is not as neat and economical as it first appears. Moreover, because the things that are surprising or profound are not the same as the things that are (supposedly) true, it has not been shown that reference to propositional contents is involved in 'That's surprising' and the like, and the lets-get-rid-of-reference-to-propositions motivation for construing 'It is true' prosententially has not been touched.

Perhaps there are other locutions where it *is* plausible to claim a pronoun is used to refer to a proposition. Consider

(33) JOHN: Some dogs eat glass. BILL: I believe it.
     MARY: You believe it, but it's not true.

It is arguable that propositions, the very entities usually taken to be bearers of truth, are the objects of belief. We are not at all sure about this, but for now we are prepared to grant that *if* 'it' in 'You believe it' is construed as a separately referring pronoun, its referent will have to be a proposition. And consequently, given the desire to treat the two occurrences of 'it' in Mary's statement as coordinate, we have the makings of an objection to our theory. But why can't we give a very different account of 'You believe it'? We suggested above that 'It is false' works like a prosentence prefixed by a negation connective, like the English* 'It-is-not-the-case-that it is true', so that the semantical connection between an utterance of 'It is false' and the statement denied is one of prosentential anaphora, not pronominal reference. We are inclined to think a parallel treatment can be given for sentences like 'You believe it'; the idea is that it works like a prosentence prefixed by a non-truth-functional connective— i.e., works like 'You-believe-that it is true', so that the semantical connection between the utterance and its antecedent statement is again prosentential anaphora, not pronominal reference. English permits us to use a special predicative phrase ('is false' in 'It is false' or 'You believe' in 'You believe it') instead of a special connective and an untouchable prosentence in the style of English* ('It-is-not-true-that it is true', 'You-believe-that it is true'). The English grammatical convention is doubtless motivated by considerations of convenience and flexibility. But the crucial point is that in neither 'It is false' nor 'You believe it' need 'it' be analyzed semantically into a referring pronominal subject with a predicate expressing a property that the speaker means to ascribe to the referent. We cannot consider all the ramifications of this approach now (see also

Prior 1971), but it seems plausible. If it is plausible, then we still have no reason to think pronominal references to propositions is a commonplace in ordinary English, or even that they happen at all.

There is another sort of "tunnel vision" with which we might be charged; namely, we haven't associated 'That's true' with 'That's right' and we haven't contrasted it in an Austinian way with 'That's exaggerated' and its cousins. A child is counting blocks on the floor and eventually looks up and says,

> I have fifteen blocks.

You remark

> That is right.

One might comment that you could just as well have said, 'That is true'. Should expressions like 'That is right' and 'That is an exaggeration' be prosentential? But isn't the point of saying 'That is right' to remark on the fact that the child has counted correctly, that something has been well done? On some occasions you can of course do this by saying, 'That is true'—in agreeing, you applaud—and to this extent there is considerable overlap. Unlike Austin (1950), we think, however, that even though sometimes one locution appears to do as well as the other, 'That is exaggerated' and 'That is right' are crucially different from 'That is true', because the point of each is different. Expressions like 'exaggerated' and 'right' fit where certain skills and techniques are in question, for example, counting or possibly language skills. When you draw a peninsula longer than it should be, we say your map exaggerates certain features, and when a child learning language says 'cow' when pointing to a cow we can say the child got the word right. But because there is no clear line to be drawn between the learning of language and simply using it, there must be tremendous overlap between 'That is right' and 'That is true'.

3.4. 'THAT' AS THE ANAPHOR

Can't you do everything you want, it might be objected, by taking 'That' in 'That is true' as the anaphor? Surely this would, at the very least, simplify the work of your colleagues the linguists. In replying to this objection, a distinction has to be made: Does or does not taking 'That' separately as an anaphor commit us to taking it as referring, presumably to a proposition, statement, or sentence, and to taking the separable 'is true' as characterizing? Suppose first it does; then we certainly could not accomplish our objectives, one of the principal ones being the demonstration that truth talk is wholly intelligible without truth bearers or truth characteristics. Of course, this is not to argue against the truth-bearer cum truth-characteristic theory or against the theory that 'That' in 'That's true' refers; such a discussion is well beyond the scope of a paper devoted to the presentation of an alternate theory.

Suppose, however, we entertain the possibility of viewing 'That' in 'That's true' as the anaphor but without commitment to a referential construal of 'That' or a characterizing construal of 'is true'; after all, it has often enough been argued that other nominal constructions are non-referring and other predications non-characterizing. Such a theory, we think, might well be viable; it might even explain how the philosophical thrust of our prosentential theory harmonizes with the linguistic details of English grammar. But we suspect it will not be easy to state such a theory clearly, and that even if it is stated the prosentential theory will be useful in rendering it intelligible. In any event further judgment on such a theory must await its appearance.

4. Consequences and Applications

So much for objections; now it is time to look at the philosophical payoff we've been promising.

4.1. Pragmatics

As we argued in the course of discussing the disappearing and repetition cases in the context of English*, the prosentential theory of truth helps explain many of the pragmatic features of our use of 'is true'. We've already harped on this a good deal—we've claimed, for instance, that the absence of plagiarism on John's part in the exchange

(3) MARY: Snow is white. JOHN: That's true.

can be understood if we view 'That's true' as a prosentence of laziness that has to anaphorize to an antecedent; and our treatment of (25) and (26) via (25') and (26') offers further illustrations.

Strawson (1950a) has drawn attention to such uses of the truth predicate as granting a point ('That's true, but . . .'), considering a point ('If that is true, . . .'), expressing agreement, and so on. Our construal of truth talk as prosentential helps explain why 'is true' does all these jobs so well. We repeat: In using a proform, one makes it explicit that nothing new is going on, that (in the case of pronouns) one is not talking about anything new, and that (in the case of prosentences) one is not articulating anything new; anaphoric prosentences must have antecedents, so using a prosentence of laziness inevitably involves acknowledging an antecedent—the core pragmatic feature of granting points, expressing agreement, and so on. Speaking of Strawson, in the course of criticizing Austin's views on truth, he remarks (1950a, p. 81), "It is of prime importance to distinguish the fact that the use of 'true' always glances backwards and forwards to the actual or envisioned making of a statement by someone, from the theory that it is needed to characterize such (actual or possible) episodes." We concur, and our conception of truth talk as prosentential provides precisely the framework needed to make Strawson's point stick, for every proform glances. Furthermore, our theory even accounts for endemic failure to make the distinction Strawson urges is of "prime importance": Reference can involve either (or both) anaphoric reference or independent reference, and because people have not seriously considered the former, the possibility that the relation between 'That is true' and its antecedent may be that of anaphoric reference has not occurred to them. In ignoring anaphoric reference, philosophers have assumed that the reference involved in 'That is true' is, through 'That', like that between a pronoun (say 'she', used independently) and its referent (say Mary). Once this picture dominates, the need for bearers of truth begins to be felt; and it is then but a small step to the claim that in using 'is true' we are characterizing these entities.

4.2. 'That' as a Prosentence

Given an account of English which includes the grammatical category of prosentences, one might find it useful to look at certain exceptional uses of words or phrases in terms of prosentences. Whereas, for example, 'that' is generally used as either an anaphoric pronoun or an independently referring pronoun, it might be that sometimes it is used prosententially, as the following example suggests:

(34) JOHN: Give me an example of a truism.
MARY: Right is right.
JOHN (to Fred): Give me an example of a truism.
FRED (nodding toward Mary): That.

The problems raised by Fred's use of 'That' in (34) are a bit tricky. It seems to us that there are two semantical approaches available, neither of which treats 'That' as an independently referring pronoun. We might view Fred's remark as elliptical for 'That is a truism', and view this on analogy with 'You believe it', as tantamount to a prosentence prefixed by a connective—'It-is-a-truism-that that is true', where the prosentential fragment 'that is true' anaphorizes to Mary's utterance of 'Right is right'. But this approach has a serious drawback, a drawback shared by the account that construes Fred's utterance of 'That' as elliptical for 'That is a truism' or 'That is an example of a truism', where the pronoun is taken as referring independently to Mary's remark. To say that Fred's utterance of 'That' is elliptical for some such statement as 'That is a truism' is to say that Fred is *asserting* something, but he isn't. He is doing what he was asked to do—giving an example of a truism. If that isn't clear, suppose John had told Fred to give an example of a truism but not to make any assertions. Even in that case, Fred would have done what he was told to do by saying 'That', with an appropriate indication of Mary's remark.

Perhaps the best account, in view of this pragmatic feature of the case, is to construe Fred's 'That' as a prosentence that gets its semantical content from its anaphoric antecedent (Mary's 'Right is right'), but which does not have assertional force. What Fred does is *like* repeating Mary's speech act, but without plagiarizing. Mary "displayed" the sentence 'Right is right' in order to give an example of a truism. By saying 'That' and indicating Mary's speech act via Mary, Fred achieves the effect of displaying 'Right is right' himself, but his use of a prosentence rather than simple repetition of Mary's performance acknowledges the fact that she was there first.

This raises some interesting questions, which we can only touch upon here. Fred's prosentential use of 'That' carries its antecedent's semantical content but adds no assertional force of its own: Mary's utterance of 'Right is right' was not an assertion that right is right, and neither was Fred's utterance of 'That'. Is it generally true of prosentences that they borrow, anaphorically, the meaning or semantical content of their antecedents *and* the illocutionary force of their antecedents as well? Perhaps prosentences depend upon their contextual antecedents for meaning and illocutionary force. Although (34) supports this view, other examples do not. Consider

MARY (arguing with somebody): Right is right.
JOHN (to Fred): Give me an example of a truism.
FRED (indicating Mary): That.

Mary *asserts* that right is right, and Fred uses her assertion as anaphoric antecedent for his "display" of a truism, but although Mary's
remark has assertional force, Fred's does not. Or consider

> JOHN: Give me an example of an asinine statement.
> FRED: Whales aren't fish. JOHN: But that's true.

In this case John's prosentential utterance, 'That's true', has assertional force—he is asserting that whales aren't fish—although its
antecedent does not. Perhaps the prosentence 'That's true' always
has assertional force, while 'That', used prosententially, never does.
But this terrain obviously needs further exploration.

4.3. PROPOSITIONAL VARIABLES

We can now return to our account of the grammar of bound propositional variables that in the Ramsey language occupy sentential positions. We shall argue that such variables have a prosentential
character, and from this fact it becomes obvious that they should
not have a truth predicate attached to them. Thus we'll finally answer the question raised long ago as to whether Ramsey's language
must for grammatical reasons contain a truth predicate. The points
are briefly presented because the topic has already been treated in
detail in Chapter 2 (Grover 1972). Our strategy, of course, will be to
show how formulas containing bound occurrences of propositional
variables can be read into English*—a fragment of English where
there isn't a separable truth predicate.

> (4′) $\forall p$(if John says that p then p)

comes over into English* as

> (4″) For each proposition, if John says that it is true, then
>   it is true.

It should be clear from this sort of case that propositional variables
and quantificational prosentences do similar jobs: They occupy sentential positions and they do the cross-referencing required of them.
Thus quantificational prosentences can be used in place of bound
propositional variables in the same way that pronouns can be used
for bound individual variables, and vice versa. Propositional variables have, so to speak, a prosentential character. But notice that
(4″) is *precisely* "the obvious candidate" for an English translation
of (4′) that we suggested (in §1.2) might seduce somebody into
thinking the Ramsey language needs a truth predicate—as in

(4‴) ∀p(John said that $Tp \rightarrow Tp$)

But (4″) is a perfectly acceptable reading of (4′) into English, and what is more important, a reading into English* (where 'true' occurs only in connectives and prosentences). So there is no basis at all for the claim that (4″) reintroduces a truth predicate or contains a separately bound nominal 'it', or in any other way suggests that we need a truth predicate in the formal language; (4‴) is chasing the wrong point.

4.4. Propositions

According to one realist tradition, we cannot have an adequate philosophical understanding of the world without recognizing that there are *propositions*—propositional contents of statements, beliefs and the like. Perhaps the most persuasive line of argument available to the realist goes like this: Any acceptable semantical theory for English will have to postulate a range of abstract entities to serve as bearers of truth, objects of belief, and so on. Though certain details may differ from theory to theory, the general semantical treatment of such sentences as 'That snow is white is true' or 'Charley believes that snow is white' will construe the former as an ascription of truth to the proposition that snow is white, and the latter as expressing a relation between Charley and the proposition that snow is white. But what is expressed by (e.g.) 'That snow is white is true' is true, so there must *be* such a thing as the proposition that snow is white.

Now we have proposed a semantical treatment of English truth talk that never construes *any* sentences involving 'true' as involving reference to a proposition, or anything of the sort. Does this give us a way of replying to the realist, a way of undercutting his argument, by showing that at least one adequate semantics for English does not have to employ propositions as objects of reference in truth talk? We really aren't sure, but we'll make some tentative suggestions.

Even if our semantics for locutions about truth makes no use of reference to propositions, there is still the matter of belief-sentences and other psychological attitudes. Perhaps any acceptable semantics for English will have to analyze 'Charley believes that snow is white' as expressing a relation between Charley and a proposition, and perhaps not. There are other possibilities—we suggested a certain line in our reply to the tunnel vision objection

(§3.3), or one might try an adverbial theory, for instance, construing 'that snow is white' as a complex adverb modifying a one-place verb 'believes', rather than as a complex nominal expression referring to a proposition. We cannot take a stand on such matters now (obviously), but suppose something like an adverbial theory *is* a viable alternative to the more traditional reference-to-proposition account. Suppose, that is, that our semantics need not introduce propositions to handle *singular* belief-sentences (or wanting-sentences, or . . .). Supposing all that—and it is a lot to suppose—have we got the realist boxed in?

Perhaps one can never do that, but one virtue of the prosentential account of truth is that *generalization* about belief and other propositional attitudes need not force us to introduce propositions into our semantical theory as objects of reference if they aren't already required by the semantics of simpler sentences. As an example, consider

(35) Everything is such that if Charley believes that it is true, then it is true.

If 'it is true' in (35) is viewed as a quantificational prosentence rather than a combination of quantificational pronoun and truth predicate, there should be no temptation to think of English sentences like (35) as analogous to first-order quantifications with individual variables ranging over propositions. It is more nearly analogous to the propositional quantification of a Ramsey language, with variables in the grammatical category of sentences. Of course, it still might happen that a semantical treatment of (35) somehow requires appeal to a domain of propositions, but we rather like the prospects of a semantics that construes (35) as, in effect, a substitutional quantification, where the truth of (35) is equivalent to the truth of all its substitution-instances ('If Charley believes that snow is white, then snow is white', etc.). So if reference to propositions doesn't happen at the level of singular belief sentences, there is no reason to think commitment to propositions somehow emerges for the first time at the level of generalizations like (35).

Although we take it to be a merit of the prosentential theory that it renders unnecessary the postulation of propositions for one of the usual reasons, we should point out that some abstract entities may need to be introduced somewhere along the line—not to account for the truth predicate but to account for general language usage. For example, we wonder if it will be possible to provide a general theory of the anaphora relation without employing the notion of a propositional content. According to us, when somebody says, 'Snow is white' and you say, 'That's true', your utterance gets its *content*, its *meaning* from its anaphoric antecedent. We leave open the question of whether that rough-and-ready characterization of what is going on in such cases can be made precise and comprehensive without appeal to some reification of the content or meaning of utterances. In such a case, we would claim an illuminating relocation of the problem of propositions.

4.5. Semantic Ascent and All That

Quine (1970, p. 11) has argued that a truth predicate is needed to obtain generality: "We can generalize on 'Tom is mortal', 'Dick is mortal', and so on without talking of truth or of sentences; we can say 'All men are mortal'. . . . When on the other hand we want to generalize on 'Tom is mortal or Tom is not mortal', 'Snow is white or snow is not white', and so on, we ascend to talk of truth and of sentences. . . ." Quine is right about this. We use the truth predicate to generalize, as in 'For every proposition, either it is true or it is not true'. But we disagree that such generalization requires reference to, or quantification over, sentences or propositions, or that it involves a characterizing or property-ascribing use of the truth predicate. We think 'It is true' functions as a quantificational prosentence. We can tell because the generalization is available already in the truth-predicate-free fragment English* as 'For every proposition, either it is true or it-is-not-true-that it is true'. In this generalization 'is true' has a double role: First, it (or some cousin) appears to be needed in order to form a connective 'It-is-not-true-that' which can exhibit the common form of those sentences on which Quine wishes to generalize, and second 'It is true' functions as a quantificational prosentence, anaphorizing to the quantificational expression 'for every proposition'. So we thoroughly agree with Quine that in English the word 'true' (or some cousin) is required for generalizing and the prosentential theory explains why; but we do not think there is anything going on here that should be called semantic ascent.

A related point: Field (1972) suggests that the "original purpose" of the notion of truth was to aid us in utilizing the utterances of others in drawing conclusions about the world. In order to make such inferences, we have to have a pretty good grasp of (i) the circumstances under which what another says is likely to be true, and (ii) how to get from a belief in the truth of what he says to a belief about the extralinguistic world. Again we agree. But again none of this demands an ascriptive use of 'is true'. Suppose we decide that Charley's assertion that there was a foot of snow in Alabama is true, and we infer that there was a foot of snow in Alabama. And for simplicity, suppose our bounds for thinking Charley is telling the truth is that everything Charley asserts under conditions C is true, and these conditions obtain. It might seem that we have here a paradigm of semantic *des*cent, a "trans-level" inference from the *truth* of the proposition that there was a foot of snow in Alabama, or the truth of the sentence 'There was a foot of snow in Alabama', to the conclusion that there was a foot of snow in Alabama. For instance we might inspect the preliminary reasoning

(36) That there was a foot of snow in Alabama was asserted by Charley in conditions C.

(37) Every proposition is such that if Charley asserts it in conditions C, then it is true.

(38) That there was a foot of snow in Alabama is true

and figure it was a valid bit of argument because the expression 'that there was a foot of snow in Alabama' in (36) and (37) works like a canonical name for a proposition, while (38) has the force of quantification over propositions, with the 'it' functioning as a quantificational pronoun. Once we take this line, the further move from (38) to a non-semantical remark about snow in Alabama obviously has to be licensed by some principle that says you're entitled to assert that it possesses truth.

But we think the logic of the situation is better represented by the following pattern of reasoning:

(36') Charley asserted in conditions C that there was a foot of snow in Alabama.

(37') Every proposition is such that if Charley asserted in conditions C that it is true, then it is true.

(38') There was a foot of snow in Alabama.

'It is true' in (37') functions as a quantificational prosentence, bound by the initial 'Every proposition is such that'. The reasoning is valid because something like universal instantiation on (37') is valid, yielding 'If Charley asserted in condition C that there was a foot of snow in Alabama, then there was a foot of snow in Alabama'. From this and (36') we detach (38'). It does not seem to us that either of these moves qualifies as a trans-level inference in any philosophically exciting sense.

4.6. PHYSICALISM

Field (1972) has suggested that Tarski's attempts to define truth predicates for various languages were motivated at least in part by a desire to promote physicalism, the metascientific principle that says every phenomenon in the world is a physical phenomenon, explicable, in principle, wholly in terms of physics (if not *our* physics, then a more sophisticated analogue that would still involve no primitive concepts that strike us as intuitively "nonphysical," like *pain* or *gene*). Despite the claimed successes of the physicalist program represented by claimed "reduction" of a wide range of biological phenomena to physical phenomena, and of chemical phenomena to physical phenomena, certain types of facts, or putative facts, have proved especially bothersome. Mental facts have received the most attention from physicalistically oriented philosophers, but semantical facts are no less problematic (the two classes may intersect in the case of "thinkings" and the like). Among the recalcitrant semantical facts are facts about truth. It is easy to believe that there are in the world such facts, or states of affairs, as *it being true that snow is white*, or *John's having just said something true*, or *'Snow is white' being true*, just as there are such facts as *snow being white* and *John's having just felt a pain*. After all, we often say that something or other somebody has just said is true, and we know what we are talking about. What could be more obvious than that people sometimes say things that are true? And what could be more obvious than that when we say 'That's true' in response to Charley's remark that snow is white, we are reporting (and correctly reporting) that a certain state of affairs obtains—the state of affairs *that snow is white is true*? That there are such states of affairs in the world is a pretheoretical datum provided by the most elementary reflection on what we say and what, intuitively, we are right in saying. But how can these semantical states of affairs, involving the *truth* of statements, be understood, explained, predicted in terms of physics? What kind of *physical* fact is the fact that some statement or other is a *true* one?

As Field points out, the physicalist can take either of two approaches. He can admit that there really are such facts in the world and show how they are, despite appearances, really physical facts. Or he can deny that there really are such facts, and can treat them the way he would treat such putative facts as *Martha the Witch having cast a spell on Charley*. Tarski, according to Field, was attracted to the first approach. A physicalist armed with the prosentence account of truth can try the second. He can insist that when we think we are (correctly) reporting the existence of one of these mysterious facts we are just buying in on a bad semantics for our truth talk. We are supposing, for instance, that the reply 'That's true' to the remark that snow is white serves to report that the statement that snow is white is a true one and thus serves to report a fact of the form: such-and-such being true. But that is not the semantical role of 'That's true'. The only fact reported by 'That's true' in this context is the fact of snow being white, and that is no special headache for the physicalist.

Of course, philosophers can come along and invent a property of "truth" that can be ascribed to sentences or statements, and they can stipulate that certain forms of words (like 'That statement is true') are to have the technical use of making such ascriptions. They can construct philosophical theories that by design permit us to ascribe this property of truth to things, and thereby report the existence of facts like *'Snow is white' is true*, where this is explicitly technical, non-ordinary discourse. How the physicalist deals with these putative semantical facts depends on the details of the philosophical theory postulating such facts.

Perhaps the theory will provide an explicit, stipulative definition of its truth property in nonsemantical terms. For example, the theory might include a Tarskian definition of a truth predicate for some fragment of a natural language, yielding a nonsemantical equivalent of the truth predicate that functions as a stipulative *definiens*, not just as an extensional equivalent for a truth predicate understood as expressing some antecedently grasped "pretheoretic" concept of truth. In that case the physicalist might well agree that statements of the theory ascribing truth to things do indeed report facts that really are in the world, but not mysterious irreducibly semantical facts.

Or perhaps the theory won't provide an easy way of eliminating 'is true' in favor of nonsemantical stuff, perhaps the truth-ascriptions that can be expressed in the theory's language will be reports of semantical facts that are prima facie nonphysical, with no obvious way to explicate them physically. In that case the physicalist can ask what it is that this theory accomplishes that could not be accomplished by a theory that uses a more physicalistically respectable truth predicate. If the theory does serve some purpose that is important enough and that could not be served if the truth predicate were explicitly defined in nonsemantical terms, then the physicalist had better start to worry. But it is hard to see what this purpose could be, because if the prosentence account is right a philosophical theory cannot have as its purpose the characterization of a predicate that expresses an ordinary truth property—a property we ascribe to things in the course of ordinary truth talk—because there is no such property. But if the theory in question is not uniquely qualified to do some reasonably important job, then the physicalist can simply tell these theorists not to bother him with their theory, which is, presumably, what he would tell a witchcraft theorist or any other proponent of a theory that insists the world is full of spooky facts that would (or might well) remain physicalistically recalcitrant if they were countenanced at all.

Physicalism can serve in this way as a guide to theory building and theory selection. But if it were really true that we find ourselves confronted by truth-facts prior to any relevant theory building at all, as it is claimed we find ourselves confronted by the facts of pain and itches, then this maneuver would not be available to the physicalist. By the lights of the prosentence account, though, truth-facts simply are not just sitting there staring at us out of our ordinary, nonphilosophical discourse about truth. We can theorize that there are such facts in the world, but if these alleged facts, as we conceive them, are not physicalistically respectable, then our theorizing had better achieve a great deal that is important and not to be achieved otherwise, or the physicalist has a right to claim that our alleged truth-facts are alleged and nothing more.

So the prosentential account of truth may be ammunition for a physicalist who worries about the reduction or "elimination" of semantical facts. Of course it will leave him with the problem of facts about referring, facts about synonymy, and whatever other semantical facts there may be in the world or may have been thought to be in the world. But it is a start.

4.7. Correspondence Theories

The prosentence account of truth forces (at least) a more complicated motivation for such philosophical enterprises as correspondence theories of truth. Correspondence theorists generally take it as noncontroversial that there are sentences (or statements, or propositions) that have the property of being true. They view the truth of sentences as resting upon some set of language-world relations that need to be spelled out, but they start with the datum that, e.g., 'Snow is white' has the property of truth and has it because snow is white, and there is some kind of connection between the sentence and the fact of snow being white (or between the sentence and *something* else in the world having to do with snow and the whiteness thereof). But if the prosentence theory is right, semantical reflection on truth talk should not cause us to think that there are sentences or statements that exemplify a property of "truth." Perhaps there are language-world relations of various kinds; perhaps 'Snow is white' does somehow picture the fact of snow being white, but on our account it is just a confusion to suppose that this has anything to do with some truth *property*.

Of course, we can construct a semantical theory introducing a property "truth" that is had by 'Snow is white' just when snow is white and that connects this property in the usual ways with relations like reference and satisfaction. But we cannot suppose that the *interest* of such a theory lies in the fact that it captures a property that we knew beforehand was exemplified by 'Snow is white' just when snow is white, and that shows us how the possession of that property by sentences depends upon referential and other sorts of connections between the sentence's parts and things extralinguistic. Its interest cannot lie there, because before we construct the theory we precisely do not know that there is a property of truth that some sentences have. We may believe it, but we believe it because we believe that the subject-predicate form of 'That is true' and its kin bespeaks property ascription rather than (as the prosentence account would have it) just grammatical convenience. We must find subtler ways to show that our correspondence theory is interesting, which is fine, because the reasons such theories are interesting are, in fact, as subtle as reasons can get.

It is interesting to speculate why traditional philosophizing about the relation between language and the world has so often taken the form of developing theories of truth. It may well be that language-world relations of various kinds need to be invoked in order to explain such phenomena as the learnability of language, the public character of language, the fact that judgments expressed in language can be confirmed and disconfirmed by observation of extralinguistic things and happenings, and so on. So why are philosophers' theories about the relation of words to reality usually (though not always) concerned with laying the groundwork for an account of how statements come to be true? Why is truth the constant theme of philosophical semantics?

We have already hinted at one answer, or one part of an answer. To wit, if you think you're ascribing a property to a sentence or statement or whatever anytime you say 'That's true', and you have a little healthy philosophical curiosity, you'll want to know what this characteristic "truth" is. And a theory about how language connects with the world might strike you as just what's needed. But although that helps explain why people may have thought there was sense to the question 'When, in general, are statements characterized by truth?' it does not help explain why so many people have thought this the central question about language-world relations. Our guess is that the main reason why a concern with language-world relations generally goes hand in hand with a concern about truth and falsehood is that our language simply doesn't let us formulate certain philosophical questions about language and reality except by using 'is true' or a cognate. For instance: It might be plausible to suppose (prima facie, anyway) that there is a certain relation that obtains between the sentence 'Snow is white' and the world when snow is white, and it is plausible to suppose that this relation would prove, upon inspection, to be of considerable philosophical interest. It is plausible to suppose this for all sorts of reasons—it is the fact of snow being white that must be observed in order to confirm directly what is expressed by 'snow is white', drawing a language-learner's attention to white snow and proclaiming 'snow is white' (in the right context) can contribute to the pupil's competence at using the words 'Snow is white' correctly (i.e., the way we all use them). 'Snow is white' (by the lights of the traditional truth-is-a-real-predicate view) is true exactly when snow is white, and so on. In short, a philosopher might want to ask the question

> What relation obtains between 'snow is white' and the world when snow is white?

for any one or more of a variety of reasons. Most of these reasons will remain in force even if the philosopher in question has been persuaded by our prosentential theory and rejects the view that there is a property of truth that 'Snow is white' exemplifies when snow is white. But suppose this philosopher wants to *generalize* his question, which he will certainly want to do if he's any good? There is only one way he can formulate the appropriate generalization in English, namely

> What relation obtains between a sentence and the world when *it is true*?

Recall Quine's observation that 'is true' enables us to frame generalizations of this kind (and recall that we agree). The point is that the interesting general question about sentences and reality simply *must* be phrased in English with the use of a (not necessarily separable) truth predicate. So it is perfectly understandable that the problem of how language connects with the world generally gets run together with some problem or other about truth. And if somebody believes that 'is true' invariably plays a property-ascribing role, it is understandable that this person will also believe that general questions about language and reality, like "What relation obtains between a sentence and the world when it is true?" are questions about the conditions under which the "property of truth" is exemplified. We, of course, draw the line at this point. We cannot formulate certain general questions about language and reality without resorting to truth talk because we speak English. But we take 'is true' in such generalizations to be a fragment of a quantificational prosentence, not an independently meaningful, property-expressing predicate. So we are not tempted to understand the question "What relation obtains between a sentence and the world when it is true?" as tantamount to the question "What is truth?" In fact, we think this last question is incoherent if it presupposes that there is a characteristic "truth" familiar to us all. Of course, taken another way, as a metalinguistic question about the role of the predicate 'true' in our talk, we find the question "What is truth?" perfectly sensible, and we have proposed an answer. Unhappily, most people haven't understood the question that way.

4.8. TECHNICAL USES OF 'TRUE'

The preceding sections indicate some connections between the prosentential theory and certain technical or theoretical uses of 'true' by philosophers, but we wish to emphasize that we have by no means tried to explain all such uses. In particular, the prosentential theory highlights the predicate's ordinary and hence nonmetalinguistic uses, whereas many technical philosophers think of themselves as using the predicate metalinguistically. Can the prosentential theory be extended to cover these technical uses? We don't know much about this. Sometimes theory precedes usage: Those who have been brought up on a particular theory, say Tarski (1936), or who have figured one out for themselves, may actually decide to use the truth predicate in accordance with that theory, no matter what happens in fluent English. (After all, it is hardly surprising that one should, when provided with a predicate, find some characterizing use for it.) And if a certain technical use originates from a theory, there is no reason a priori why the prosentential theory should cover it. But we leave open, or at least for another occasion, the question of just what such a theoretically based truth property could be, and how it might be related to the ordinary—i.e., prosentential—uses of 'true'. We do, however, hope that those which are in the spirit of ordinary usage will be accommodated in the prosentential theory.

4.9. REDUNDANCY

Is it a consequence of the prosentential theory that truth is redundant? We divide the question.

In the first place, we certainly do think that all uses of 'true' in English except in the connectives and prosentences of English* are redundant; that is simply an alternative statement of our thesis that English can be translated into English* without significant residue. We noted in §2.6, however, that though redundant, a separable predicate is of enormous convenience.

The second and more interesting question is whether 'true' is redundant in English* itself. Recalling the special nature of English*, this amounts to asking for the result of subtracting from English* on the one hand its prosentences and on the other its connectives such as 'It is not true that' (and any equivalent like 'It is not the case that' which logicians often invoke partly to conceal from themselves, we think, that there is truth talk lurking). To answer these questions, we need to talk a bit more about the functions of prosentences and connectives in English*—and hence in English.

First prosentences. From the literature on pronouns, one gathers that it might plausibly be argued that pronouns of laziness can be eliminated in "the deep structure"—though (a) not without introducing ambiguities, as we mentioned, and though (b) also not without pragmatic loss, and though (c) the evidence is in any event far from conclusive. But let us put the laziness cases to one side; the literature certainly suggests that it is extremely doubtful that quantificational pronouns can be similarly eliminated. This suggests, we suppose, that quantificational pronouns give us ways of saying certain things in English which we'd not otherwise be able to say. But notice that the new things we can say with quantificational pronouns and cannot say without them are new in a special sense: They are not *topically* new, allowing us now to discuss new topics;

nor *ascriptively* new, affording us new noncomposite properties or relations, nor *categorically* new, giving us a brand new conceptual framework within which to work. Rather, the newness of the things we can say is like that of the things we can say with 'or' that we cannot say without 'or'; let us say that the newness is *logical*.

Our suggestion is that quantificational prosentences are in this respect like quantificational pronouns: They are absolutely irredundant in English, allowing us to say things we could not say without them, but the irredundancy is logical, like that of 'or'. And to turn the coin over, they are (contrary to those who view truth as a characteristic) topically, categorically, and—especially—ascriptively redundant.

Now for the role of 'true' in forming connectives: We argued above, we think conclusively, that if we are to have quantificational prosentences, then we must have these connectives. But we also conjectured that they are independently irredundant, though we now add that the irredundancy is logical rather than any of the other sorts. Remember the example we used in §2.5: Meaning by the "contradictory" of a sentence one that has exactly the opposite truth-conditions, we conjectured that there are in English sentences for which one cannot find a contradictory without using a connective such as 'It is not true that'.

These remarks are of course sketchy and deserve expansion, but the upshot is clear: 'True' is far from redundant, but its role in English is logical rather than ascriptive. According to Frege (in Klemke 1968, p. 512):

> It is also worthy of notice that the sentence 'I smell the scent of violets' has the same content as the sentence 'It is true that I smell the scent of violets.' So it seems, then, that nothing is added to the thought by my ascribing to it the property of truth. And yet is it not a great result when the scientist, after much hesitation and careful inquiry, can finally say "what I supposed is true"? The meaning of the word 'true' seems to be altogether unique. May we not be dealing here with something which cannot, in the ordinary sense, be called a quality at all? In spite of this doubt I want first to express myself in accordance with ordinary usage, as if truth were a quality, until something more to the point is found.

Our aim has been to provide "something more to the point."

4

Inheritors and Paradox*

Those who hold the traditional view that the primary role of the truth predicate is property ascription encounter problems when they try to determine the truth or falsity of sentences such as 'This is false' (the Liar sentence), which appear to be true if false and false if true. In order to save the truth property, it has been customary to seek ways of excluding such sentences from the extensions of 'true' and 'false'. The source of the problem, and also a way out of the seeming ascription of inconsistent properties, has been seen to lie sometimes with self-reference, sometimes with category mistakes, sometimes with natural language itself, and so the list goes on. But there is another avenue to explore. In this paper I discuss the status of sentences such as the Liar from the point of view of a theory in which the use of 'true' and 'false' in English can be understood without supposing that these predicates ascribe properties. On such a theory, because there is no ascription of properties, the Liar sentence cannot—at least for the reasons usually given—be paradoxical.

The prosentential theory of truth (see Chapter 3—Grover, Camp, and Belnap 1975—for details) is a theory of truth in which 'true' has a "prosentential" role. In Grover 1976 I briefly explain the prosentential account of 'This is false', showing that whatever strangeness it does have can be found in many other sentences and also in terms involving "proforms." Because the prosentential account sketched there explains a number of intuitions we have concerning the Liar and because it is important to see how certain conceptual confusions have led to the construal of similar sentences and predicates as paradoxical and to the development of inconsistent formal languages, I extend that account here to

* I am indebted to Nuel Belnap, Charles Chastain, Susan Haack, Hide Ishiguro, and Robert L. Martin for their comments on earlier drafts. Also helpful were critical comments made in discussion of the paper when I read an earlier version at the University of Illinois at Chicago and at Wayne State University.

cover sentences that are like the Liar but have different subject
terms, strengthened versions of the Liar, and I also explain—from
the point of view of the prosentential theory—why such sentences
have been thought to be paradoxical. In Chapter 8 I discuss Berry's
paradox.

I will not devote space in this paper to either motivating or explaining in detail the claim that 'true' and 'false' have prosentential
roles in English. The reader is referred to Chapter 3 for that. With
respect to certain points, reference will be made to sections of
Chapter 3. However, as a brief introduction to the theory, I will say
a bit about what a prosentence is (Chapter 3, §2.1).

Prosentences were introduced in Chapter 2 (Grover 1972) to provide natural-language readings of formulas containing bound propositional variables. Pro*sentences* (also pro*verbs* and pro*adjectives*)
were introduced by analogy with pro*nouns*. Prosentences are like
anaphoric pronouns in that they can be used both in the *lazy way*,
as the pronoun 'he' is used in

(1) John is tall and *he* is heavy.

and *quantificationally*,[1] as 'it' is used in

If a number is even, *it* is evenly divisible by 2.

Pronouns[2] are different from prosentences in that pronouns occupy
positions in sentences that singular terms can occupy; prosentences
occupy positions in sentences that declarative sentences can occupy. Part of the claim that 'true' has a prosentential role is that it
is used in forming prosentences, as in 'That is true', which is used
in English as a prosentence of laziness (Chapter 3, §2.3). Just as 'he'
in (1) has 'John' as its antecedent,[3] so 'That is true' in

MARY: Chicago is large.

JOHN: If *that is true*, it probably has a large airport.

has 'Chicago is large' as its antecedent. In each case the tie is grammatical. (In the case of 'That is true', although the tie derives from
an anaphoric 'that', it is the whole of 'That is true' which is the
prosentence.) Semantically, just as the referent of 'he' in (1) is the

---

[1] Although I assume here a distinction between lazy and quantificational uses of
pronouns, I don't mean to suggest that an adequate theory of pronouns must make
the distinction. For the moment, the "distinction" is useful.

[2] See Partee 1970 for a helpful discussion of pronouns.

[3] The word 'antecedent' is a bit misleading. Even though an antecedent usually
occurs earlier in the discourse than does a dependent proform, it doesn't have to.

same as the referent of its antecedent 'John', so the propositional content (or simply "content") of 'That is true' is the same as that of its antecedent, 'Chicago is large'.

The prosentential account of 'That is true' captures features of 'true' which have hitherto been noticed but left unexplained. The connections that obtain between prosentences of laziness and their antecedents establish connections required in communication between what the speaker is saying and what someone else has said. When a pronoun of laziness is used, we know that in the simple cases no new object is being referred to, and, in the case of prosentences, that nothing new is being asserted or entertained. This last is a fact about 'true' that the redundancy theorists drew attention to. Furthermore, an antecedent is explicitly acknowledged when a proform (i.e., a pronoun, prosentence, or proadjective, etc.; Chapter 3, §2.1) is used, and so it is made clear that the speaker is not plagiarizing. So also, as Strawson (1950a) has pointed out, 'true' is used in expressing agreement, granting, or considering a point.

Proforms are also used to obtain generality. One way is through the prosentence 'It is true'. Consider, for example, a generalized form of

If the pope says that snow is white, snow is white.

Namely,

If the pope says something, *it is true.*

W. V. Quine (1970) has also pointed out that 'true' is needed in generalizing, but his account differs from the prosentential account, because on his account 'true' is metalinguistic. A prosentential 'true' is in the object language.

Prosentences can be modified (Chapter 3, see §2.6 and §3.1), as in 'That was true', 'That might be true', etc. Modified prosentences inherit as their content a modified form of their antecedent's content. In most formal languages, connectives do the work of such verb modifications. 'That is false' is a modified prosentence that inherits as its content the contradictory of its antecedent's content.

The prosentential account of 'This is false' goes something like this:[4] Pronouns and prosentences of laziness, along with some other expressions in our language which I will mention later, acquire their referents or content—as the case may be—from antecedent ex-

---

[4] Strawson (1949) gives an account of the Liar in terms of his non-property-ascribing account of 'true'. The account of the Liar given here is very much in the spirit of what Strawson has to say.

pressions. I call such expressions "inheritors." If, for some reason, the antecedent either fails to denote, if it is a term, or fails to have propositional content, if it is a sentence, the inheritor fails to acquire an appropriate referent or content. There is such a failure in the case of 'This is false': As a modified prosentence, it relies on its antecedent for content, but it is, unfortunately, its own antecedent and, as such, fails as an independent supplier of content. So 'This is false' lacks content.

1. Grounded Pronouns

Pronouns of laziness are often used for stylistic reasons and perhaps also for lazy reasons, but, in addition, they (together with quantificational pronouns and other proforms) are useful semantically for the way in which they facilitate connections between one piece of a discourse and another. In the simple cases, a pronoun of laziness has the same referent as does its antecedent, and so, when such a pronoun is used, we know the same object is referred to. The connections can also be more complex: There are pronouns that resist treatment by coreferentiality theories (Partee 1970) and there are cases where a pronoun has as its antecedent an expression that belongs to a different grammatical category, as in

John visited us. It was a surprise.

No matter how complex the connections, however, the fact is that a pronoun of laziness, in acquiring a referent from another expression—or in "bringing" a referent forward—depends on another expression for the referent it has. And because of this, pronouns of laziness must be connected by the anaphoric relation to an expression that can *supply* a referent. Terms that can supply referents must acquire their referents in other ways: as proper names do, according to the causal theory of reference, or, as with demonstratives, by means of a demonstration. A term such as a pronoun of laziness that, in a given context acquires its referent from another expression will be called an *inheritor*. Terms such as proper names which acquire their referents in other ways (i.e., independently of another expression having a referent, or another expression having propositional content, as in the case 'John visited us') will be said to acquire their referents *independently*. A pronoun of laziness is *grounded* if it is connected to an expression that acquires its referent or propositional content independently, if at all.

Note that groundedness does not guarantee a referent. Consider 'he' in

The King of France is bald, and he is wise.

2. Inheritors

In the case of pronouns, the anaphoric relation locates the antecedent from which a referent is inherited, but there are limits to the connections that can be made by means of such grammatical ties. Where there are several candidate antecedents, ambiguity can arise when a pronoun is used, and grammatical ties are not available for distant pieces of discourse. When a name is available, it can often be used, but sometimes, in order to convey the fact that the same person or thing is being talked about, reference must be made in other ways. Consider

> SUSAN: I have a student in my class who says that his father works in the National Park. He has some good suggestions about places to visit.
> TIM: I don't know *the student you are referring to*, but I think he is someone Mary has in her class too. I'll get her to talk to him.

A definite description is used here to refer to someone who has been referred to in another place. The occasion I have in mind is one where the point for Tim is not to talk about Susan herself and what she was doing in using 'he', but to say something about the student Susan is talking about. Descriptive phrases such as 'just mentioned', 'been talking about', 'are referring to', which ostensibly describe discourse, may often be used merely to locate an antecedent piece of discourse from which a referent is inherited. What is sought is a way of making connections with other parts of the discourse so that it becomes clear—as it is with pronouns—that, say, the person talked about in this place is the same as the person talked about in that other place. Thus, insofar as each depends on another expression for its referent, Tim's 'the person you are referring to' and 'he' are on a par.

Occurrences of definite descriptions that acquire their referents from other expressions are also *inheritors*. Like pronominal inheritors, an occurrence of a definite description inheritor is *grounded* if it is connected to an antecedent that can acquire a referent independently.

3. Ungrounded Inheritors

In normal (perhaps all) circumstances, successful communication requires that inheritors be grounded. However, in order to evaluate the Liar, I must consider some circumstances in which inheritors are ungrounded. I consider cases where the grammatical picture is complete, that is, there is an antecedent wherever there ought to be one—but the antecedent fails to supply a referent. Ungroundedness can happen this way. A referring term purports to acquire its referent from another referring term, and this in turn purports to acquire its referent from yet another term, and things continue in this way, with each term an inheritor, yet there is no term in the sequence that acquires a referent independently. Such cases arise when there is either a circle or an infinite sequence of inheritors. Consider, for example, the problem of determining the referent of the italicized terms in

> (2) MARY: *The person you are going to refer to in your next sentence* is someone I know.
> FAY: *She* is not.

Given the "universal availability" of definite descriptions, circles can be very small, as in

> (3) The person I am now referring to is tall.

And, if we forget that definite descriptions are sometimes only inheritors, we may suspect inconsistency in

> (4) The oldest living person to whom I am not now referring is tall.

An infinite sequence can be generated as follows:

> (5) S_0: The person referred to in S_1 is tall.
> S_1: The person referred to in S_2 is tall.
> .
> .
> .
> S_n: The person referred to in S_{n+1} is tall.

In each of the above cases, the definite descriptions purport to acquire referents from other (not necessarily distinct) expressions. Because there is no independent supplier, they fail to have referents. The result is a set of sentences with nondenoting subject terms.

4. Grounded Prosentences

Other proforms of laziness share with pronouns the feature that they inherit from antecedent expressions. Prosentences are no exception: 'That is true' has the same content as does 'Snow is white' in

(6) TOM: Snow is white. FAY: That is true.

Thus prosentences are *inheritors*, and so also are modified prosentences (Chapter 3, §2.6) that inherit a modified form of their antecedent's content. A sentence that does not inherit its propositional content from another must acquire it *independently*—in some such way, for example, as 'Snow is white' does. An occurrence of a prosentence is *grounded* if it is connected to an antecedent that acquires its content independently. 'That is true' is grounded in (6). (The distinctions outlined, both here and in §1, are made only intuitively.)

5. Sentential Inheritors

Just as pronouns are not the only term inheritors, so also prosentences are not the only sentence inheritors: 'True' is used to form inheritors. In the case of 'That is true', an anaphoric 'that' provides a grammatical tie between it and an antecedent sentence. If there is a desire to make connections with more distant pieces of discourse or if for some other reason 'that' won't do, then, as with the case of terms, another way must be employed. Consider, for example, the use of 'The first paragraph of this paper' in

(7) If the first paragraph of this paper is true, then . . .

which might on some occasions of use be construed as locating the antecedent discourse from which content is inherited. The antecedent part of (7), construed as an inheritor, is in effect "standing in" for a conjunction of (roughly) the sentences of the first paragraph. [In §8 I indicate treatments of (7) appropriate for other occasions of use.] Proper names can be used to locate antecedents and so also can numerals, as in

(8) Snow is white.

(9) (8) is true.

The antecedent can also be "displayed":

(10) 'Snow is white' is true.

In (10) the antecedent is a proper part of the inheritor. As inheritors
with 'Snow is white' as antecedent, (9) and (10) are about whatever
the sentence 'Snow is white' is about, and not about the sentence
'Snow is white'. In all these cases, *the truth predicate is the clue
that we have an inheritor on our hands.*

The use of 'true' to form inheritors is clearly a natural extension
of the prosentential 'true', even though such inheritors are not
themselves prosentences. They are not prosentences because the
ties they have with their antecedents are not grammatical (Chapter
3, §2.1). We need an anaphoric 'that' for that.[5] The role in providing
us with a sentence that can "stand in" for another is (at least a part
of) what is in question here.

Like prosentences, these inheritors can be modified and should
then be thought of as standing in for a modified form of the antecedent. A sentential inheritor is *grounded* just in case it is connected by an "inheritance chain" to an antecedent that can acquire
its content independently.

6. Ungrounded Inheritors

Contexts similar to those in which we found ungrounded terms provide us with ungrounded sentences. The same kinds of circles and
sequences are possible, with similar semantic problems. An example like (2) in which there is a content circle is

(11) (a): (b) is true.
     (b): That is true.

In this case (b) purports to acquire its content from (a), and (a) from
(b). There is no independent supplier of content in the circle of antecedents. Very small circles such as we had in (3) are also possible:

(12) This is true.

and also

(13) (13) is true.

---

[5] In the examples discussed, 'that' in 'That is true' has always been anaphoric.
However, an antecedent might sometimes be located by means of a demonstrative
'that'. In such a case, 'That is true,' although still an inheritor, is not a prosentence.
The same applies for 'This is true'.

Sequences can be generated:

(14) S_0': S_1' is true.
   S_1': S_2' is true.
   .
   .
   .
   S_n': S_{n+1}' is true.
   .   .   .

In this case each inheritor is standing for the next, but, because there is no supplier of content, all lack content. Modified forms of inheritors yield the familiar

(15) (c): (d) is false.
   (d): That is true.
(16) This is false.
(17) (17) is false.

And variations of the infinite sequence are also possible. As before, these inheritors all lack content—a consequence of their ungroundedness. The circles might be well called *circles of discontent*!

7. Paradoxes

We have at last arrived at those sentences which undermine the thesis that 'true' and 'false' are, on every occasion, property-ascribing predicates. What is the prosentential alternative? As inheritors, the Liar and its related versions [e.g., (17)] depend on their antecedents for content. But these inheritors are ungrounded: They are not connected to antecedents that can acquire content independently. The problem of a simultaneous ascription of inconsistent properties doesn't arise: The "paradoxical" sentences lack content. *Lack of propositional content is a problem, but it is not an isolated problem that only "paradoxical" sentences have*: Sentences such as (11) lack content, in similar circumstances terms lack referents, and I will show in §9 that the same problem can arise with definitions.

8. Generalized Versions of the Liar

I have discussed so far only "lazy inheritor" versions of the Liar. There are also generalized versions like

(18) Anything that is identical with this sentence is false.

Quantificational uses of 'true' were explained in Chapter 3 by means of translations into a language containing bound propositional variables, and then natural-language paraphrases were provided in English* (Chapter 3, §2.3 and §2.4) using 'It is true' as a quantificational prosentence capturing the bound variables. Thus 'Everything John says is true' was translated

∀p(If John says that p, then p)

if the point was not just to assert what John had asserted, but to explicitly tie it to John's saying it. The conditional '/', introduced by Nuel Belnap (1973) in his analysis of conditional assertion, was used when there was no desire to say anything about John. Thus

∀p(John says that p/p)

Similar analyses can be given of (7) and are appropriate when, for example, the speaker doesn't actually *know* what has been said in the first paragraph.

So, following the program of English* analyses suggested in Chapter 3, (18) can be rendered—making the modified quantificational prosentence explicit—as

(18′) Anything that is identical with this sentence is such
        that it is false.

The propositional content that a quantificational prosentence contributes to the sentence it occurs in, comes from the *possible* contents of the prosentence's substituends (sentences that yield substitution instances[6]). Often the propositional content of the whole sentence can be determined if we know only what the possible contents of the prosentence's substituends are, even though we don't know which contents the substituends actually have. In these cases the problem of ungroundedness does not arise. A problem can arise, however, when, in determining the content of the whole, the specific content of a given substituend must first be determined.

Insofar as quantificational prosentences contribute content acquired from substituends, they are *inheritors*. A substituend is *crucial* if excluding it from the set of the prosentence's substituends would alter the propositional content—if any—of the whole sen-

_____

[6] See Chapter 2 (Grover 1972), §2.1.

tence.[7] Clearly, a quantified prosentence is *ungrounded* if it has a crucial substituend that is ungrounded. It is also ungrounded if the crucial substituend is the quantified sentence: The prosentence purports to acquire content from the quantified sentence and the quantified sentence from the prosentence. This is the case with (18'). The modified prosentence occurring in (18') has (18') as a substituend. The substituend is crucial because it is the only sentence identical with (18'), and so *the* sentence whose content (if it had any) would be denied by means of 'It is false'. So (18') lacks content—it is not inconsistent.

9. Grounded/Ungrounded

The grounded/ungrounded distinction separates those occurrences of inheritors which have content from those which don't. Included in the former are grounded occurrences of inheritors like (9) and (10), and included in the latter are ungrounded inheritors such as (11)–(17). The set of occurrences of sentences that are useful in communication includes those which acquire content independently (e.g., 'Snow is white') and grounded inheritors. This set corresponds, roughly, to that set of sentences to which Kripke (1975) has assigned a truth value at the smallest fixed point, and of which he says, "The smallest fixed point is probably the natural model for the intuitive concept of truth." (p. 708) Presumably he has in mind a concept having to do with a truth property, but never mind that. There is agreement that the grounded inheritors are the inheritors we care about: They are the ones we use for successful communication.

There is another respect in which there is agreement between this prosentential account and Kripke's theory. Consideration of examples like

DEAN: Everything Nixon said about Watergate is false.
NIXON: Everything Dean said about Watergate is false.

led Kripke to the following moral: "An adequate theory must allow our statements involving the notion of truth to be risky: they risk being paradoxical if the empirical facts are extremely (and unex-

---

[7] 'Crucial' has to be extended to cover cases where a family of substituends is crucial. And various alternatives must be considered, like those which arise in §11, before the grounded/ungrounded distinction can be made clearly here. A similar model is presented in R. L. Martin and P. W. Woodruff (1975).

pectedly) unfavorable." (p. 692) Because the context of an occurrence of a sentential inheritor determines what content it has (or what it contributes to a quantified sentence), and thereby whether it is grounded, empirical facts do have a role, on my account, in determining whether an utterance is risky—as they should.

Kripke goes on to say, however, "There can be no syntactic or semantic 'sieve' that will winnow out the 'bad' cases while preserving the 'good' ones." (p. 692) The cases Kripke has in mind are sentences. Because the content of an inheritor changes from one context to another, my cases must in contrast be utterances. On my account, the good cases are separated from the bad whenever an analysis of the content of a sentential inheritor is given. Sensitive to the effects of context, this (informally developed) account provides a sieve.

10. A Cause of "Paradox"

I have defined an inheritor as an expression that acquires either its referent or its content from another expression, and I've claimed that 'true' is used in the construction of sentential inheritors.

Suppose a sentential inheritor is not recognized as such. That is, its content is not recognized as acquired from another expression. In that case the content will be assumed to be acquired independently. In languages like English, sentential inheritors can be connected to (and so purport to inherit from) any sentence, including themselves—that is, sentential inheritors are "universally available." Also, in such languages, inheritors can be modified so that they inherit the contradictory of their antecedent's content. Then inconsistencies arise *if* content is also acquired by inheritors in some way independently. Suppose, for example, it is not thought that 'true' is used in inheritors, but that both 'true' and 'false' are property-ascribing predicates. Then sentences containing 'true' and 'false' are thought to acquire their content independently, and not from other expressions. That might be all right on its own, but it is also generally assumed that (roughly) 'X is true' can be replaced by X, and 'X is false' by the contradictory of X. This fits with a prosentential 'true', but combined (without restriction) with the other, it leads to a problem. I'll try to give a picture of what is going on:

Suppose α is a sentential inheritor, and suppose, also, that we write as a suffix the antecedent α has in a particular context. Thus the case where α has 'Snow is white' as its antecedent is represented by

$$\alpha_{'snow\ is\ white'}$$

Given this way of representing the situation, one easily envisages the possibility of combinations like

(19) (a) α_α (b) $\alpha_{\sim\alpha}$ (c) $\sim\alpha_\alpha$ (d) $\sim\alpha_{\sim\alpha}$

So far as the prosententialist is concerned, none of the occurrences of α is connected to an expression that can acquire content independently, and so, in each case, the inheritor is ungrounded—(19a)–(19d) yield more circles of discontent. So α fails to have content.

Suppose, on the other hand, the role of the inheritor has not been recognized, and it is assumed that α has propositional content. If, in addition, the inheritor is still cashed in for its antecedent, there is a problem. No matter what content α is assumed to have, (19b) and (19d) are inconsistent: They both allow the simultaneous affirmation and denial of α. (19b), for example, expresses the proposition that α. But α also acquires content from $\sim\alpha$, so α is cashed in for $\sim\alpha$. So we then have (19b) expressing the proposition that $\sim\alpha$! The Liar sentence has the form of (19d).

Because it is impossible for universally available modifiable inheritors to consistently acquire content independently, *inheritors must not go unrecognized.*

These inheritance problems arise for definitions also. Because in a definition the definiendum acquires its content from the definiens, that occurrence of the definiendum is an inheritor. In this case the problems are well recognized. The definiendum must not occur in the definiens—otherwise the definiendum is ungrounded. It is also realized that there are cases such as

$$H = {}_{df}\sim H$$

where, were the "definition" taken seriously, an "inconsistency" arises. But of course H hasn't really been defined, because the expression it is supposed to acquire content from does not have content independently.

11. A Strengthened Version of the Liar

Are inheritors—properly understood—free from inconsistency? Obviously I have no proof that they are, but I can show that some problems that arise for property-ascribing theories do not arise on this account.

Consider, first, a version of the Liar sentence, Let X be 'X is false'. According to (syntactical) inheritance properties, it seems that if X is false, X is true, and that if X is true, X is false. These have the "form" of contradictories, but there is no contradiction because each lacks content.

One might think that talk of *ungroundedness* and *lack of content* lands this account in the class of third-value "solutions." If this is true, the account faces the usual objection: Paradox has not been eliminated; it has been relocated. Consider

(20) (20) is false, or (20) is ungrounded.

According to the property-ascribing view, if (20) has one of the mutually exclusive properties true, false, and ungrounded, it also has another of those properties: Thus, if (20) is true, it is also either false or ungrounded! Because 'ungrounded' does not introduce a third property, this problem does not arise for a prosentential 'true'. '(20) is true' and '(20) is false' are only inheritors. There is no conflict between '(20) is true' and (20) because '(20) is true' has the same content as does (20): To suppose that (20) is true just is to suppose that either (20) is false or (20) is ungrounded. The part of (20) that supplies content is '(20) is ungrounded', so that could be the only source of inconsistency. I will use the three-valued Weak and Strong valuations of S. C. Kleene (1952) to picture what is going on. As 'X is true' is an inheritor, the value of 'X is true' should be the same as that of X, and the value of 'X is false' the complement of the value of X.

The grounded/ungrounded distinction has been made so far only for inheritors with simple antecedents. It will have to be extended to cover sentences like (20) and inheritors with such mixed antecedents. I consider only conjunctions and disjunctions. The point of the grounded/ungrounded distinction was to separate occurrences of inheritors which have content from those which don't. In the case of sentences like (20), one might decide—depending, presumably, on where the distinction is to be used—either that a sentence is ungrounded if its content cannot be completely determined or that it is ungrounded if no content at all can be determined.

To begin with, I will say that an occurrence of an inheritor is *grounded* if it is connected to an antecedent with conjunctive (disjunctive) parts that can acquire content independently, or, if any of those parts are inheritors, then those inheritors must be grounded$_1$; a conjunction (disjunction) is *grounded*$_1$ if all its conjuncts (disjuncts) that are inheritors are grounded$_1$.

Consider now

(20$_1$) (20$_1$) is false, or (20$_1$) is ungrounded$_1$.

According to the definition, (20$_1$), '(20$_1$) is true' and '(20$_1$) is false' are ungrounded$_1$. So '(20$_1$) is ungrounded$_1$' is assigned the value t. When using Weak Kleene, ungrounded$_1$ inheritors will be assigned u (are undefined); on Strong Kleene, an ungrounded$_1$ inheritor has the value u unless its antecedent has a conjunct with value f, or a disjunct with value t. In these cases an inheritor either inherits those values, or, if it is modified by 'false', it has the values t and f, respectively. I believe (20$_1$), '(20$_1$) is true', and '(20$_1$) is false' are assigned unique values on each of these valuations.

> WEAK KLEENE. Because '(20$_1$) is true' and '(20$_1$) is false' are ungrounded$_1$, they have the value u. Because one disjunct of (20$_1$) has the value u, (20$_1$) has the value u.

> STRONG KLEENE. Because '(20$_1$) is ungrounded$_1$', has the value t, (20$_1$) and '(20$_1$) is true' do too; '(20$_1$) is false' will then have the value f.

The second alternative is to say that an inheritor is *ungrounded*$_2$ if it is not connected to an antecedent with a conjunct (disjunct) that can acquire content independently; a conjunction (disjunction) is *ungrounded*$_2$ if it contains only ungrounded inheritors. Consider now

(20$_2$) (20$_2$) is false, or (20$_2$) is ungrounded$_2$.

(20$_2$) is grounded$_2$, so '(20$_2$) is ungrounded$_2$' has the value f. On both Weak and Strong Kleene (20$_2$), '(20$_2$) is true' and '(20$_2$) is false' have the value u.

A third "alternative" is to say that a sentence is *grounded*$_3$ if it is either true or false. But then 'grounded$_3$' is a disguised inheritor. If X has no content, 'X is true' and 'X is false' don't either. So 'X is grounded' will lack content also. If 'true' and 'false' are to be used in definitions, care must be taken to see that the inheritors they occur in are grounded.

12. Semantic and Logical Paradoxes

If this account of the Liar is successful in the way I think it is, the distinction between the semantic and logical paradoxes collapses. I believe that in each case the problems stem from ungrounded modified inheritors. Formal-language variables are very like quantificational proforms: The ungrounding problems that arise for inheritors are problems that variables can have also.

5

Prosentences and Propositional Quantification:
A Response to Zimmerman*

In Chapter 3 of this book (Grover, Camp and Belnap 1975), we propose an alternative to the simple subject-predicate grammatical analysis of sentences containing 'true' and 'false'; we then develop an account of the semantic and pragmatic roles of 'true' and 'false' which is suggested by that alternative. If the prosentential theory is right, ordinary truth talk can be explained without making the assumption that 'true' and 'false' have as their (primary) role, property ascription. In Part I of his paper, Zimmerman (1978) gives a good summary of our prosentential characterization of 'true'.

Although we recognize that the semanticist may need to introduce some abstract entities to explain other aspects of language usage, we see it as a merit that the prosentential theory promises an account according to which propositions do not need to be introduced as the bearers of truth, so that to make reference to such entities would not be a commonplace of ordinary truth talk. Another advantage of our theory is that it provides good explanations of a number of intuitions concerning truth that have been articulated by Ramsey, Strawson, and Quine (see Chapter 3). I have also shown, in Chapter 4 (Grover 1977), that the prosentential theory provides a good account of the Liar and related sentences as lacking propositional content, and that the theory can motivate, beyond simply the desire for one consistent truth concept, the truth model with its minimal fixed point as presented in Kripke (1975). Other semantic paradoxes can also be explained.

Other than to say that it is suggested by the subject predicate analysis, we did not seek (in Chapter 3) to explain the intuition that 'true' and 'false' have property-ascribing roles. It is now clear, however, that (to the extent that others can obtain extensions) ex-

---

* See Zimmerman 1978.

tensions for 'true' and 'false' can be derived on the prosentential account. I investigate the possibility that this leads to property-ascribing uses in Chapters 6 and 7.

In Part II of his paper, Zimmerman raises questions concerning the role of our atomic prosentence 'thatt' in English + 'thatt', the acceptability of propositional quantification in explanations of English, and the (possible) irredundancy of connectives of English* containing 'true' and 'false'. Accordingly, this response has three sections. I will restrict discussion to the more important points that Zimmerman raises.

1. Prosentences

Zimmerman claims that the prosentential theory has not been shown plausible. One aspect of our account he finds fault with is our employment of 'thatt' as an atomic prosentence. His complaint appears to be that 'thatt' cannot be understood unless a reading in colloquial English is provided for it; but to 'interpret' it as either 'That is true' or 'It is true' as he claims we do is, he says, to beg the question.

'Thatt' was introduced in Chapter 2 (Grover 1972) as an atomic prosentence to provide readings in an extension of English of bound propositional variables that occupied sentential positions in formulas of certain formal languages. An informal account of the grammar and semantics of prosentences was given both there and in Chapter 3. (Because the possibility that 'It is true' might function as a prosentence had not yet been explored, I had no good reason at that time to believe that there were any expressions in English which functioned as generally available prosentences. Zimmerman misleadingly describes the situation I was in when he says that I "admit" in the early paper that there are no good readings available in English.) Because Zimmerman's comment that "it is not implausible to assume that certain terms in English function as prosentences" suggests that he *does* understand what a prosentence is—at least the "lazy" kind—it is puzzling that he thinks 'thatt' should be interpreted. In fact, Zimmerman is confused in thinking that we try to give what he calls an interpretation of 'thatt'. In Chapter 3, §2.2, we clearly say we are using 'thatt' merely as a heuristic device, to illustrate the functioning of prosentences. It was not introduced— as he suggests—to "bolster" the claim that 'That is true' and 'It is true' function as prosentences. The point was to help the reader understand what such a claim would come to: We hoped that the association of 'That is true' and 'It is true' with an atomic prosentence would help break habits suggested by the subject-predicate/property-ascribing analysis. Perhaps this expository move was a mistake: Because 'thatt' does not have the form of an English declarative, it may not be sufficiently suggestive. We have, for example, Wittgenstein's (1953, Part I, p. 134) comment on the failure of 'p' to give the "general form of propositions":

> We may say, e.g.: "He explained his position to me, said that this was how things were, and that therefore he needed an advance." So far, then, one can say that that sentence ['That is how things are'] stands for any statement. It is employed as a propositional schema, but only because it has the construction of an English sentence. It would also be possible here to use a letter, a variable, as in symbolic logic. But no one is going to call the letter the general form of propositions. To repeat: "This is how things are" has the position only because it is itself what one calls an English sentence. But though it is a proposition, still it gets employed as a propositional variable. . . .

Prior sees Wittgenstein as suggesting a prosentential role for 'This is how things are'. (Judy Walter has pointed out to me that this interpretation is found especially in Prior 1967.) An *atomic* prosentence is not as much in the spirit of English grammar as is one with the structure noun-plus-verb-phrase. We should have emphasized this point more strongly than we did in Chapter 3, §2.6.

Be that as it may, how do we bolster our claim that 'That is true' and 'It is true' function as prosentences? Do we have an argument? Yes, but not a conclusive argument. We describe how prosentences would function if there were any in English and also show what it would be for 'That is true' and 'It is true'—if we abandoned the standard analysis—to function in that way. We show that the division into the "lazy" and "quantificational" uses, as well as the concept of an antecedent, fit the prosentential account. Further support for accepting the analysis comes from the fact that important features of usage can be explained, and also the Liar and other paradoxes. But more work needs to be done before the theory can be properly evaluated against the standard analysis; so we don't claim to have shown that 'That is true' *must* be construed as a prosentence, only that it might be so construed.

Another worry that Zimmerman has concerning prosentences in English arises when he discusses the connectives of English. He questions our assumption that there are many modified prosentences.

It is widely acknowledged (by linguists at least) that English contains a great variety of anaphoric devices. And if, instead of focusing on single sentences, semanticists had considered sets of sentences which comprise discourses, and the varieties of ways in which semantic connections are established between discourses, we would have a better understanding and appreciation of the variety of these anaphoric devices. Anaphoric devices are used (at least) to establish connections between one piece of discourse and another, and for generalization. Because it seems reasonable to assume that we should wish to establish connections with what others say, no matter what the grammatical category, we might expect natural languages to contain a variety of proforms. Furthermore, given that we have modified forms of other sentences, we should expect modified forms of prosentences. In the light of these considerations, it is not clear we should be impressed by Zimmerman's claim that he found our suggestion that there are many modified prosentences "hard to swallow."

2. Propositional Quantification

Zimmerman's principal objection to the prosentential theory is directed at our assumption that some parts of English involve propositional quantification. We are not, of course, in a position to either claim or conjecture that propositional quantification will feature in "the final analysis" of English, but that is not what is at issue. Zimmerman appears skeptical that it is even prima facie plausible that propositional quantification occurs in English.

Quine (1970, p. 11) appears to assume that just as we have a desire to generalize with respect to the noun places in 'Tom is Tom', so also we have a desire to generalize with respect to the sentence places in 'Tom is mortal or Tom is not mortal' and 'Snow is white or snow is not white'. That seems right. Given we have the desire, why should speakers of English not in fact generalize with respect to sentence positions? Is there a reason why we shouldn't? Quine and presumably Zimmerman assume that only individual quantification is involved in the resulting generalization. But to assume this because 'it' or some other nominalization appears in the generalization is not a sufficient reason. If Wittgenstein is right, we should expect a prosentence to have the form of an English "proposition" and so, given the centrality of the noun-plus-verb-phrase structure, we might expect a prosentence to contain a noun such as 'it': An anaphoric 'it' would then signal merely some kind of anaphoric device, not a specific one. Philosophers should investigate analyses that, in assuming the employment of some kind of *sentential* anaphoric device, respect the desire to generalize with respect to sentential positions. (Prior proposes such an analysis of 'However he says things are, that's how they are'.)

A reason Zimmerman gives for his skepticism is his claim that whereas we haven't shown that propositional quantification functions properly in English, he knows that individual quantification does. I am not sure what it is that is known about the one that is not known about the other, because a formally correct semantics has been given for each as it occurs in formal languages. Perhaps he means that there is a fairly comprehensive account of individual quantification as it occurs in English which we do not have for propositional quantification. But then his claim is false. What account (with what domain?) would he give of sentences like 'Anything you might say about Mary is either true or false'? (And what would he do with 'There are Greek gods that Robert Graves doesn't know about'?) In the case of both kinds of quantification, our understanding—such as it is—derives pretty much from attempted translations into formal languages. There is one difference: Whereas there is general—not universal (see Montague (1970) for example)— agreement that there are at least some sentences in English which involve something close to individual quantification as it occurs in first-order logics, there is no such general agreement concerning sentences in English and propositional quantification logics. But a majority vote isn't a good reason for supposing that one kind of quantification "functions properly" in English while the other doesn't. Is there a reason for rejecting an account of English which assumes propositional quantification?

There are some—perhaps Zimmerman—who would *prefer* an analysis of English which did not assume that propositional quantification is a part of English. A reason is that they do not want an analysis of language to presuppose the existence of abstract entities like propositions. Because I doubt we can get by without propositions (all semanticists assume a domain or lattice containing at least 1 and 0), I will not discuss that point. Another reason someone might have for objecting to propositional quantification is that it would have the object language user—as well as the semanticist— referring to propositions. This position is hard to evaluate because it is not clear what determines that a language user has referred to a proposition. We tried, in cautioning about "range over" talk, to at least draw attention to some things that have been run roughshod over (Chapter 3, §2.2). Because the question of the acceptability of propositional quantification is important, I will take up that discussion here.

We cautioned about "range over" talk because such talk often goes hand in hand with a tendency among philosophers to assimilate propositional quantification to individual quantification. Along with this assimilation is then the worry that certain expressions in English (e.g., sentences) must be construed as names of propositions (Quine 1970, p. 74; Suppes 1957, p. 128). But is the assimilation reasonable?

Because of a desire to provide uniform treatments and models, logicians have associated a denotation, or both an extension and an intension, with all expressions, irrespective of their grammatical categories. Although there are many advantages to doing things this way, there are disadvantages: Important differences are ignored. Thus, for example, the relation between a sentence and the proposition it expresses is not the same as the relation between a proper name and its bearer.

Propositions have been introduced as the intensions of sentences but, just as Prior (1967) says, " 'What a sentence says' . . . is misleading . . . when it means anything, it means 'how a sentence says things are' or, better, 'how we say things are' when we use the sentence in question," so also the reification of propositions as set theoretic entities is misleading. In ordinary English we would usually give what a sentence means or expresses by means of another already understood sentence—that's how we say how things are. Set theoretic reifications of propositions have point to the extent that we can recover from them how things are said to be. We should keep an eye on such facts when trying to determine what a semantic analysis tells us about the object language user's use of language. (I take it that Clark [1970] has in mind a similar point. See especially the last couple of sentences.)

Now what of generalizations with respect to sentential positions? From the point of view of the standard semantic accounts given of individual and propositional quantification as they occur in formal languages, I think there is reason to believe that although the semanticist assumes and talks about—what he considers to be—appropriate domains or lattices in each case, in the one case the object language user says something about the objects that happen to be in the semanticist's domain, and in the other he doesn't. The proposition expressed by, say, a universal generalization, is the intersection—or some associated operation, depending on how propositions are reified—of propositions that may possibly be expressed by substitution instances. In the one case instances contain terms that are used to *refer* to objects in the domain, and in the other, sentences that *express* propositions belonging to the domain—given the reification. In the latter case, the instances, and so, I believe, the generalizations, are about things like Tom and snow, not propositions. Others disagree: Propositional variables, like individual variables, are said by semanticists to have "a domain as their range," and this implies reference (by the object language user) to propositions. But to draw such an implication from what the semanticist does ignores the fact that the point of the presence of the "objects" in the domains is different: In the one case the objects are referents of terms in the object language, and in the other they are reifications of what sentences are said to express. Given such complications, the move from what one understands the semanticist to be doing, to the claim that the object language user refers to propositions, is too swift. The issues are clearly complex, more complex than I have been able to present here. I conjecture, however, that, if the semanticist does need propositions, more careful thinking may well reveal that a semantic account that assumes that only individual quantification occurs in English will have to portray object language users as commonly referring to, or talking about, propositions.

3. Irredundant Uses of 'True'

In our description of the syntax of English (Chapter 3, §2.4), we say that English* does not contain 'true' in any interesting sense, meaning, as we explain, that the truth predicate is not isolable. Because Zimmerman takes us to be claiming that 'true' does not have any interesting uses in a much broader sense, I think he must have missed our explanation. Of course the uses of 'true' in prosentences and connectives are interesting. All anaphoric devices are interesting!

The most important question Zimmerman raises with respect to English* concerns our conjecture that some of our connectives (e.g., 'It's false that') may be irredundant. Is there a problem here for the prosentential theory?

In Chapter 3, §4.9 we conjecture that quantificational prosentences, like quantificational pronouns, are "logically" irredundant in that they enable us to say things (by way of generalizations) that we would not otherwise be able to say in English. We also point out that some "lazy" pronouns may, for all we know, be logically irredundant. But the fact that pronouns cannot always be replaced either by their antecedents or modified forms of their antecendents (e.g., 'her' in 'the woman with a ribbon in her hair') does not make pronouns, as we say in §4.9, either "topically," "ascriptively," or "categorically" irredundant. They do not introduce new topics, properties, or conceptual frameworks. Similarly, some of our connectives may be logically irredundant in that the connective-plus-sentence cannot be replaced by a modified form of the component (i.e., antecedent) sentence. The function of such a prosentential connective is to provide us with a modified form of a given sentence when simple tinkerings with verbs would fail to do the trick. (See, e.g., Zimmerman's footnote 9.) Given that modified prosentences provide us with ways of asserting modified forms of antecedent sentences, it seems natural that a language user, when wanting a way of constructing a modified form of a complex sentence, should employ the appropriate modified prosentence in connective form. The connective-plus-sentence yields the required modified form of the sentence in question. On this account, the connectives remain topically, ascriptively, and categorically redundant, because, if we know the propositional content of the component sentence, we can figure out the content of the connective-plus-sentence: just as modified prosentences have as their propositional content an appropriately modified form of their antecedent's content, so also a connective-plus-sentence has as its propositional content an appropriately modified form of the component sentence's content.

Prosentences thereby become useful not only for pragmatic punch and generalizations, but also in that they provide modified forms of sentences. Perhaps the more occurrences there are of irredundant proforms, the more useful they are, and so the more interesting.

The reader of Chapter 3 may have noted that in §4.9 we claim that quantificational prosentences are ascriptively redundant in that they do not introduce "new noncomposite properties." This correctly describes what I have called the primary role of 'true', because, according to the prosentential theory, English truth talk can be explained without beginning with an assumption that 'true' and 'false' are property ascribing. However, in view of the fact that extensions for 'true' and 'false' can be derived from a prosentential 'true', the implied claim that 'true' in no way introduced a new noncomposite property must be withdrawn. The issues are complex. This last topic is discussed in Chapters 6 and 7.

6

Truth*

On the one hand it seems that 'It is true that snow is white', ' "Snow is white" is true', and 'Snow is white' all seem to say the same thing: Proponents of some theories of truth claim 'true' is redundant; yet on the other hand, if we ask what the sentences are about, different answers come to mind: Proponents of other theories claim 'true' is used to ascribe a property or relation to sentences or propositions. Despite the apparent conflict between these positions, each appeals to intuitions that most of us have; our understanding of 'true' would be enhanced if we had a theory that explained the source of each intuition. In this paper I will discuss, from the point of view of the prosentential theory of truth (presented in Chapter 3, originally published as Grover, Camp, Belnap 1975)—both aspects of 'true'. Because it has already been shown that the prosentential theory incorporates the idea motivating the redundancy theory, the emphasis will be on the property-ascribing aspect. I will investigate the possibility that a property-ascribing 'true' derives from a prosentential 'true' and, in discussion of occasions in which a predicate might prove useful, draw attention to the interplay between the basic prosentential aspect of 'true' (which, so to speak, has 'true' at the "object language level") and the derivative property-ascribing ("metalinguistic level") aspect of 'true'. In the final section of the paper, I will argue that a substantive assumption of the prosentential theory, that propositional quantification into sentence place occurs in English, is a plausible one. Because Strawson argues against a similar claim by Prior, I will address his argument.

* I have benefited from many discussions with Herbert Heidelberger and other members of the University of Massachusetts and Smith College philosophy departments during the preparation of this paper. I thank Anil Gupta for drawing attention to some confusions in an earlier draft of §3.1. Also helpful have been comments made on an earlier draft by Kent Wilson and other colleagues at the University of Illinois, Chicago. The research was supported in part by an NEH summer grant.

Below is a brief summary of the prosentential theory. The reader
is referred to Chapters 3 and 4 for further details.[1] It will be seen
that, although the analysis provided by the prosentential theory of
sentences containing 'true' borrows heavily from Ramsey, much of
our understanding of the utility of the truth predicate in colloquial
language has been inspired by Strawson's perceptive and stimulat-
ing remarks on truth.

Because we felt a need for a better understanding of our employment of 'true' and 'false' in colloquial language, and in recognition
of the fact that a given grammatical analysis of a sentence can
sometimes mislead, we proposed, in Chapter 3, an alternative to the
standard subject-predicate analysis of sentences containing 'true',
according to which the subject term must refer and the predicate be
property-ascribing. The semantic and pragmatic roles of 'true' and
its cognates that are suggested by our alternative were explored.
Our alternative employed the concept of a *prosentence*. *Prosentences* were introduced by analogy with pronouns. However,
whereas pronouns occupy positions in sentences that singular
terms occupy, prosentences occupy positions that declarative sentences occupy. Pronouns and prosentences are alike in that both can
be used anaphorically. A central claim of the prosentential theory
is that 'That is true' and 'It is true' are used as prosentences. Just as
'he' in

Tom is on the left, and *he* is wearing Dad's old hat.

is anaphorically related to its antecedent, 'Tom', from which it acquires its referent, so 'That is true', construed as a prosentence in

MARY: The school year has started.
JANE: If *that's true*, then he's probably away at college now.

has 'The school year has started' as its antecedent, from which it
acquires its propositional content. When an anaphoric pronoun is
used in this "lazy" way, we know no new object or person is being
referred to. Similarly, in the case of prosentences, when a prosentence of laziness (Chapter 3, §2.1) is used we know nothing new is
being said or entertained. This is a feature of 'true'—although not
so described—that the redundancy theorists took account of.

The prosentential theory does not claim that 'true' is redundant,
however. Use of a prosentence can carry pragmatic force that mere

---

[1] The reader is also referred to Prior (1967), who similarly suggests a prosentential
role for 'true'.

repetition of the antecedent sentence would not effect. When a proform (i.e., a pronoun, prosentence, proadjective, etc.) is used, an antecedent is explicitly acknowledged. By using a prosentence, a speaker can make it clear that he or she is agreeing with, considering, or granting a point that has already been made or might be made.

Like pronouns, prosentences are also used in generalizing. Just as we have, for example, a quantificational 'it' in

A melon is ripe if *it* feels soft.

so, also, 'it is true' can be used as a quantificational prosentence to obtain a generalization of

If the doctor says that smoking is bad for you, then smoking is bad for you.

A colloquial reading of a generalized form is

(1) All that the doctor says is true.

Such uses of 'true' were classified as quantificational (Chapter 3, §2.1) and explained—in part—by paraphrase into a language containing bound propositional variables. A translation of (1), appropriate for at least some occasions of its use, is, following Ramsey (1927),

$\forall p$(If the doctor says that p, then p)

For other occasions of use, (1) might be better captured using the conditional, '/', of Belnap (1973)

$\forall p$(the doctor says that p/p)

The former suggests the following paraphrases of (1):

Anything that might be said is such that, if the doctor says that *it is true*, then *it is true*.

or the more colloquial

Whatever the doctor says, *it is true*.

The quantificational prosentence 'It is true' is the analogue in English of a bound propositional variable. This example illustrates both how 'It is true' is used as a quantificational prosentence and what a prosentential analysis of a sentence such as (1) comes to.

We conjecture that just as pronouns seem not to be eliminable from English without loss, so also quantificational uses of 'true' cannot be eliminated without loss. Like variables of formal languages, proforms of natural languages allow us to say things, by way of generalizations, that cannot be said otherwise.

In Chapter 3, §2.5, we noted another feature of prosentences: Like other sentences, prosentences can be modified. We have, for example, 'That was true', 'That is probably true', and 'That is false'. Modified prosentences acquire as their propositional content an appropriately modified form of their antecedent's content. And connectives such as 'It was true', 'It is probably true that', and 'It is false that' can be used to construct modified forms of the ("antecedent") sentence to which they are attached. Such connectives are especially useful—perhaps essential—when simple tinkerings with the available verbs do not provide the required modification. The contradiction, for example, of the counterfactual

If the switch is up, the light is on.

which cannot be expressed by either

If the switch is not up, the light is on.

or

If the switch is up, the light is not on.

can be expressed by

It is false that if the switch is up the light is on.

With such cases in mind, we argued that 'true' is "logically" irredundant (Chapter 3, §4.9, Chapter 5, §3). So, although with the redundancy theorists we claim 'That is true' says the same thing as its antecedent, we do not claim 'true' is redundant: We conjecture that 'true' and its modified forms are needed for generalizing and modifying sentences. We have also seen that prosentential constructions are useful pragmatically. Indeed, anaphoric devices of various kinds may be essential for successful communication, not just for the accompanying pragmatic force that their use may carry, but as providing a way of making needed semantic connections between discourses and parts of discourses.

A substantive claim of the prosentential theory (see Chapter 3, §2.4) was that all uses of 'true' in colloquial English "can be viewed as involving only prosentential uses of 'true'." This was how we thought theory should be formulated, even though we hadn't given anything like a conclusive defense of the claim, and even though there are occurrences, as in 'true likeness', that we had not said anything about. The considerations of this present discussion call for a slight modification of this thesis (see §4.1 below). Until now, the question as to whether the prosentential theory might provide an explanation of philosophers' technical or theoretical uses of 'true' has been left open (see Chapter 3, §4.8). The principal purpose of this paper is to discuss some of these uses.

The principal merits of the prosentential theory, as it has so far been developed, lie (I believe) in the explanation it provides of our understanding of 'true' as it is used in colloquial language. As I have already pointed out, the theory explains why it is that 'true' seems to "add nothing" to the antecedent sentence[2]: Prosentences of laziness acquire as their propositional content the content of their antecedents. The theory also explains why sentences containing 'true' are used with the kind of performatory force Strawson suggests they have (see Strawson 1949, 1950a). Strawson in one instance compares 'That is true' with 'Ditto.' Although there is a lot more to prosentences than to 'Ditto', there are in some occurrences some important similarities, which Strawson's remarks draw attention to. On p. 91 of Strawson (1949), we have "When somebody has made an assertion previously, my saying 'Ditto' acquires a point, has an occasion: and, if you like, you may say that I am now making a statement, repeating in a manner, what the speaker said. But I am not making an additional statement, a meta-statement" and on p. 93, "In using such expressions we are confirming, underwriting, admitting, agreeing with, what someone has said." We believe that Strawson is right about all of this and, furthermore, that a theory of 'true' should explain this usage. However, as the quote from p. 91 continues with "It would perhaps be better to say that my utterance is not a statement at all, but a linguistic performance," it is unclear whether Strawson would want to endorse our suggestion that 'That is true' has as its propositional content the content of its antecedent. But perhaps some finer distinctions are needed. I fully expect our construal of the functioning of prosentences will have to be substantially revised when a more rigorous account is provided, their

---

[2] Redundancy theorists, by the way, are not the only philosophers who are inclined to say that 'true' "adds nothing." Frege (1918–19) says: "The sentence 'I smell the scent of violets' has the same content as the sentence 'It is true that I smell the scent of violets'. So it seems, then, that nothing is added to the thought by my ascribing to it the property truth."

syntactic structure accounted for, and more of their nuances are isolated.

Why is it that sentences containing 'true' can be used to confirm,
underwrite, and express agreement? Consider the case of agreement. A person may express agreement by saying, 'I agree'. He or
she might also express agreement by in some way indicating a will-
ingness, perhaps even a desire, to assert whatever it is that is agreed
upon. On some occasions, simple repetition of what the other has
said will do the trick. But sometimes it won't. The context may not
make it clear that the speaker is aware (for example) that someone
else has already said the same thing. The expression of agreement
is not then recognized. And this is where a prosentence may prove
useful, because when a prosentence of laziness is used, an antecedent is explicitly acknowledged. Because those who espouse a
property-ascribing role for 'true' (in colloquial English) *also* provide
a tie with the antecedent sentence ('that' refers to the antecedent,
or what is expressed), it has been objected that the prosentential
theory does not provide a better explanation of this feature of our
use of 'true'. My reply is that whereas on the prosentential theory
agreement is expressed by "saying the same thing", on the property-
ascribing view, use of 'That is true' changes the topic—to sentences,
or propositions, or whatever. It must then be explained how, under
such circumstances, an expression of agreement is conveyed. By
comparison the prosentential account is a simple one.

I have also argued, in Chapter 4, that the prosentential theory provides a nice account of the Liar and related sentences as sentences
that fail to express a proposition. It is interesting to note further
agreement with Strawson's account of 'true' and 'false'. His suggestion is that such uses of 'true' and 'false' are spurious. There is a
failure to make a statement. On my account prosentences of laziness must rely on other sentences for their content. As Strawson
(1949) says on p. 91, "The words 'true' and 'false' normally require,
as an occasion for their significant use, that somebody should have
made, be making or be about to make (utter or write), some statement." (Of course this doesn't hold for all quantificational uses of
'true' but does for most "lazy" uses.)

The prosentential theory also explains why it is that 'true' is
needed—as Quine (1970) points out—in generalizing: That just is
one of the principal functions of proforms. Because Quine is not
inclined to accept our substantive assumption that natural languages contain something like propositional quantification, our ex-

planation of this fact differs from his, of course. Quine's account is in terms of linguistic ascent and first-order quantification.

1. Two Sources of Scepticism

Should the prosentential theory be pursued any further? I think there are some who think that the project may be basically wrongheaded. Their scepticism arises from considerations like the following:

OBJECTION. What you have said about a prosentential role for 'true' is interesting, but something important about truth seems to be missing. We talk of people seeking the truth and contemplating the truth. Frege (in Klemke, p. 507), says: "The word 'true' indicates the aim of logic as does 'beautiful' that of aesthetics or 'good' that of ethics. All sciences have truth as their goal." Truth as the goal of the sciences, or the aim of logic, is highly valued. Now all you seem to have given us are prosentences. And although prosentences may well constitute an important feature of natural languages, it is not clear that such an account of the role of 'true' in English can account for the fact that Truth is regarded in these significant ways.

REPLY. Although, needless to say, I am not in a position to give a complete analysis of our use of the word 'truth', I doubt the prosentential theory is in a worse position than any other theory in this respect: Seeking the truth or contemplating the truth is hardly a matter of seeking or contemplating a *property truth*.

Surely our interest is primarily in such matters as whether it will snow again this month, whether an ice age is imminent, whether honesty is a virtue, and perhaps even whether there is a truth property. When we are concerned with truth, these are the questions we seek answers to and the matters we contemplate. And the prosentential theory has its place here. For example, a modified quantificational prosentence may be used to formulate the relevant general questions

> For anything you may consider, is it true?

or simply

> What is true?

which has as instances

Is it going to snow again, and will my garage roof collapse?
Is honesty a virtue?

Now it might be thought, by someone who assumes the primary role of 'true' is property-ascription, that seeking or contemplating the truth is a matter of seeking or contemplating sentences or propositions that have the property truth. But this in itself doesn't explain the degree of interest there is in truth. And that is what is in question here. Why should there be an interest in sentences or propositions that are said to have the property truth? I suggest the reason, relevant to the above objection, is that we have an interest in such questions as whether an ice age is imminent. Just how that interest might account for an interest in sentences that have the property truth should become clear in the discussion in §3 of the utility of a property-ascribing 'true'.

Another worry about the prosentential theory arises from those who consider a property-ascribing 'true' to be essential in philosophical inquiry. In the case of one who has an interest in utilizing formal semantic theories, doubts may arise in something like the following way:

OBJECTION. The prosentential theory, in construing 'true' as having a prosentential role, seems to leave no room for property-ascribing uses of 'true'. This clearly conflicts with the semantic theory of truth, which assumes that 'true' is property-ascribing. Because model theory is an indispensable tool of logicians and semanticists, a requirement on any theory of truth must be that it leave the essentials of Tarski's semantic theory intact. If, because of the non-property-ascribing prosentential role, the prosentential theory is in serious conflict with the semantic theory, the prosentential theory must either be rejected or significantly modified.

Furthermore, what more could we want than the riches of Tarski's kind of theory? Tarski provided us with a formal definition of truth, of which even more attractive versions have been developed by Kripke (1975) and Martin and Woodruff (1975). In all of these we've been shown how to avoid paradox.

REPLY. There is an assumption here, encouraged to some extent in Chapter 3, that if all uses of 'true' in colloquial English involve only prosentential uses of 'true', or in some way are to be explained in terms of a prosentential 'true', then the possibility that 'true' may sometimes be used in important ways to ascribe a property is excluded. This is not quite right. Given—at least for simple languages—that prosentences (like bound propositional variables) can be used to define "appropriate extensions for 'true' and 'false'," it would seem reasonable to speculate that in natural language also prosentences may bring with them "appropriate extensions." If that is the case, a prosentential 'true', rather than excluding the possibility of an extension being associated with 'true', might well introduce it. Just what this would mean in terms of a truth property is the principal topic of this paper.

In the present inquiry I will ignore questions of conflict between Tarski's project and the prosentential and focus, instead, on the problem of explaining something of the source of our interest in uses of the truth predicate that Tarski had his eye on.

There is also an assumption in the above objection that our understanding of 'true' as it is used in natural languages is not very important, or at least not important if one's main concern is with formal languages and the resources of formal languages. Perhaps underlying this is an acceptance of Tarski's despair regarding natural languages when he says (Tarski 1936, §6), "The considerations of §1 prove emphatically that the concept of truth (as well as other semantical concepts) when applied to colloquial language in conjunction with the normal laws of logic leads inevitably to confusions and contradictions." But should things be left at this? Clearly those who are interested in the phenomena of language, especially colloquial languages, will want a theory of 'true' which reveals something of what these confusions and contradictions come to. But I think such a theory is of interest beyond that.

Although various techniques have been developed for avoiding paradox in formal languages, it is still unclear what conceptual confusions led to the construction, initially, of languages that contain contradictions. It is possible we will acquire a better understanding of formal languages as we get a better understanding of the natural languages from which they derive. Moreover, might one not want to know something more than that a concept is clear and precise? Why, for example, does the concept of truth feature in discussions of (formal) languages?

Philosophers are faced with a labyrinth of theories of truth. Besides the semantic theory we have, of course, the correspondence, coherence, and pragmatic theories of truth. According to some versions of these (or other theories), truth is a property; according to others it is a relation; according to some, sentences are the primary bearers of truth, and according to others, propositions are. And so the list goes on. Surely we should try to find some way of getting these conflicting suggestions into perspective. One thing we might do is see whether a theory that explains our understanding of 'true' will lead us to a better understanding of what philosophers are saying about truth and related things.

2. Extensions for 'True' and 'False'

Suppose, for a minute, there is someone who has been brought up on the prosentential theory and who also has no knowledge of a past history of truth property talk. That is, until now this person has always thought of each use of 'true' as prosentential. What might lead this person to start thinking of 'true' as a predicate with a property-ascribing role, other than the observation that predicates usually have such a role?

Equipped with the quantificational prosentence 'It is true', the prosententialist can ask certain general questions. One place to start would be with

Q1 Are there sets of sentences S_1 and S_2 such that for each sentence x, x is in S_1 iff it is true and x is in S_2 iff it is false?

The condition stated in the question has instances like

'Snow is white' is in S_1 iff it is true, and 'Snow is white' is in S_2 iff it is false.

which in turn, if we now interpret 'It is true' as a prosentence of laziness, has as its "instance"

'Snow is white' is in S_1 iff snow is white, and 'Snow is white' is in S_2 iff snow is not white.

Even a prosententialist will agree that sets such as S_1 and S_2 would be good to have.

We can anticipate many of the problems our prosententialist will encounter in trying to construct the sets S_1 and S_2 in this way for sentence types of a natural language. In many cases, context (at least partially) determines the propositional content, if not the meaning, of a sentence. And then the condition stated in (Q1) is not uniquely determined for a given s. For this reason it may be better to work with a domain of tokens (or "possible tokens," if that idea can be coherently articulated). But a domain of all well-formed tokens won't do either, because sentence tokens that are semantically deviant will be included. A referring term in a token may, for ex-

ample, fail to refer; or a token may contain an "ungrounded" proform (Chapter 4): In the simple case, a prosentence is *ungrounded*
if it is not connected (by the anaphoric relation) to a sentence that
acquires its content—as 'Snow is white' does—independently. Because prosentences of laziness acquire their propositional content
from their antecedents, they can fail to express a proposition if ungrounded. (When taken "self-referentially," 'This is true' is an example of an ungrounded prosentence that *fails* to express a proposition.) If 'It is true' in the above condition fails to acquire
propositional content from its antecedent, the "condition fails to
state a condition on membership in S_1 and S_2." For this reason the
prosententialist must begin with a domain of (possible) sentence tokens that have determinate propositional content.

Suppose, for the purposes of this discussion, the prosententialist
has successfully divided (possible) tokens in this way. He or she
might then entertain the idea of introducing a couple of predicates,
say 'True' and 'False', which have S_1 and S_2 as their extensions. Because the addition of 'True' and 'False' has given us some new sentence tokens, the question arises

Q2   How might 'True' and 'False' be added to the language?

It would be fortunate if, by this time, the prosententialist had
come across the work of Kripke (1975) or Martin and Woodruff
(1975). Their results suggest answers—at least in the case of formal
language analogues—to Q2. The prosententialist, in contemplating
the addition of 'True' and 'False', might consider proceeding in
pretty much the way suggested by Kripke on p. 701 and p. 705. The
natural place to stop will be at the minimal fixed point. Beyond that
point, 'It is true' fails to be properly grounded and so the "condition" again fails to state a condition on membership in the sets.

Of course the idea here is a familiar one and is stated succinctly
in a language containing bound propositional variables and quotes.
For an appropriate substitution range of sentence tokens, we have

For any p, 'p' is True iff p.

3. Would a Property-Ascribing 'True' Be Useful?

Suppose the prosentence 'It is true' generates an extension in such
a way. Where does this leave us with respect to the role of 'True' in
English, including philosophical discourse?

An extension seems to justify the claim that there is a truth property. But we need more than that. It is one thing to introduce an adjective and assign it an extension, and another to find occasions in which to use it. The property is a little odd: The sentence (or sentence token) 'Snow is white' has this property truth just in case snow has a certain property, 'There is life on Mars' is True just in case there is life on Mars, and so on. Could I just as effectively introduce an adjective 'blah', with letters of the alphabet in its extension, as follows?

'a' is blah iff snow is white.

'b' is blah iff there is life on Mars.

'c' is blah iff an ice age is imminent.

'd' is blah iff no further cases of smallpox are isolated.

It is doubtful, isn't it, that 'blah' would find its way into ordinary discourse? For it is hard, though not impossible, to imagine what interest might prompt someone to use it—not any interest speakers presently have in 'a' or 'b', anyway.

Suppose, however, the unlikely happens: A highly respected biologist says, in all seriousness, " 'b' is blah." Our interest might well be captured. However, it is clear that it is not 'b' we are curious about, but (if not the oddity of the utterance) the question of life on other planets. And we remain puzzled as to whether all the scientist intends to convey is that there is life on Mars and, if so, why he or she chose to use the sentence 'b is blah'. Similarly, we might try to explain any interest aroused by an utterance of a sentence containing 'True' by the curiosity we have in extralinguistic matters. But, again, this doesn't explain why someone should use a sentence such as " 'There is life on Mars' is True" rather than the sentence 'There is life on Mars'. Because semanticists and logicians (at least) think they can put a property-ascribing 'True' to good use, there is, somewhere here, an important difference between 'True' and 'blah'. Presumably the difference lies in the fact that the extension seems, in the one case, to be arbitrarily determined while, in the other, the expression quoted is the sentence used in the condition determining the extension. What might prompt the use of a property-ascribing *linguistic* predicate that has its extension determined by *extralinguistic* facts in the way the extension of 'True' is determined?

Presumably the occasions in which the predicate is used, if at all, will be ones in which there is some reason to talk of sentences.

Quine argues, of course, that there is such a need when generalizing, but a prosententialist doesn't need a property-ascribing 'True' for that. In the sections below on Meaning and Truth (§3.1), and Logic and Truth (§3.2), I suggest a couple of occasions in which there seems to be point in using a property-ascribing 'True'. I leave open such questions as whether types, or tokens, or something else, should or can be in the extensions of 'True' and 'False'.

Although this prosententialist approach to the topic of a truth property is different—it has been described as a "backwards approach" but might, for all that, be a move towards the right approach—I do not claim that the following sketch of the possible utility of a property-ascribing truth predicate can be given only on the prosential theory.

3.1. MEANING AND TRUTH

It is often assumed that a property-ascribing 'true' is used in accounts of meaning that appeal to the truth conditions of sentences. For a statement of the truth conditions of a sentence is assumed to be a statement of the conditions in which the sentence has the property truth and those conditions in which it has the property falsity. I am not going to discuss the question of the extent to which a theory of truth conditions might contribute to a theory of meaning, nor what form such a theory should take. What I wish to consider is why it should seem even initially plausible that, say, a statement of the truth conditions of sentences, as presented for example in the recursive clauses of Tarski's truth definition, gives at least something of the meaning of the logical connectives; or, why it seems plausible that truth conditions represented by, say, mappings from circumstances (possible words) and contexts into truth values capture the meaning (or part of the meaning) of a sentence (Lewis 1972).

What is it about the property *truth* that makes it a candidate in an account of *meaning*? And, if someone is said to know the truth conditions of a sentence, does that mean he or she knows *that it has the property truth* in such and such conditions, and *that it has the property falsity* in other conditions? That is, does this person have that propositional knowledge?

A theory of meaning is presumably intended as a constituent in an explanation of the phenomena of language. As language is something that is used, a theory of meaning must contribute to an account of the function of the various expressions of the language in linguistic activities. It is therefore expected that a theory of meaning will play some part in accounting for the knowledge that a competent speaker has, or perhaps might have. Speakers acquire a certain facility with language: A speaker knows *how* to perform and respond to a variety of linguistic acts, and in particular *how* to use sentences in different communicative situations. It is on the basis of such performances that we seem to make claims about *what* a speaker implicitly knows. (The question of when we are justified in making such claims is one I hope to avoid.) So, insofar as a theory of meaning provides an account of what a speaker might know, it must capture something of a speaker's facility with language. How might a theory of truth conditions become a part of this? Consider the following:

Suppose that at one time an adult says to a child, 'The milk has curdled', and at another, 'The milk hasn't curdled'; suppose, further, that what the adult says is true. Suppose also that the child has some linguistic skills: He or she can perform and respond to a variety of linguistic acts, can assert, deny, and so on. The adult might then have provided this child with one of two kinds of learning situation. (The distinction is probably not in general as sharp as I will describe it, but that won't matter for this discussion.) Suppose in the first case—which I will discuss later—the child has not been observing the milk in question but does understand the sentences. Then he or she learns something about the milk—something extralinguistic about the world. The second case is the one I wish to examine at this point. Suppose the child has been observing the milk but doesn't understand the sentences—perhaps he or she doesn't understand the word 'curdled'. Then the child may learn something of the meaning of the sentence: The child observes that when the milk is in one state the adult says, 'The milk has curdled' and when the milk is in another state the adult denies that it is curdled. The lesson continues, of course, as the child learns how to use the sentence, how to respond to utterances by others of the sentence, form questions, embed it in other sentences, and so on. At some stage the child's facility with the sentence 'The milk has curdled' demonstrates that he or she knows the meaning of the sentence. This example illustrates that appropriate use a sentence can serve to convey the meaning of a sentence. In accordance with this idea one might, in an account of meaning, try to capture the meaning of a sentence in a description of the following kind:

> In conditions (possible world) C_1, the milk has curdled.
> In conditions (possible world) C_2, the milk hasn't curdled.
> . . . .

Such sets of conditions can be given a general description if we use the prosentences 'It is true' and 'It is false'.

> An account of the meaning of a given sentence must give (at least) the conditions in which it is true and the conditions in which it is false.

The instance that leads to the above set is

> An account of the meaning of the sentence 'The milk has curdled' must give (at least) the conditions in which the milk has curdled and the conditions in which the milk hasn't curdled.

But there are difficulties here. Like the language-learning situation, the sentence whose meaning is being conveyed is used rather than mentioned. When the meaning of a sentence is being taught in the way described here, it is crucial that *that* sentence be used—a translation won't do. The sentence is, in effect, simultaneously both used and displayed. This feature is not incorporated in the present formulation. As formulated, the set of conditions is ambiguous in the way that the learning situation is ambiguous: Without help from the context, it is unclear whether the intention is to draw attention to the sentence 'The milk is curdled' or to the milk. Indeed, outside of very special contexts, our expectation would be that milk is the topic. In the presentation of a theory of meaning, some way must be found to make it quite explicit that the sentence is the topic.

The obvious way to make the point clear is to *refer to* (or display) the sentence—and then find some way of capturing the use. Of course there can be many reasons for wanting to draw attention to features of the syntax as when, for example, the meaning of a complex sentence is said to derive in some way from the meaning of its parts, or when language-world relations are discussed. So linguistic reference is needed, but in this particular case a special property would be useful also. What is wanted is a pair of properties such that a sentence has one of them just in case it is true, and the other, just in case it is false. For if we have that, a statement of the conditions in which a sentence has one or other of the properties will capture the information contained in the above list, except this time it is made explicit that the intention is to draw attention to the sentence in question. An account of the meaning of a sentence along these lines can now be expressed in Carnap's formal mode:

> In conditions (possible world) C_1 'The milk has curdled' is true.
> In conditions (possible world) C_2 'The milk has curdled' is false.
> . . . .

And this has taken us to what is usually referred to as the *truth conditions* of a sentence, where

> A statement of the truth conditions of a sentence specifies the conditions in which it has the property truth—in which case it is true—and the conditions in which the sentence has the property falsity—in which case it is false.

(As before, I assume that only sentences that have propositional content will be in the extensions of these properties.)

In summary, those who wish to explain language must, in accounting for the functioning of linguistic expressions, talk about those expressions. Furthermore, in the case of sentences, the theory must capture distinctions that are believed to underlie the use of sentences in linguistic practice. One way of doing this is to see to it that there are properties available of the sentences in question, properties that reflect the distinctions that are assumed. It is clear that 'True' and 'False' might well serve such a purpose, if their extensions are determined through the use, in the statement of the condition on the membership in the extensions, of the sentences in question. For in that case, what falls in the extension of 'True' and 'False' is *thereby* tied to the language itself in practice.

Do sets of truth conditions capture knowledge that a competent speaker has? Although someone has demonstrated facility with the sentence 'The milk has curdled', has appropriate milk experiences, and can be said to have the propositional knowledge that the milk has curdled, he or she may not have the propositional knowledge—under this description—that 'The milk has curdled' *is true*, because 'true' or some equivalent may not be in the speaker's vocabulary. So, such truth conditions do not represent—in any straightforward sense at least—the propositional knowledge that a competent speaker has. The observations of the last paragraph suggest that truth conditions may, however, represent some aspect of knowing *how* rather than knowing *that*. And this seems appropriate if a theory of meaning is to contribute to an explanation of the phenomenon of language.[3]

3.2. LOGIC AND TRUTH

Philosophers of language are not the only people who might find a truth property useful. It is generally assumed that a truth property is involved in logicians' talk of "truth preserving rules," sentences that are "true on an interpretation," and the truth table account of the logical connectives. A possible alternative to the ascription to sentences of a truth property, or truth values, is to employ a higher-order logic with quantifiers binding variables that occupy sentence positions, or else quantificational uses of a prosentential 'true'. Thus, instead of things like

If x is True and $x \to y$ is True, then y is True.
x is True in interpretation I.

we could have

If p and $p \to q$, then q.
On interpretation I, p.

where 'x' and 'y' take names of sentences as substituends and 'p' and 'q' take sentences as substituends.

But this is not the way things are usually done: A truth predicate is almost always used. I believe this fact is not to be explained simply by the desire many have to keep away from higher-order logics, but rather by the part that details of syntax play in the presentation of theories. A brief look at some things logicians care about will reveal some further reasons those who construct theories have for drawing special attention to the syntax of the language being discussed.

It is well known that logicians have provided us with an abundance of formal languages. Although much of their data and inspiration come initially from natural languages and linguistic acts performed by speakers of those languages, the product of the work of logicians is generally found in the languages they construct for the perspicuous presentation of their theories. These languages yield formal systems that in their turn become objects of study by mathematical logicians.

---

[3] To repeat, I am not making any suggestion as to how a theory of truth conditions should be formulated if it is to provide an adequate (partial) theory of meaning. All that is in question is how truth talk enters in at all. The point is to understand our use of 'true' and 'truth' here.

The reasons for constructing formal languages are many. Sometimes the point is to use the language in the presentation of a theory as when, for example, a theory of inference is presented or when a formal language is used to explain features of a natural language. However, logicians have also sought (not necessarily as a separate goal—indeed it is not clear this can be a separate goal) to provide us with useful tools: They have tried to provide us with good languages in which to draw inferences, ask and answer questions, etc. Whatever the reason for the language, its syntax is important.

That the syntax of a language can be utilized in significant ways is well illustrated by the way numerals help us perform certain tasks. A person can add a "column" of numbers without understanding the process involved. Frege (1884) points out that what made such a mechanical procedure possible was the thought that went into the selection of the numerals: "It only becomes possible at all after the mathematical notation has, as a result of genuine thought, been so developed that it does our thinking for us, so to speak." Logicians have similarly designed languages that make possible the replacement of certain complex or intuitive procedures by mechanical procedures. We have propositional logic with its truth tables, for example.

There are a couple of reasons for arranging things so that syntax does as much work for us as possible. First—so long as needed riches are not lost—things are just simpler that way. The other reason arises from a desire for objectivity. To continue with Frege, he claims one of his goals is to account for certain moves in argument that mathematicians say are obvious. He sought principles that would justify those moves. To the extent that such principles can be applied in a routine manner, the so-called obvious moves are replaced by mechanical procedures, and subjectivity is removed. For this reason, if the process of applying the theory can be reduced to symbol-pushing maneuvers, a desire for objectivity provides a reason for seeking the right syntax.[4]

Where does 'true' come in? I will make a suggestion about one case.

Most of us have our curiosity aroused by extralinguistic matters. We want to know whether the milk has curdled, whether an ice age is imminent, whether triangle *ABC* has a right angle, and so on. That is, we want to know what is true. In trying to find answers to

---

[4] I have not tried to sort out to what extent logicians can provide at the same time, both good explanations and useful systems. I believe that, to date, logicians have, for the most part, had an eye on both goals. I am mostly concerned, in this context, to discuss some of the ways in which useful systems might be developed.

such questions, we produce arguments. Because inference is one of the linguistic acts logicians seek to explain, they have sought theories that in their application will help us determine whether, from certain assumptions, a given conclusion follows. If, for the kinds of reasons given above, the expressions of the language are to be manipulated in applying the logical theory, the expressions need to be given properties that mirror features of the data being explained. In the case of a theory of inference, because the relevant data include language activity involving sentences, sentences must be given (or have) properties, or denotations, or something, that can be utilized in the application of the theory.

Suppose we want to know whether triangle ABC has a right angle. We have been told

> Triangle ABC has two 45° angles.
> If a triangle has two 45° angles, it has a right angle.

Now if (1) there is a property T that the sentence 'Triangle ABC has a right angle' has just in case it is true, and, furthermore, every declarative sentence has T just in case it is true; and (2) we had a way of calculating whether the sentence 'Triangle ABC has a right angle' has the property T, given that the sentences stating our two premises have the property T also, then we could, by using the algorithm, determine whether triangle ABC has a right angle.

Of course the truth property is the candidate for satisfying (1), and logicians have suggested ways of doing the calculating called for by (2) and similar cases.

For these kinds of considerations a truth property proves useful to logicians. So also, of course, may some other properties or denotations (like propositions) be useful, especially for doing the calculating along the way.

4. Review

It is easy to see that if there are prosentences in a language the idea of a truth property might soon follow. What doesn't follow (obviously, anyway) is that such an idea will be a coherent one. If it is assumed, for example, that a predicate, which happens in fact to be a prosentence-forming predicate, is a property-ascribing predicate in all its occurrences, the idea is incoherent—if the prosentences are "universally available." This point is discussed in detail in Chapter 4, §10. The question of the coherence of the truth property concept arises also in the case of a language in which no success has been achieved in defining an appropriate extension (be it only approximate) for 'true'. Suppose, however, something along the lines just now sketched in §2 is successfully carried out for English; what does the prosentential theory come to?

4.1. The Prosentential Theory

I have entertained the idea that 'true' has two "complementary" roles, yet there is just one word in English. So 'true' has two aspects: the prosentential and the property-ascribing. Although the fact of the matter (if there is such) may be determined only after we know much more about linguistic behavior and speakers' intentions, I am inclined to believe at this point that most uses of 'true' in colloquial discourse are (between the two) best explained in terms of a prosentential 'true'. I have a number of reasons for thinking this, most of which have been given in other places. For example, the prosentential theory explains very nicely why 'true' can be used in the way Strawson (1950a) describes. Furthermore, speakers usually talk about extralinguistic things, rarely about language. The prosentential role gets this bit right: It keeps 'true', appropriately, in the object language, so to speak. To the extent that speakers in ordinary discourse engage in inchoate theorizing, however, a property-ascribing 'true' will be more to the point.

Because it is not uncommon for people to engage in inchoate theorizing, and the considerations of §3 show that the use of 'true' in such contexts can be explained in terms of a property-ascribing use of 'true', the claim in Chapter 3 that all colloquial uses of 'true' involve only prosentential uses of 'true' must be revised. However, as the property-ascribing use derives from a prosentential 'true', there is a closely related claim that can be retained in a statement of the prosentential theory: All uses of 'true' in colloquial English either involve only prosentential uses of 'true' or are to be explained as derivative in some way from a prosentential 'true'. (This second disjunct accommodates not only the possible property-ascribing uses, but also the use of 'true' in connectives: Connectives like 'It is true that' and 'It is false that' are not strictly speaking prosentences. What they have in common with prosentential uses of 'true' is discussed in the last section of Chapter 4.)

If I am right in claiming that a property-ascribing 'true' comes into its own in the context of language-connected theory construction, it is not surprising that many semanticists and logicians have thought that a property-ascribing 'true' is at the heart of the matter. For then, however, both aspects are crucial, because not only is a property-ascribing 'true' used, but its "origins" are exploited. (This is, of course, the reason that schema [T] is given a centrally important place.) If we continue with the picture provided by the object language/metalanguage distinction, it is seen that the two aspects of 'true' are in an important sense complementary, connecting, as they do, two significantly related modes of speaking. The considerations of §3 show something of this interplay of the two aspects, and how it may be utilized in the development and application of a theory.

All of this suggests that the prosentential theory might be able to provide an account of both the use of 'true' in colloquial discourse and philosophers' property-ascribing uses. Furthermore, explanations are forthcoming, not only of how a property-ascribing 'true' might suggest itself, but also of the utility of such a predicate. There is, however, one use of 'true' that has been completely ignored, and that is the use of 'true' in 'neither true nor false'. As an explanation of that use calls for further investigation into the peculiarities of this strange predicate, that discussion is left for another time. (See Chapters 1, §3.1; 7, §7; 9, §5.2.)

4.2. Ambiguity in 'True'

On this account 'true' has both a prosentential role and a property-ascribing role. It has been suggested that this feature is sufficiently complicating as to count against acceptance of the theory. Briefly, the objection goes like this:

Objection. Because 'true' has, according to the theory, both a prosentential and a property-ascribing role, 'true' is ambiguous. Isn't this implausible? It's not apparent that speakers have struggled with ambiguity, yet when someone says 'That is true', how do we know whether the 'true' is prosentential or property-ascribing?

Reply. As I said in the last section, I am inclined to think that non-theorizing uses of 'true' are prosentential. To a large extent, it will be clear from the context whether a linguistic predicate is intended. (Difficult cases to get agreement on will include sentences like 'That's true, but not surprising.')

Insofar as there is ambiguity, however, the ambiguity is not novel, nor does it count against the theory. The situation with 'true' is rather like that described in my adult child story. In such a situation, it is often unclear which of the two learning situations the child is in, whether something is being learned about things linguistic or things extralinguistic. Similarly, it may be unclear whether the adult has one or the other in mind. Often there is a bit of both. To my knowledge, whatever ambiguity there is, is harmless and usually unnoticed. It is even possible that is an advantage here: Such ambiguity might well be a feature of language that makes learning it possible.

In addition, I think it is worth noting that ambiguity makes for easy application of the kinds of theories considered. It is helpful to be able to recall, at any time, that 'true' can be taken as either property-ascribing or prosentential. Because of similar kinds of considerations, it is a common practice of mathematicians and logicians to make a deliberate effort to generate and then exploit such ambiguity in the presentation of a theory.

5. Propositional Quantification in English

As I mentioned earlier, the prosentential theory was said in Chapter 3 to make two substantive claims: The first claim was that propositional quantification into sentence place occurs in English, and the second claim was that all uses of 'true' in colloquial English involve only prosentential uses of 'true'. Although I think the second of these should be revised in the way suggested in §4.1, I continue to think there are some good reasons for thinking the first is true. I have also frequently claimed that the prosentential theory provides a good explanation of features of 'true' that Strawson has drawn our attention to. Strawson, however, may disagree, because he has claimed that propositional quantification into sentence place does not occur in English. Can the assumption of the prosentential theory be defended against Strawson's arguments?

Strawson argues against such a construal of English when he argues (1974) that the evidence goes against Prior's claim that propositional quantification (in English) should be viewed as quantification into sentence place and not into singular-term-place. Although I find the distinctions Strawson makes in the whole discussion particularly illuminating in a number of respects, I have some questions concerning the force of his argument against Prior. The fact that we begin with different assumptions as to what is to be included in "the apparatus of quantification"—I include prosentences of course—may well explain any difference of opinion.

Supporting evidence for the claim that sentential propositional quantification occurs (in some form) in English would come from the prosentential theory itself, should it turn out, indeed, to provide a good explanation of our understanding of 'true'. But Strawson has his eye on some arguments that arise from the consideration of certain aspects of the syntax of English. And that is what I will consider here. I take it, however, that what is in question does not simply concern the syntax of words like 'something', 'whoever', and 'it', but something like the following:

> Does English contain generalizations, with respect to the sentence places, of sentences like 'Either snow is white or snow is not white' and 'Mary believes that Tom shoveled the sidewalk'?

Strawson's argument against Prior has two parts. He begins with an argument to show that propositional quantification into singular-term-place does occur in English. What Strawson takes as relevant evidence is the fact that "the language is full of what are traditionally classified as noun-phrases specifying propositions (e.g., 'that it is raining', 'this doctrine', . . .)," and "it is full of what appear to be proposition predicates (. . . like 'true' and 'false', . . . 'believe', . . .)" Furthermore, "when we quantify, the apparatus of quantification is regularly attached to these apparent predicates and replaceable by those apparent noun-phrases."

In the second part of his argument, although not denying either the intelligibility or usefulness of Prior's analyses of the sentences in question (e.g., 'Tom said (asserted) something incompatible with everything William said (asserted)'), Strawson denies that *sentential* propositional quantification occurs in English. Evidence cited in this case is that "there just are no sentences in English which the Priorese versions [∃p (Tom said that p. ∀q (William said that q → (if p, then ~q)))]], with sentential quantification, can be taken as representing in the way in which sentences with quantification over propositions can be taken as representing the two readings of the ordinary English sentence we started out with." (p. 75) In these passages Strawson is assessing Prior's claim about English for "realism"; So I take it that what is at issue in the second part of his argument is whether English contains sentential propositional quantification in the form in which it is utilized by Prior in his paraphrases. Given that Strawson's answer is no, one wonders how the prosentential construal of English would fare when similarly assessed for realism. Strawson seems to assume that his arguments show that no form of quantification into sentence place occurs in English. But let's take a look at what he says of Prior's versions.

Strawson says that there are no sentences in English which can be taken as representing Prior's versions *in the way* in which "sentences with quantification over propositions [that is, into singular-term-place] can be taken as representing . . ." Before trying to locate the failure in Prior's versions, I think it is important to note that in neither case are there sentences in English which serve as *exact* representations of the quantified formulas in question, for English does not contain anything exactly like the bound variables of formal languages, be they individual or sentential. Proforms are the closest analogues. So grammatically exact matches are presumably not required by Strawson for realism. Other passages indicate that what Strawson is looking for are representations that keep membership in the other grammatical categories the same, so that, for example, a one-place predicate of the formula is also a one-place predicate in English; this should hold also for the instances of the quantified formulas. So, allowing for the slight variable mismatch (and consequential quantifier mismatch), Prior's versions are to be assessed relative to a grammar of English. Which grammar is adopted becomes important and we might consider some alternatives. I am going to consider the one I'm familiar with, and which might be reached through the question, What might the syntax of English look like if it were to have propositional quantification with respect to sentence positions?[5]

I have argued elsewhere (Chapter 2) that, just as pronouns provide us with readings in English of formulas that contain bound individual variables, so also prosentences—if we had any—would provide us with readings of formulas containing bound (sentential) propositional variables. This suggests a place to start. Is there any reason to believe (other than the reasons provided by the prosentential theory itself) that English might contain prosentences?

Because the idea of quantification into sentence place seems (at least to some of us) both useful and natural, that alone makes it plausible that prosentences might, in some form, occur in English. But there are other considerations. One reason for using a pronoun is to make it clear that the same person or object is being referred to as was referred to in another place. And, in general, a reason for using any kind of proform or other kind of anaphoric device is to establish semantic connections. Reflection on the need to make connections between one discourse and another, and different parts of a discourse, leads one to expect that natural languages might well

---

[5] The discussion that follows overlaps, to some extent, with some things I say in another context. See Chapter 5.

contain a variety of anaphoric devices. Given the wide variety of complex anaphoric devices (including deletion) that are being unearthed by linguists, there is evidence supporting this claim. So perhaps there are prosentences. Suppose there were; what would they look like? Would they be atomic or complex?

In another part of his paper, and in connection with another topic, Strawson makes the pertinent remark "What is wanted in all sentences is the indication of propositionality, the verb-form or whatever does its duty." Because prosentences are sentences, Strawson's observation would seem to make an atomic prosentence unlikely, for in such a case there would be no indication of propositionality. (This agrees with some remarks of Wittgenstein [1953, Part I, 134] on the failure of 'p' to give the "general form of propositions".) So, if there are prosentences in English, we might expect them to have the form Subject-Predicate. In this respect prosentences will be different from pronouns, which are atomic. And there would clearly be advantages to language users if things did develop in this way, because features of the language that have been developed to accommodate the subject-predicate form in other sentences may be resorted to in the construction and employment of prosentences. For example, the anaphoric relating capabilities of pronouns (like 'that' and 'it') might be utilized in the construction of an (anaphoric) prosentence, and expressions that serve to provide modifications of other sentences of the language might be used to provide useful modifications of a prosentence. It could also happen that quantifier expressions that had been used for quantification into singular-term-place might be used to accomplish quantification into sentence place. It has often been observed (e.g., Chapter 3, §2.1) that 'yes', 'so', and 'ditto' have some of the features of prosentences. The above considerations show, however, that they do not have the potential, in terms of adaptability and availability, that a prosentence with more structure would have. Locutions like 'These things are so' are better candidates, and so also is 'That is true', of course. If we assume a grammar in which 'That is true' and 'It is true' are prosentences, Prior's claim begins to look plausible.

In Chapter 3 we separate off a portion of English that we call English* (see §2.4 for details). English*'s special feature is that the truth predicate is not isolable. 'True' either occurs in the prosentences 'That is true' or 'It is true', or else it appears in connectives like 'it was true that'. In effect, the prosentences and connectives are atomic. Because the truth predicate is not isolable, English* does not contain sentences of the form 'What Plato said is true'. The point of English* was to show that English "could" have been constructed so that it had the structure—in the relevant respects—of the kind of language Prior and Ramsey appealed to.[6] We claimed that English* provides readings of the paraphrases Prior supplies us with, provided we have enough prosentences. Thus for the Priorese version cited above, we have

There is something such that Tom said that it$_1$ is true, and for anything such that, if William said that it$_2$ is true, then, if it$_1$ is true, it$_2$ is false.

(Much of what is cumbersome in this reading is a problem, also, for complex formulas involving quantification into singular-term-place.) A similar reading can be given of a Priorese version of 'Mary believes something'.

There is something such that Mary believes that it is true.

If it is assumed, as we do in the case of English*, that English contains prosentences, readings satisfying Strawson's conditions are available. So, given the assumption, the claim that sentential propositional quantification occurs in English may be assessed positively for realism. However, although English* is in some sense a part of English, English isn't English*. Similarly, although Prior uses atomic propositional variables, prosentences are not atomic despite English*. If attention is to be paid to that point, Prior's versions fail a more demanding realism assessment.

The situation for the prosentential theory is not quite the same because our prosentences are not atomic. Nevertheless, we have done little more than provide the reader with English*. Beyond that, all there is, is some speculation as to why English is constructed the way it is. What is lacking is lacking for most of English: an explanation of why English has the syntactic features that it does. In particular, I think the case for sentential quantification is not much different from that of quantification into the predicate place that Strawson thinks does occur in English. Consider his example

Tom does whatever William does.

which has as an instance

If William hops, Tom hops.

---

[6] There may be a problem for English* as a possible natural language on its own, if the prosentences and connectives were strictly atomic, for there would then have to be only a finite number of modified forms.

A formal language with quantifiers that bind variables occupying predicate positions does not explain all that is going on in 'Tom does whatever WIlliam does', for it doesn't account for the structure of 'does whatever'. The point is, I think, as Strawson says, 'does whatever' or 'does something' "exhibits the form of the verb necessary for sentencehood (propositionality)." And that seems to be just the reason prosentences have the structure they do. With that structure, the resources of the rest of the language can be utilized in using the prosentences.

7

Truth: Do We Need It? *

In a recent paper (Chapter 6 of this volume) I considered the possibility that prosentences may be used to define "appropriate extensions" for 'true' and 'false'. The case I considered was one in which meaningful sentence tokens were the candidates for membership in the extensions of 'true' and 'false': A sentence token belongs to the extension of 'true' just in case it is true, and it belongs to the extension of 'false' just in case it is false. For example, 'Snow is white' belongs to the extension of 'true' just in case it is true. ('It is true' and 'It is false' are used here as prosentences—see Chapter 3 for details.) My project was not to provide the extensions for 'true' and 'false' but to consider the following: Suppose well-defined extensions derive from prosentences in the way suggested, and make available property-ascribing roles for 'true' and 'false'. *Why* might it be useful to have such predicates available?

In Chapter 6, I said that "an extension seems to justify the claim that there is a truth property" and proceeded from there. I am now disinclined to accept an extension as justifying the claim that there is a truth property. A reason is given in §2. However, I will show (§6) how the extensions that are available are useful, and I will provide (§4) an explanation of a characterizing role that 'true' and 'false' seem sometimes to have. It is in virtue of these two features that I will refer to truth and falsity as "quasi-properties." The question remains, What do we need 'true' and 'false' for? I now think that for those occasions in which I argued it would be useful to have properties available, with the features that the supposed properties would have had, the prosentential 'true' and 'false' are more to the point: The properties either take us through an unnecessary detour or introduce a problem. So, I shall take another look at what it is that semanticists and others working with languages want of 'true' and 'false'. Among the issues discussed will be the connections be-

* This paper was written while I was on a Mellon Postdoctoral Fellowship, for which I thank the University of Pittsburgh.

tween Meaning and Truth (§5), a logician's use of 'true' and 'false'
(§6), and whether we need to be able to say of questions, or 'The
king of France is wise', or the Liar sentence, that they are neither
true nor false (§7).

1. Problems of Expressibility

What's wanted of a truth predicate?

(1) 'Snow is white' is true iff snow is white.
(2) 'Snow is white' is false iff snow is not white.

Facts such as these have led some to espouse the redundancy theory
of truth. However, with an eye on uses that semanticists, logicians,
and other philosophers have for the truth predicate, others argue
that the truth predicate is essential; furthermore, it is supposed that
the usefulness of the predicates 'true' and 'false' is to be accounted
for by a property-ascribing role that the predicates have. One version of this account of 'true' and 'false' then construes facts like (1)
and (2) as capturing the essential feature of the properties of truth
and falsity. In conversation the opinion has been expressed to me
that this just is what the properties come to. Is such a property view
either necessary or viable?

But of course such a brief account of a truth property is not adequate, for simply saying that facts such as (1) and (2) give the essentials of the truth property does not explain the nature of the problems raised by sentences such as

(3) (3) is false.

Nor does the view as outlined explain how 'not true' can be employed by Strawson and others to say of sentences containing nondenoting subject terms that they are neither true nor false, as in, for
example,

(4) 'The king of France is wise' is neither true nor false.

The problem here—as Heidelberger (1968) has pointed out in another context—is that (4) seems to reduce, with the aid of (1) and
(2), to

The king of France is not wise and the king of France is
wise.

which is either a contradiction or is itself neither true nor false. (4), on the other hand, is taken by many to be true.

Then there are those who like to be able to say of paradoxical sentences that they are *not true*. What account is to be given on the property view of

(5) (3) is not true?

The paradoxical sentences force a reexamination of intuitions: The intuitions that are considered relevant are usually weighed in the context of some assessment of what should count as constituting the centrally important uses of the predicates. As a result, a modified description of the truth property is forthcoming, according to which the contradictions that appear inherent in sentences such as (3) are avoided.

The feature of such views I wish to focus on is the fact that what is held onto in the face of difficulties is the assumption that there is a truth property in some sense underlying our truth talk. But can such an assumption be held onto? In the next section, I sketch the details of what I think is a reason for holding that the paradoxes themselves show that 'true' and 'false' are not property-ascribing.

2. Is Truth a Property?

In §2.1, I show that there is a reason for thinking that properties should "partition" domains that are theory-recognized categories or sorts.

My attention in this paper is directed toward some uses that philosophers have for 'true' and 'false' in which they are predicated of sentences—rather than propositions. If we are to have the expressibility desired, we would have to require that property-ascribing 'true' and 'false' partition at least the domain of all linguistic expressions, if the partitioning requirement is right. On this way of looking at the issues, the Liar provides a reason for thinking that neither 'true' nor 'false' partition such a domain, and so a reason for thinking that truth and falsity are not properties. These points are made in §2.2.

2.1. If a primary reason for talking about properties or the characteristics of things connects with the need in any theory to individuate and make comparisons between objects—that is, if dictums such as

Two objects are identical iff they have the same properties.

reflect some crucial interplay between what counts as a property and what counts as an object—then it would seem that the question as to whether a given object has a property should always be significant. If not, a comparison between objects cannot be made with respect to the candidate property. Suppose, for example, an object a has P, but no significance attaches to the claim that b either has or doesn't have P; that is, there is no condition that b must satisfy or fail to satisfy for it to have P—then it is not possible to make a comparison of a and b with respect to P. P cannot be appealed to in providing explanations of the similarities and differences between a and b. One might try to explain things by saying they belong to different categories or sorts, but suppose a and b belong to the same category.

For a given predicate P, let the set of objects satisfying 'x is P' be the *extension* of P, and the set of objects satisfying 'x is not P' be the *anti-extension* of P. P will be said to *partition* a domain just in case the set containing the extension and the anti-extension (completely) partitions the domain. Similarly, if a predicate is said to be property-ascribing, the candidate property P *partitions* a domain just in case its extension and anti-extension partition the domain.

The requirement that I am suggesting for properties can now be put as follows: In the context of a given theory, a predicate should count as property-ascribing only if it partitions a domain, that is, a theory-recognized category or sort, and of which the extension and anti-extension of the predicate are subsets.

I am supposing that theory-recognized categories or sorts are—in the case of fairly well developed theories—sets of objects that are identified by a theory for the articulation of lawlike generalizations. (The whole domain of discourse is included.) A reason that properties identified by the theory as explanatory should partition an appropriate category or sort is that there should be a determinate answer, for each instance of a lawlike generalization, as to whether the generalization is true or false.

2.2. Suppose one wishes to defend the assumption that the uses semanticists and other philosophers have for 'true' and 'false' are to be explained by the fact 'true' and 'false' are property-ascribing predicates. Then the ontological question as to what the bearers of truth are requires an answer. If the above considerations are to the point, the question is challenging, for the difficulties raised by paradoxical sentences (and other features of language also) make unlikely the possibility that one of the seemingly easier options—sentence types or tokens—are the bearers of truth and falsity. The particular problem I have in mind is, of course, the fact that there are tokens like 'This is not true' that seem to neither have the property truth nor fail to have the property, and there are tokens like 'This is false' that seem to neither have the property falsity nor fail to have it: Truth and falsity don't provide—through their extensions and anti-extensions—partitionings of the set of sentence tokens of natural language. Recent work on the paradoxes might be utilized here in seeking a response to this problem.

One response would be to propose that the bearers of truth are propositions and then hope (or believe) that an adequate theory of propositions will be a theory that posits a set of propositions that will be partitioned by truth. There is also, of course, (i) the task of saying how a property of *propositions* will explain those occurrences of 'true' and 'false'—in descriptions of languages—that occur as predications of sentence types or tokens, and (ii) the task of accounting for the peculiarities of 'This is not true' while, on the other hand, allowing expressibility of the kind that makes it possible to say of the Liar sentence that it is *not true*. Although I think this alternative should be developed and investigated, we cannot be sure of its success, for as yet there is little detail: Indeed it is far from clear, at this stage in our investigation of language, just what, and how, propositions should feature in an account of language.

A second response, on the assumption that predicates are category-restricted, might be to seek an appropriate domain of sentence tokens for 'true' and 'false'. One might, for example, take up Martin's (1967) suggestion that 'true' and 'false' are restricted to meaningful tokens. But if that is the domain partitioned by 'true' and 'false', then we do not have the required expressibility: We would not be able to say of a meaningless string that it is not true. There is also a question concerning the domain. Is the Liar sentence a meaningful sentence? Martin says no, but it's not clear his argument is conclusive. (I shall be returning to these issues in §8.)

Such considerations lead me to think we should hesitate in making the assumption that either truth or falsity are properties—of sentence types or tokens, at least. But more importantly, there are alternatives to be explored that make it seem doubtful such properties are needed to explain the use of 'true' and 'false' in explanations of linguistic practice, where they are predicated of sentences.

3. The Prosentential Theory

Because I shall be arguing, in later sections, that semanticists and logicians employ prosentential 'true' and 'false' in their theories of language, it is necessary that I give a brief description of prosentential constructions. I will not, however, devote space to either motivating or explaining in detail the claim that 'true' and 'false' have prosentential roles in English. The reader is referred to Chapters 3–6 for that. The following is a brief survey of the basic points.

3.1. Prosentences were introduced in Chapter 2 to provide natural language readings of formulas containing bound propositional variables. Prosentences (also proverbs and proadjectives) were introduced by analogy with pronouns. Prosentences are like anaphoric pronouns in that they can be used both in the—so-called—*lazy way*, as the pronoun 'she' is used in

(6) If *she's* encouraged, Sarah will do well.

and *quantificationally*, as 'it' is used in

If a number is even, *it* is evenly divisible by 2.

Pronouns are different from prosentences in that pronouns occupy positions in sentences that singular terms can occupy; prosentences occupy positions in sentences that declarative sentences occupy.

Part of the claim that 'true' has a prosentential role is that it is used in forming prosentences, as in 'That is true' and 'It is true'. Just as 'she' in (6) has 'Sarah' as its antecedent, so 'That is true' in

(7) JANE: New Zealand has little industry.
    BILL: That's true; nevertheless, there are many polluted rivers and bays.

has 'New Zealand has little industry' as its antecedent. (Note that, although the tie derives from an anaphoric 'that', the whole of 'That is true' is the prosentence.) Semantically, just as the referent of 'she' in (6) is the same as the referent of 'Sarah', so the propositional content of 'That is true' in (7) is the same as that of its antecedent 'New Zealand has little industry'. Prosentences can be *modified*, just as other subject-predicate sentences can. Examples are 'That was true', 'That is false', and 'That might be true'. A modified prosentence acquires as its content an appropriately modified form of its antecedent's content: 'That is false', for example, will have as its content the contradictory of its antecedent. Prosentences can also be used to obtain generality. Thus, 'It is true' can be used to obtain a generalized form of

> If the theory says that there is life on Mars, then there is life on Mars.
> If there is something such that the theory says it is true, then it is true.

When pronouns and prosentences are used in the lazy way, they are *inheritors* (Chapter 4, §1 and §2), for they acquire their semantic content from other expressions. The contrast is with expressions that acquire their content *independently* as, for example, 'Mary' and 'Mary swims' do. In the case of a pronoun or prosentence, the tie with its antecedent expression, from which content is inherited, is grammatical. Other inheritors locate their antecedents in other ways. A definite description or name might be used. Thus, for example, the following may be used in certain contexts as sentential inheritors:

(8) The first sentence is true.
(9) 'Snow is white' is true.

If the first sentence is '2 + 3 = 5', then the content of (8) in the given context would be the same as that of

> 2 + 3 = 5

and the propositional content of (9) is the same as that of

> Snow is white.

The function of the subject terms 'That', 'The first sentence', and 'Snow is white' is only to locate the antecedent sentence from which the propositional content of the inheritor is inherited. We might think of the locating of an antecedent as work done off to the side—in a "working column"—for the subject terms do not, themselves, directly contribute to the propositional content of an inheritor. Where we have available the referential resources of English, and 'true' and 'false' are prosentential, modifiable sentential inheritors are *universally available* (Chapter 4, §3) for, for any sentence token, an inheritor (or modified inheritor) can be constructed that will have that token as its antecedent. This includes the possibility of an inheritor having itself as antecedent, as in the case of 'This is true'. Clearly, for a lazy inheritor to have content, it must have as its antecedent a sentence that can supply content.

The semantic connections that obtain between proforms of laziness and their antecedents establish connections that seem to be required in communication between different parts of a discourse. When a pronoun of laziness is used, we know that in the simple cases no new object is referred to, and in the case of prosentences, that nothing new is being asserted, denied, or considered. This last is a fact that the redundancy theorists drew attention to. The prosentential theory is not a redundancy theory however; just as pronouns seem to be essential for successful communication, so, we conjecture, prosentences are an essential part of our language: Prosentential constructions are required, not only for establishing connections between various parts of a discourse, but also "logically," for generalization and for modifying sentences—when modification of the verbs in a sentence itself won't do the trick, a connective (like 'it is false that' and 'it was true that') can be used.

The reader should note shortcomings of this account. All I have tried to do is provide a description sufficient for an intuitive understanding of how prosentences and inheritors might be used in a language. Not only does this description of pronouns and prosentences ignore the variety of constructions that proforms can occur in (see, for example, Chapter 3, Partee 1970, and Wilson 1980), but it also suffers—along with other accounts—from being based on an inadequate understanding of the significance of these constructions in natural language. Some suggestions concerning the functioning of pronouns in the network of language are made in Chastain's (1975) paper on reference: One becomes persuaded that a unified theory of pronouns (or proforms in general) cannot be developed so long as, in conformity with standard practice, theories take as data only isolated sentences considered one or two at a time.

3.2. In determining the merits of the prosentential theory, it is necessary that we know what we *need* the predicates 'true' and 'false' for, for the pragmatic and semantic accounts we provide must be adequate for the tasks in question. As I frequently contrast the prosentential theory with a theory in which 'true' and 'false' have property-ascribing roles—often to show in a given case that we don't need to assume that truth and falsity are properties—I will briefly explain what I take to be the difference between their respective semantic accounts of basic subject-predicate sentences containing 'true' and 'false'.

According to the prosentential theory, a token of a sentence like 'That is true' or ' "Snow is white" is true', has as its propositional content—in a given context—the content of its antecedent. (If the predicate had been 'false', the propositional content would be the contradictory.) By contrast, on the kind of property view I have in mind, the propositional content of such sentences is (typically) different from that of their antecedent's, because 'true' and 'false' would, like other property-ascribing predicates, have their own characterizing content. Furthermore, on this view, ' "Snow is white" is true' says something about the sentence 'Snow is white'. A correspondence theorist, who *also* believed 'true' is used to (explicitly) affirm for a given sentence that the correspondence relation holds, might be represented as having such a view. (By contrast, in the next section I discuss a "quasi" characterizing role that 'true' and 'false' seem to have.)

These are not the only accounts according to which 'true' and 'false' are irredundant, for there is Quine's (1970) description of 'true' as a "disquotational device" that cancels "linguistic reference". Though Quine's disquotational device is closer in some respects to the prosentential, in that it suggests a "logical" role for 'true' and the truth predicate "restore(s) the effect of objective reference," there are important differences; but the idea needs to be worked out for a proper comparison to be made.

4. A Bit of Characterizing

In §4.1 I consider an objection according to which the generation of extensions for 'true' and 'false' would seem to require characterizing roles for 'true' and 'false'. 'True' and 'false' are also sometimes used in the expression of either approval or disapproval of people. In §4.2 I consider the force of the claim that people are commended for saying what's true.

4.1. In a discussion of Russell's paradox, Prior (1976, p. 94) says the following about 'is not a member of itself' (see also Prior 1954): "To say that the characteristic of not being a member of itself cannot define a class is to say in effect that there is no such characteristic (for what sort of characteristic would it be which could not divide the universe into things that possess it and things that do not?). And this seems a strange thing to say; for is there not such a characteristic and does not the class of men, for example, possess it? For the class of men, surely, is not a man; it is not a member of itself."

A similar dilemma arises for 'true' and 'false': on the one hand they do not seem to characterize because they don't partition appropriate domains, and on the other, there are circumstances under which 'true' and 'false' seem to be used to characterize. Would it be possible to generate extensions for 'true' and 'false' if they are not property-ascribing?

The challenge has been presented very forcefully by Kent Wilson (1980). Briefly, and ignoring several other issues Wilson raises, I will put it this way: We can ask someone to (systematically) divide a set of sentences into two groups by asking of each, 'Is it true?' Because decisions *are made* as to whether 'Snow is white' is true and whether 'Birds are fish' is true, characterizing must be going on; because 'true' is used in each case to ask the appropriate question, we must be asking whether 'true' *applies* to the sentences 'Snow is white' and 'Birds are fish', and so we must be asking whether 'true' correctly characterizes the sentences 'Snow is white' and 'Birds are fish'. A property-ascribing 'true' rather than a prosentential 'true' seems to be required to explain the use of 'true' here.

It suffices, for a set of sentences to be systematically divided into two, that there is, for each sentence, a membership condition that the sentence must satisfy. If 'true' had an independently acquired characterizing role, then 'true' could be used to state the condition in each case, but that's not the only possibility, as the following project will show:

Suppose our performer, instead of being told to ask of each sentence, 'Is it true?' is given the following instructions: "Take each sentence in turn, put it in interrogative form, and then ask the question as formulated: 'Is snow white?' 'Are birds fish?' If the answer is yes, put the original sentence in the extension of 'true'; if no, put it in the anti-extension." Clearly, the same sets are generated, yet in this case *the sentences in question* state the membership condition. But isn't that what in effect happens when we ask, 'Is it true?' How would the question 'Is it true?' be explained if the performer were a young child? We would probably explain that he or she should ask, 'Is snow white?' 'Are birds fish?' and so on. We don't need first to explain what it means for a sentence to have the property truth. Indeed, a truth property need not be assumed to explain 'Is it true?' for there is a prosentential account that gets to the point directly. 'Is it true?' is the interrogative form of the prosentence 'It is true': 'Is it true?' can be used to ask questions anaphorically (while at the same time accommodating indexicals in the antecedents) and serves to give the general form of the questions to be asked, for, with one antecedent 'Is it true?' has the force of 'Is snow white?' and with another, 'Are birds fish?' To ask whether a sentence has the property truth takes us through an unnecessary detour. The prosentential reading suffices to explain how the extensions are generated, but it also explains a "quasi" characterizing role that we might sometimes want to say 'true' and 'false' have.

Providing a token of an inheritor ' "S" is true' is well grounded, the inheritor has propositional content, and so we can speak (neutrally) of 'true' as either 'applying' or 'not applying'—'true' *applies* to 'S' just in case 'S' is true. (A "lazy" inheritor is *grounded* if it is connected through antecedents to a sentence that can acquire content independently, and it is *well grounded* if the sentence that can acquire content independently does indeed have, in the context, propositional content.) Even though 'true' is "really" an incomplete symbol, this introduces the possibility of characterizing talk because, providing 'S' has propositional content, there is a condition on the application of 'true'. Because 'Is it true?' is parasitic (i.e., it acquires its content from an antecedent expression), 'true' does not itself state the condition on the application of 'true'. It is the antecedent 'S' that states the condition. The generation of extensions and anti-extensions for 'true' and 'false' is made possible by the fact that inheritors supply, through their antecedents, the conditions of application. It is for this reason that 'true' and 'false' can be viewed as having extensions and anti-extensions, and so truth and falsity might be said to be *quasi-properties*, and 'true' and 'false' to have quasi-characterizing roles.

The fact that the conditions of application of 'true' are stated by other expressions is not sufficient to show that truth isn't a full-blooded property—we might want to give such an account of 'even' or 'bachelor', if they were introduced by definition. It's the kind of dependence that causes the problem. Whether 'true' applies (or "characterizes") depends on the context, for, if an antecedent fails to supply propositional content (as in the case of 'This is true' or, for the Strawsonian, 'The king of France is wise'), the inheritor is not well grounded, and so *no* condition is provided that determines whether 'true' applies. So 'true' doesn't always characterize, and this is why 'true' and 'false' fail to partition appropriate sets.

The question remains open as to whether other paradoxical predicates, e.g., 'is not a member of itself', that seem to characterize in some contexts, do so only because of content inherited by them or by expressions of which they are a part. If that is the case, it might well turn out that the associated paradoxical expressions are ungrounded inheritors lacking content, rather than expressions that harbor incoherence.

4.2. We commend or recommend an adviser because he or she will say what's true; we complain if we're told something that's false. Is a person commended because he or she says something that has a certain property, truth, and is a person criticized because what he or she says has another property, falsity? If that were the case, it would seem the prosentential 'true' and 'false' wouldn't suffice for such commendings and criticizing; 'true' and 'false' would have to ascribe properties. But *why* do we value people who tell us things that are true? Valuing being told the truth must derive from the fact that we seek knowledge, with discourse playing an important part in that co-operative venture; and it might be suggested that it's *the truth* that we want to know about.

But that can be a misleading description of what we seek to know, if it is taken to suggest that what we seek is knowledge of a *property* truth or of which *sentences* (or propositions) are true, and it provides, at best, only a partial account of what's valued here. Surely, what we usually want to know about are extralinguistic things: We want to know whether a certain reactor is safe, whether the prices of automobiles will go down, and whether a growth is malignant. So we seek experts who will tell us that a reactor is safe only when the reactor is safe and that automobile prices will go down only when they will go down. And what we value are people who, *because* they have the knowledge, ability, and inclination, tell us what is true. In commending such people, we *do not* have to say they tell us things that *have the property truth*. They tell us what's true, certainly, but a prosentential 'true' is all that seems to be needed here: 'True' is needed for generality. What we want to generalize on are sentences like

> Smith is a good investigator; she won't tell you the reactor
> is safe if the reactor isn't safe.

and not sentences like

> Smith is a good investigator; she won't tell you 'the reactor
> is safe' is true, if 'the reactor is safe' is false.

As in Chapter 3, 'It is true' and 'It is false' can be used to make explicit the fact that prosentential constructions can be used to provide the required generalizations

Smith is a good investigator; if there is something such that it is false, she won't tell you that it is true.

Although, usually, we'd say something like

Smith is a good investigator; she'll only tell you what's true.

5. Meaning and Truth

I have argued that the use of 'true' and 'false' facilitates connections between a description of linguistic practice and the practice itself. This suggestion begins to seem plausible if the form of (T) sentences is considered. In

'Snow is white' is true iff snow is white.

for example, a sentence is *mentioned* on the left-hand side and used on the right. This point, which was made in Chapter 6, is right; but the suggestion that property-ascribing roles for 'true' and 'false' are needed to establish the required connections is not. In this section, I will show why prosentential 'true' and 'false' might be used in a theory of meaning, and, in §6, why logicians use 'true' and 'false' in setting up models.

My project in Chapter 6 was not to discuss the question of the extent to which a theory of truth conditions might contribute to a theory of meaning, nor what form such a theory should take, but to consider why it should seem even initially plausible that a statement of the truth conditions of a sentence might capture the meaning (or part of the meaning) of a sentence. That is the question I'll address here also.

5.1. Because a language is something that is used, a theory of meaning must contribute to an account of the function of the various expressions of the language in linguistic activities; furthermore, insofar as a theory of meaning provides an account of what a speaker must know, it must capture something of the speaker's facility with language. How might a theory of truth conditions become a part of this? Consider the learning situation I described in Chapter 6, §3.1:

Suppose, at one time, an adult says to a child, 'The milk has curdled', and at another, 'The milk hasn't curdled'; suppose, further, that what the adult says is true. Suppose, also, that the child has some linguistic skills: He or she can perform and respond to a variety of linguistic acts; can assert, deny, and so on. The adult might then have provided this child with one of two kinds of learning situation. (The distinction is probably not in general as sharp as I will describe it, but that won't matter for this discussion.) Suppose in the first case the child has not been observing the milk in question but does understand the sentences. Then he or she learns something about the milk—something extralinguistic about the world. The second case is the one I wish to look at. Suppose the child has been observing the milk but doesn't understand the sentences—perhaps he or she doesn't understand the word 'curdled'. Then the child may learn something of the meaning of the sentence: The child observes that when the milk is in one state the adult says, 'The milk has curdled', and when the milk is in another state, the adult denies that it is curdled. The lesson continues, of course, as the child learns how to use the sentence and how to respond to utterances by others of the sentence, form questions, embed the sentence in other sentences, and so on. At some stage the child's facility with the sentence 'The milk has curdled' demonstrates that he or she knows the meaning of the sentence. This example illustrates that appropriate use of a sentence can serve to convey the meaning of a sentence.

Those considerations lead one to suppose that the meaning of a sentence might be given by a set of conditions of the following form:

In circumstances C_1, the milk has curdled.
In circumstances C_2, the milk hasn't curdled.
. . .

where the meaning of the sentence 'The milk has curdled' is given, so to speak, by example—that is, through the practice of language. This is how it is done in the language-learning situation in Chapter 6, for there, as here, the sentence in question was used. But there's a problem with presenting the meaning in this particular way, for it does not succeed in drawing attention to the sentence in question. The problem is highlighted by the fact that, if translated, the sentence 'The milk has curdled' drops out of the picture. (This might, of course, simply reflect an inadequate translation, for it doesn't recognize that—at least in learning situations—the sentence used is implicitly on display also.) The fact that we need, in giving the meaning, to draw attention to the sentence actually used pushes us either to specific reference to the sentence, or display. A prosentential 'true' can help us do this. The above set of conditions can be recast as follows:

> In conditions C_1 'The milk has curdled' is true.
> In conditions C_2 'The milk had curdled' is false.
>
> . . . .

where 'true' and 'false' are used to generate inheritors. Because inheritors acquire as their propositional content the content (or modified content) of their antecedents, ' "The milk has curdled" is true' can stand in for 'The milk has curdled', and ' "The milk has curdled" is false' for 'The milk hasn't curdled'. Thus, whereas in the language-learning situation the sentence whose meaning was being given was explicitly used and only implicitly displayed, here the sentence is explicitly displayed and only—so to speak—implicitly used. (Of course, the inheritors don't capture every aspect of the use of their antecedents, only their assertional or propositional content.)

The conditions must be stated in a slightly different form if the sentence whose meaning is being given contains indexicals. Something along the following lines would do:

> Consider the sentence 'I am a New Zealander' uttered in conditions C_1 and context O_1: It is true. In conditions C_2 and context O_2, it is false.

I am assuming the context will contain information concerning the speaker, audience, time, etc. Again we don't have the sentence in question explicitly used, but we have a prosentence that captures what would be said and a modified prosentence capturing the contradictory of what would be said, if the sentence in question had been used. This allows the theorists to capture use: The theorist's task is to supply a (nontrivial) characterization of those conditions in which the sentence is true and those in which it is false.

Quantificational proforms are used, of course, to state the general case:

> A statement of the truth conditions for a sentence must state, for each set of conditions and each context, whether the sentence is true or whether it is false.

What's captured on this approach is an aspect of knowing *how* rather than knowing *that*. And this seems right if a theory of meaning is to contribute to an explanation of the phenomenon of language.

5.2. Dummett (1978, p. xxi) expresses concern that there have been many who are not "vividly aware" of the incompatibility of two generally held theses: that a "grasp of meaning consists in a grasp of truth conditions" and that an outright stipulation of the equivalence thesis, or a Tarski truth-definition, yields a complete explication of the concept of truth. As part of this, Dummett claims that, if the redundancy theory is accepted, truth has "no central role to play in a theory of meaning."

Although the prosentential theory is *not* a redundancy theory, it may be considered sufficiently like the redundancy theory that acceptance of it would preclude the possibility that 'true' and 'false' play a central role in a theory of meaning. The foregoing discussion has shown that view mistaken. In a way, Dummett allows for such a possibility, for his argument rests on a claim that *the point of 'true'* must be given prior to its use in a statement of truth conditions, if the truth conditions are to provide an account of meaning. Although it is not clear that the general principle in this is right, the prosentential theory provides, anyway, an independent account of 'true'. A prosentential 'true' can also be used to "give the meaning" of the logical connectives in the manner of Tarski. But there is a further point to be made: Tarski's definition can be viewed as simultaneously providing extensions for 'true' and 'false'. The situation is as follows:

For any language in which we are presenting a theory of meaning, we must assume that it comes equipped with connectives and other "logical" items like quantifiers and pronouns. A prosententialist will, in the same spirit, assume that prosentences are available. The use of 'true' and 'false', in prosentential constructions, can therefore be assumed understood when they are used in providing an account—as described in §5.1, or along the lines of Tarski—of the meaning of sentences that belong to an object language. Now, once 'true' has been used, in inheritors, to "give meaning," we can think of a sentence like 'Snow is white' as providing the condition on the *application* of 'true' to the sentence 'Snow is white' (as explained in §4.1), and so we can then view the truth definition as defining an extension for 'true'. The statement of truth conditions is thereby viewed in two ways—as a statement of truth conditions, and as a so-called truth-definition. The connections between the two will come up again when, in §6.1, I describe a situation in which it is useful to have extensions for 'true' and 'false'.

6. Logic and Truth

Most of us have our curiosity aroused by extralinguistic matters. We want to know whether the milk will curdle, whether Pittsburgh has more hours of sunshine than it used to, and whether triangle *ABC* has a right angle. In trying to find answers to such questions, we produce arguments.

Inference is one of the linguistic acts logicians have sought to explain. Why is it that 'true' and 'false' seem to play a "central role" in the theories logicians have produced? In §6.1, I shall show how 'true' and 'false' can be used in inheritors to facilitate connections between the practice of inference, and the systems that logicians have, in their theories of inference, supplied us with; in §6.2, I show that if inheritors are what logicians need, then 'true' and 'false' cannot be property-ascribing.

6.1. Logicians provide explanations, but they also try to help us determine whether, from certain assumptions, a given conclusion follows. Because a part of the logician's project has included an attempt to replace intuitive moves by objective procedures, and complex procedures by simple ones; wherever possible, inference has been replaced by a mechanical process. A mechanical process is normally based on a formal system, that is, a structure of objects with functions and relations defined in terms of it. So those seeking to produce a theory of inference in this way have been faced with the task of representing the essentials of the linguistic activity of drawing inferences, as a formal system. How is this done?

The move to the formal system involves a move from the normal use of expressions involved in linguistic practice, to treating those expressions as (only) objects, for one aspect of the project has been to get the syntax of a language to do as much work for us as possible. Suppose that in an inference it is affirmed, for example, that triangle *ABC* has a right angle. In inference the sentence 'Triangle *ABC* has a right angle' is used in the usual way—its declarative form is in force. But then in applying, say, an axiomatic system, we treat the sentence as an object—as an item in a deduction. If in addition we further simplify by having sentences name themselves, the sentence 'Triangle *ABC* has a right angle' will have become involved in three different ways: From one vantage point, its declarative form is in force; from another it is an object of reference; and sometimes it also serves as a name. We have become experts at "double-talk." It will be helpful to draw a comparison with the role syntax plays in arithmetical computation.

Frege (1884) has pointed out that the reason that a person can add a "column" of numbers without understanding the process involved is the thought that went into the selection of the numerals: "It only becomes possible at all after the mathematical notation has, as a result of genuine thought, been so developed that it does our thinking for us, so to speak." But let's look a little more closely at this. A reason that the numerals simplify certain procedures is that they've been selected so that they can be read in different ways—on different occasions. In adding a set of numbers that includes 598, for example, there is one stage at which we read '598' as designating the number 598 (that's what it "really" designates), and we sometimes read '5', '9', and '8' separately, as designating 5, 9, and 8, respectively. Although problems arise if the two modes of speaking are confused and we don't always understand how it all works, it is clearly to our advantage to generate such double-talk.

I claim something similar goes on in the systems logicians provide us with. There is the case above, in which for a given sentence we think at one stage of the form of a declarative sentence as being in force, and at another stage we use it as a name of itself in "symbol pushing maneuvers." Then, for those cases in which a distinction is drawn in a theory between whether something is to be affirmed or denied in an inference, logicians sometimes supply us with ordered pairs, a sentence and a truth value. Thus we might have either

<'Triangle ABC has a right angle', 1>

or

<'Triangle ABC has a right angle', 0>.

We need to understand that extra-model-theoretically we use the first of these to affirm that triangle ABC has a right angle, and the second to deny that triangle ABC has a right angle. (This is what the ordered pairs "really" say.) On the other hand, in the discourse of the model, these expressions name ordered pairs.

The extra-model-theoretic reading requires the ordered pair expression to be a sentential inheritor, for consider the general pattern: For any declarative sentence 'S' that might be used in an inference, we are using something of the form "<'S', 1>" to affirm that S, and "<'S', 0>" to deny that S. For a given sentence, the values 1 and 0 provide a way of distinguishing between the circumstances that it is true and that it is false. This is where 'true' and 'false' come in. The effect of the ordered pair notation is the same as that of ' "S" is true' and ' "S" is false', for as in the case of giving truth conditions (§5), although there is a need to capture the force of a sentence in use, there is also a need to draw explicit attention to the sentence used, because here the sentence is to be mapped into an element of a lattice. Thus, again, there is a move from linguistic practice where a declarative sentence is used in its normal way and is only implicitly displayed, to explicit display of the sentence, with its use only implicitly (so to speak) given.

Now what happens in the model? A Tarski-style "truth-definition," insofar as it provides a statement of truth conditions, might be viewed as providing a (partial) account of meaning, along the lines suggested in §5. The definition also provides invaluable models, however. We wish to draw inferences because we want to know whether the milk will curdle, and so on: We want to know what is true. Tarski has provided us with a basic model that provides us with both a better understanding of which inferences are valid, and help in determining what follows from what. This topic requires more attention than I can give it here, but perhaps, by oversimplifying a bit, we can make two points: First, the definition—for certain languages—of extensions for 'true' and 'false' warrants the kind of mapping of sentences into truth values that we want from the extra-model-theoretic perspective. The kind of mapping we want is one in which a sentence 'S' is mapped into 1 iff it is true; that mapping preserves the required inheritor reading of the ordered pairs. Second, in defining the truth value of one sentence in terms of the truth values of others, Tarski has defined pertinent interconnections of truth value that provide help with "calculating," an explication of "validity," and so on. Thus 'true' and 'false' make it possible to have certain of the moves in the model parallel moves in inference, because assertion of membership or nonmembership in the extensions of 'true' or 'false' carries our extra-model-theoretic (inheritor) reading.

In sum, my suggestion is that, if we wish to be able to draw a distinction between saying that something is true, and that it is false, while drawing attention to the sentence used in each case, inheritors are needed. Furthermore, if a sentence is treated in a model as an object, and extensions are defined for the predicates 'true' and 'false' in the inheritors (thereby defining appropriate mappings from sentences into a two-element domain), then we have double-talk, for each inheritor can be read in two ways: as affirming or denying the "antecedent" sentence, and as an ordered pair.

6.2. Suppose, because there are reasons for wanting to say things in the formal mode that we usually say in the material mode, inheritors are what semanticists and logicians need; then 'true' and 'false' cannot be property-ascribing. If 'true' and 'false' were property-ascribing, then extra-model-theoretically an ordered pair like "<'S', 1>" would say both that S—on the inheritor reading—and that 'S' has the property truth—on the usual reading—and this leads to trouble when we want inheritors to be modifiable and universally available. (Inheritors are *universally available* if an inheritor can be formed with *any* expression of the language as antecedent.) For, if modifiable inheritors are universally available, then inconsistency results if inheritors, in all their occurrences, acquire content independently. Briefly, the argument in Chapter 4 went as follows: Suppose α is a sentential inheritor, and that we write as a subscript the sentence from which it acquires its content. Then if any sentence can be an antecedent, α could have $\sim\alpha$ as its antecedent. Consider $\alpha_{\sim\alpha}$ and $\sim\alpha_{\sim\alpha}$. If it is assumed that α acquires content independently, then incoherence results, for each of $\alpha_{\sim\alpha}$ and $\sim\alpha_{\sim\alpha}$ appear to simultaneously express both that $\sim\alpha$ and that $\sim\sim\alpha$. Indeed, in these cases, incoherence results if α is supposed to have acquired content in *any* way.

On the assumption that if 'true' and 'false' were property-ascribing, they would be so in every occurrence, *each* inheritor formed by 'true' and 'false' would have content independently. It is for this reason, given the above considerations, that we cannot simply "turn" 'true' and 'false' into property-ascribing predicates by (arbitrarily) completing the partitioning of sentence tokens, *unless* we give up (at least part of) the inheritor-forming role of these predicates. I should also point out that although this argument supports the claim that truth and falsity are not properties (of sentence tokens) it does not affect the claim that truth and falsity are quasi-properties, for then we do not require 'true' and 'false' to characterize in each and every occurrence.

In Chapter 6 I assumed that logicians had available property-ascribing roles for 'true' and 'false' and suggested that, given the kinds of properties these would be, they would supply the bridge required between practice and our models. I believe I have now shown that the assumption of properties is not needed. (Fortunately) all that we need from 'true' and 'false' in this context are the inheritor features and, for the models, appropriately defined extensions for 'true' and 'false'.

Finally, as in the case of arithmetical computations, it is important the double-talk (the two modes of speaking) that yields useful models not be confused. One concern here is that we should not too hastily make assumptions concerning the extra-model-theoretic significance of things that we might want to say in or about a model. The kind of case I have in mind is one in which, in a model, a given sentence 'R' is not assigned either the value 1 or 0 ('R' doesn't have a truth value). Although an assignment of 1 by the model to a sentence 'S' will be read extra-model-theoretically as a claim that S, there will not be a corresponding extra-model-theoretic reading in the case of 'R'. It is only when a sentence has a truth value in a model that there is an inheritor reading—that is the point of the truth values: In only those cases do we move to the affirmation or denial of what's said by the antecedent sentence.

Just how a claim according to which a sentence 'R' is said *not* to have a truth value in a model is to be understood extra-model-theoretically, is something that should emerge from the considerations of the next section.

7. On 'Neither True nor False'

It is often said of nondeclaratives, such as questions and commands, and of certain declaratives that falter in some way, like 'The king of France is wise', that they are neither true nor false. And it is generally required of a theory of truth that it accommodate expressibility of this kind. Those who think of 'true' as property-ascribing also think—unless consideration of the paradoxes forces some compromise—that we should be able to say of a sentence like the Liar that it is not true. Providing room for this kind of expressibility has proved a recalcitrant problem.

What point is being made when it is said of a sentence that it is *neither true nor false*? or, when it is said of the Liar that it is *not true*?

A "truth claim" or "judgment" is said to be "something that is either true or false." Is something not a judgment just in case it is neither true nor false? A careful consideration of the status of this way of introducing 'truth claim' and 'judgment' will show that it is a mistake to make the move to "neither true nor false" here; furthermore, this fact undermines the belief that most of us have had that we need 'true' and 'false' for the kind of expressibility described above.

7.1. The practice of language involves the performance, by speakers of language, of a variety of linguistic acts. Speakers are said to refer, characterize, assert, deny, ask questions, command, and so on. The performance of any of these acts involves not only the speaker as a member of a community of people who participate together in these practices but also, for each kind of act, the use, typically, of a particular kind of expression. For example, although a declarative sentence can be used—if the context and intonation is right—to ask a question or to command, it is typically used to make a truth claim. However, mere utterance of the appropriate kind of expression does not generally suffice for the performance of the linguistic act, nor does a speaker, when referring, always refer to the denotation of a given singular term, etc. But these are complexities of language use that I hope to be able to avoid, and I will sometimes simplify further by talking as though it is (a token of) a declarative sentence that makes a truth claim, or a singular term that refers, even though the making of truth claims, and referring, are things that only speakers do.

Although use of a declarative sentence normally has a speaker making some kind of reference, and characterizing, these acts are—so to speak—only constituents of another for which we need the declarative form, and that is the making of a truth claim. What are truth claims?

It might be suggested, initially, that the making of a truth claim involves explicit predication of 'true' (or 'false'). But that's not correct. Consider, for example, Frege's (1892) point about the making of a truth claim in his argument against the suggestion that the relation of a thought to its truth value is like that of subject to predicate "understood in the logical sense." Frege (1892) is comparing '5 is a prime number' with 'The thought, that 5 is a prime number, is true': "The truth claim arises in each case from the form of the declarative sentence, and when the latter lacks its usual force, e.g., in the mouth of an actor upon the stage, even the sentence 'The thought that 5 is a prime number is true' contains only a thought." and in "The Thought" (Frege, 1918–19), we have "We declare the recognition of truth in the form of an indicative sentence. We do not have to use the word 'true' for this. And even when we do use it the real assertive force lies not in it but in the form of the indicative sentence, and where this loses its assertive force the word 'true' cannot put it back again.''

Although Frege's primary concern is with a certain aspect of the conditions under which a truth claim is made, that the form of the declarative sentence be in force, it is clear that the other point he makes, that the making of a truth claim is not (usually) a matter of predicating 'true' of something, is also right.

So why is it that *truth* comes in here? Truth claims, propositions, judgments, and thoughts have been variously described in the literature as "capable of truth and falsity." Prior (1976, p. 17) provides us with a summary of one such tradition: "There is the tradition . . . All its spokesmen agree that a proposition is a form of speech, a sentence, though not any sort of sentence—it must be in the indicative mood, capable of truth or falsehood, and somehow connected with 'judgment'." The tradition Prior describes seems to justify claims like the following:

(10) A truth claim is something that is either true or false.

And so to "neither true nor false," for presumably a sentence fails to be a truth claim if it is neither true nor false.

So, if we assume it is important to distinguish in the practice of language between those acts that involve the making of a truth claim and those that don't, we can see why, given *this reading* of (10), the neither-true-nor-false expressibility indicated above is required: If we wish to say of a question, or 'The king of France is wise', that it is not used in making a truth claim, we need to be able to say of it that it is neither true nor false.

Unfortunately, problems arise if such expressibility is assumed. I gave a brief indication of these in §1. (The reader is referred to Dummett 1973, p. 445; Heidelberger 1968; and Wilson 1980 for detailed presentations and discussions of the problems, especially for the case where 'neither true nor false' is predicated of a sentence like 'The king of France is wise'. For a discussion of some difficulties that 'The Liar is not true' raises, the reader is referred to Chihara 1979, and for critical surveys of suggested formal approaches and their failure to provide well-motivated systems, the reader is referred to Parsons 1974 and Burge 1979.) The problems arise for those theories that accept certain forms of the equivalence (or redundancy) thesis. The thesis states, in its simplest form, that 'S' and 'S is true' are interchangeable, and similarly for '$\sim S$' and 'S is false'. Although the prosentential theory does not subscribe to quite this version of the thesis (Chapter 3 explains in some detail differences between the redundancy theory and the prosentential theory of truth), the differences do not affect the force of the argument. The problems also arise for the Tarski- and Kripke-style models in the following way: Because Tarski's Criterion of Adequacy requires derivability of all instances of schema (T), it also subscribes (if 'false' is treated as 'not true') to the equivalence thesis. Now although, in one sense, the problems outlined do not arise, because the Tarski-style model does not include cases in which S is a nondeclarative, or problematic in some way, the problems *do* arise in the sense that it is not known how the models might be extended to accommodate the required expressibility and yet avoid the problems.

But what do we think we want to be saying? Let's consider (10) again, to see what its status is, in an account of truth claims. It will be helpful to make some comparisons with reference: Because both are assumed basic to the practice of language, we might expect some similarities. What kinds of accounts do we have?

A theory of reference like a causal, or historical, theory of reference, seeks to provide an account of the conditions that make reference possible, and as a part of that, to provide an account of how a speaker, in using a singular term, succeeds in referring to the particular object that is referred to. There are similar projects concerning truth claims: Under what conditions are truth claims made? What determines that different truth claims are made? It is presumably as part of such an inquiry, or related inquiries, that philosophers have been prompted to provide analyses of the propositional, or declarative form, to isolate those circumstances in which the form is in force, to provide us with theories of reference, and predication, and so on.

No matter how these projects are characterized, I think it is clear that there is one thing that they are not: Their goal is not to teach us how to refer or make truth claims, nor to provide us with explicit definitions or paraphrases of 'refers' or 'truth claim'. The practice is acquired in other ways, and the use of 'refers' and 'truth claim' is probably learnt—in the context of a theory or an explanation of linguistic practice—through some kind of ostensive definition, some kind of "pointing" to the practice. With these points in mind, I will consider something else that seems to tell us something of 'refers' or reference. Carnap pointed out that

(11a) 'a' refers iff $\exists x(a = x)$

(11b) 'a' refers to b iff $a = b$

There's a problem here if 'a' doesn't refer. Suppose, for example, 'a' is 'runs'. Then neither of the following instances is well formed:

'runs' refers iff $\exists x(\text{runs} = x)$

'runs' refers to b iff runs $= b$

So (11a) and (11b) must be understood as coming with a proviso. If the proviso is that 'a' refer, they might be written as

Providing 'a' refers/'a' refers iff $\exists x(a = x)$

Providing 'a' refers/'a' refers to b iff $a = b$

where '/' is interpreted along the lines of Belnap's (1973) restricted assertion operator: The only instances that count will be those in which 'a' refers.

(11a) had the appearance of being a definition that stated necessary and sufficient conditions for an expression 'a' to refer. But if the point of such a definition is to determine which members of a domain the predicate applies to, then (11a) fails to be such a definition; in the case in which 'a' doesn't refer, the right-hand side fails to state a condition that must be satisfied for the predicate to apply. The ineffectiveness of (11a) and (11b) in this regard is especially made clear when the assumed proviso is stated. (It might be suggested that the proviso should restrict the instances of 'a' to only singular terms. But that won't do if we want to say that 'runs' doesn't refer; furthermore, the right-hand side would remain semantically problematic—consider the case of 'Pegasus'—in a way that the left-hand side is not.)

The similarity with the problem raised (§1) for 'neither true nor false' should, I think, be obvious. Consider

(12) 'p' is a truth claim iff either p or not p.

If we provide a reading of (12) in English, using 'it is true' and 'it is false' as prosentences, we get

(13) Something is a truth claim iff it is true or it is false.

which is very close to what we began with, (10). (Note that [13] has an advantage over [12] with respect to perspicuity, for the use of the [nonatomic] prosentences, by contrast with the letter 'p', features the declarative form in use—our vehicle for making truth claims.) As in the case of 'refers', (12) and (13) are not definitions. To treat them as such would require that all expressions be covered, including instances like

'Runs' is a truth claim iff either runs or not runs.

It's clear that isn't what is (or should be) intended by (10). A proviso is presupposed or implicated. In most discourse, satisfaction of the proviso by any 'p' that might appear in something of the form 'p or not p' is taken for granted, and so we simply endorse any sentence—belonging to the discourse—of the form 'p or not p'. But if we are in a discourse in which such an assumption is not being made, the proviso must be made explicitly, so that instead of (12) and (13) we have

Providing 'p' is a truth claim/'p' is a truth claim iff either p or not p.

Providing an expression is a truth claim/It is a truth claim iff it is either true or false.

The move from (10)

A truth claim is something that is either true or false.

to

Something fails to be a truth claim if it is neither true nor false.

is now blocked.

Thus, although (on present theories at least) we do seem to want the truth claim/nontruth claim distinction, and we *do* want to say of a sentence like 'The queen of England is wise' that it is either true or false, we do *not* need to say of a sentence like 'The king of France is wise' that it is neither true nor false. I have also shown that the kind of problem to which discussions of the equivalence thesis have drawn attention is not isolated: The problem may arise whenever a sentence containing a proform is taken out of context, for then certain assumptions that are usually made concerning likely antecedents may not obtain.

I have said more about what status (10)–(13) do not have than about the status they do have. (10)–(13) have returned us to the subtle connections that seem to occur inevitably between the language in which we describe linguistic practice (on the left-hand side) and the practice itself (the expression in question is *used* on the right-hand side).

A peculiarity of having the expression in question (only) used on the right-hand side is that the right-hand side doesn't say anything *about the expression*. So what's the connection between the left-

and right-hand sides? Because instances of the right-hand sides of (10)–(13) provide pertinent samples of linguistic practice, we might do well to think of (10)–(13) as providing *ostensive* definitions.

7.2. Strawson and Frege have been criticized for both holding that there are sentences (or uses of them, or thoughts) that are neither true nor false *and* for believing in the equivalence thesis. I think it might reasonably be suggested that it is the truth claim/nontruth claim distinction that is assumed in their discussions.

The critics have emphasized the use of 'neither true nor false', but attention should be paid to some other locutions that are used by these philosophers. (I haven't, in fact, found a place where Frege uses 'neither true nor false'. He does say that there are sentences that don't have truth value, but that is another matter, for there is not a corresponding equivalence thesis [see §6].) A frequent concern of each critic is whether "the question of truth (or falsity) arises." Consider, for example, these pieces from "The Thought" (quoted in Klemke 1968, p. 511): "Without wishing to give a definition, I call a thought something for which the question of truth arises." and "A thought is something immaterial and everything material and perceptible is excluded from this sphere of that for which the question of truth arises." And in "On Referring" (Strawson, 1950b, p. 183) we have "When . . . we say . . . 'There is no king of France' we should certainly not say we were *contradicting* the statement that the king of France is wise. We are certainly not saying that it is false. We are, rather, giving a reason for saying that the question of whether it is true or false doesn't arise." Sometimes Strawson hyphenates 'true-or-false'. I presume he does this to get the right contrast. Consider "Mentioning, or referring to, something is a characteristic of *a use* of an expression, just as "being about" something, and truth-or-falsity, are characteristics of *a use* of a sentence." (p. 180) I take it that the point is not that truth and falsity are each characteristics of uses of sentences, but that truth-or-falsity alone is, as if the "making of a truth claim" is a characteristic of a use of a sentence.

But back to the question of truth arising. For either a prosententialist or someone holding a property view, it is assumed, I believe, that the question of truth arises for only those sentences that can be used to make truth claims. So, in the terminology that I have been using, the point that Frege and Strawson seem to be making is that a sentence like 'The king of France is wise' does not make a truth claim. If this is the distinction that is in question, then 'neither true nor false' is not needed.

So much for the distinction. Are Frege and Strawson any better off with questions of truth arising? Consider, for example, 'The question as to whether it's true (or false) doesn't arise'. Instances will look like

> The question as to whether Odysseus was put on shore doesn't arise

and

> The question as to whether the king of France is wise, or whether the king of France is not wise, doesn't arise.

It seems that a Strawsonian could hold these to be semantically acceptable while rejecting

> The king of France is wise and the king of France is not wise.

This disparity provides one reason for favoring "question of truth arising" talk over "neither true nor false," but only as long as the context restricts the substituends to sentences. There is a problem, for example, with

> The question as to whether runs doesn't arise.

Similar kinds of disparities arise for 'refers'. Corresponding to (11b) we can say

> The question of which object it is doesn't arise.

but only with a struggle might we introduce

> The question of which object runs is doesn't arise.

So, unless the grammar of our language is particularly accommodating, the formal mode should probably be adopted.

7.3. It does not follow from the fact that 'neither true nor false' does not have to be used in capturing the truth claim distinction, that there is no place for 'not true' and 'not false': 'not true' and 'not false' are sometimes used in modified prosentential constructions. Related matters that will arise concern some differences between 'That's not true' and 'That's false'.

Wittgenstein (1974, §21) says: " 'Not' is a gesture of rejection. To grasp negation is to understand a gesture of rejection." 'That is false' is generally used to (anaphorically) affirm the contradictory of an antecedent sentence. But sometimes we reject what someone has said without knowing exactly what we would like to put in its place, perhaps because 'not' can modify a sentence in more than one way. And sometimes, although we know what modification we would accept, we don't need to make that clear when expressing our disagreement. In either case, perhaps in order to suggest or implicate open possibilities, 'That's not true' might be used. Thus, someone responding to an utterance of 'Smith's dishonest' with 'That's not true' need not be prepared to affirm that Smith is honest, but only that, for example, Smith is devious. 'That's not (quite) true' can also be used when only a part of what was said is false.

But it would also be consistent with a prosentential 'true' for 'That's not true' to be used when the reason for rejecting what's said is no longer a matter "merely" of disagreement. Suppose someone says, 'Green eyes sleep furiously' or 'The king of France is wise.' Then, as Strawson (1950b) points out, we would normally respond with something like 'I'm afraid you must be under a misapprehension.' But we might also respond with 'That's not true', and a cooperative speaker will add a rider explaining why what was said is being rejected, for the discourse may not be able to proceed successfully without a correction of beliefs.

What account can be given of such a use of 'That's not true'? The intention might sometimes be (for the reasons discussed in §7.1 and §7.2) to deny that the antecedent sentence makes a truth claim; but sometimes 'That's not true' might be used as only a *gesture* of rejection—the antecedent sentence is rejected as not belonging to the discourse. As a gesture of rejection, use of 'That's not true' becomes a limiting case among prosentential constructions, in the sense that the antecedent is modified "out of existence," for no modified form of the antecedent is accepted in place of 'That is not true'. And this is why neither 'That is false', nor any other modified prosentence, will do as well. As a "modified prosentence," 'That is not true' retains, here, only its function of providing a response to what someone else has said. In terms of assertional content, it will convey (at most) the implicature that some presupposition of what was said is false. By contrast, if 'That's false' is used, the understanding will be that the intention is to affirm the contradictory of the antecedent.

7.4. A very clear statement of a challenge, presented by a line of reasoning we seem to engage in when reflecting on the status of paradoxical sentences, is presented in Burge 1979. (Burge includes references to earlier discussions of the reasoning in question: Prior 1971, Herzberger 1970, and Parsons 1974. See also Chihara 1979.)

Burge puts it this way (p. 178): "In all the variants of the Strength-ened Liar so far discussed, we started with (a) an occurrence of the liar-like sentence. We then reasoned that the sentence is pathologi-cal and expressed our conclusion that it is not true, in the very words of the pathological sentence. Finally, we noted that doing this seemed to commit us to saying (c) that the sentence is true after all."

His assessment is that "there seems to be no change in the gram-mar or linguistic meaning of the expressions involved. This sug-gests that the shifts in evaluation should be explained in pragmatic terms. Since there is . . . a shift in truth value without a change of meaning—there is an indexical element at work." Parsons had his eye on the same phenomenon when he argues that the use of 'true' and other semantical expressions can involve shifts in the domain of discourse. On the other hand, Kripke (1975) claims that the move to (b) is made at a later stage in the development of natural lan-guage.

There *is* a move to be made, for there are things that we want to say about pathological sentences, but if the account I've been giving of how 'true' functions is right, the inference as formulated by Burge is not valid.

The move to (b) has the form

'S' is pathological, therefore 'S' is not true.

and I assume the move is assumed to be justified by

If 'S' is pathological, it doesn't make a truth claim.

and

If 'S' doesn't make a truth claim, 'S' is neither true or false.

for then

(14) If 'S' is pathological, 'S' is not true and 'S' is not false.

Now if 'true' and 'false' were property-ascribing, with one of 'true' and 'not true', and one of 'false' and 'not false', applying to each expression of a language, then we *must* be able to move to ' "S" is not true'. And whether or not we think of 'true' and 'false' as prop-erty-ascribing, if we treat (14) as stating a necessary condition for an expression to be pathological, then we should again be able to con-clude that 'S' is not true. And so Burge would seem to be right.

But perhaps 'true' and 'false' are not property-ascribing, and per-haps (14) does not state a condition that pathological expressions must satisfy. Having in mind the considerations raised in earlier parts of §7, we can then argue that, instead of

If '*S*' is pathological, then '*S*' is not true

for any expression '*S*', we have only something like

Providing '*S*' is not pathological: either *S* or not *S*.

and so the expressibility thought to be required is not needed. What I am suggesting is that considerations like those raised in earlier sections of §7 show that reflection may lead us to conclude that liar-like sentences are pathological, but *that* conclusion can be arrived at *without* also concluding that liar-like sentences are not true.

(I suggested, above, that a move to ' "*S*" is not true' would be "invalid," but I'm not certain we should say that there is *reasoning* here at all, either valid or invalid. I'm equivocating because in such a case—if 'true' is prosentential—' "*S*" is not true' fails to express a proposition. We have been so well trained to identify inference with certain symbol-pushing maneuvers that, so long as a *pattern* of the right kind is followed, we say we are reasoning—but if we're not asserting or denying anything in the process, all we're doing is following the pattern, or at best tracing out the form of an argument.)

If this approach is taken, we must look somewhere else for an account of 'pathological'. In §7.1, I very briefly reviewed ways in which we have tried to come to grips with the conditions under which we make truth claims. I did not address, specifically, the task of determining the conditions under which *inheritors* can be used to make truth claims; that's what is in question here, if we are thinking of liar-like sentences as inheritors that are pathological. How and why can things go wrong when inheritors are used? We need to develop theories that explain when and how inheritors are well grounded; that means we need an account of how the referent, propositional content, or whatever, of the use of one expression may be determined by, or help determine, that of another.

In Chapter 4 I pointed out why it can be a mistake to use 'true' and 'false' to define *grounded*: With 'true' and 'false' in inheritors that are not grounded, the defined 'grounded' becomes, itself, a disguised inheritor and not grounded. Investigations of the Chastain 1975 kind need to be investigated. And Kripke-style models could be modified to further help us understand, and so utilize, the "logic" of inheritors: Such models help us *pick out* or *identify* the grounded or nonpathological sentences containing 'true' and 'false', because (for the reasons given in §6) such models could be used to *exhibit* the grounded sentences of a language. (Note that "mere" exhibition of, say, the grounded sentences of a language does not turn the construction of such models into a trivial exercise, for the challenge is to draw attention to the grounded sentences in a truly useful and informative way.)

Perhaps a further remark should be made. Philosophers, thinking of a truth property, have looked (frustratingly) for an all-encompassing explicit truth definition. By contrast, it does not seem reasonable to begin with a comparable demand in the case of prosentences. Just as a theory of pronouns is going to have to assume the use of pronouns understood, so, it would seem, a theory of prosentences will have to assume the use of prosentences understood.

In Chapter 4 I provided some reasons for thinking that inheritors may not be paradoxical—pathological sentential inheritors only lack propositional content. Perhaps the issues I have raised in this paper will help us determine whether we might be able to have, also without paradox, the expressibility we would like in describing linguistic practice.

8. Properties Reconsidered

It will have occurred to the reader that if we do not require from 'true' and 'false' the expressibility outlined in §1, then we do not have to require that truth and falsity, as candidate properties, partition the set containing all expressions of the language. It would suffice if truth and falsity partitioned the set of tokens used to make truth claims. According to such a view, ' "Runs" is true', ' "Runs" is not true', and (I assume) 'It's false that "runs" is true' would all fail to make truth claims, because each use of 'true' and 'false' breaks the category restriction. Furthermore, it will be argued, if truth and falsity are restricted to such a category, the property theory will no longer be required to explain why each of the following,

'How are you?' is not true.

This is false.

The Liar is not true.

seems not to be equivalent to the result of applying the equivalence thesis. If the application of truth and falsily is restricted to those tokens which make truth claims, none of these three is equivalent to anything.

This suggestion raises some controversial issues. For example, the suggestion would have to be supplemented by a defense of the more general claim that properties are category-restricted, i.e., the union of the extension and anti-extension of a property is restricted to a category or sort. Granted, in a large number of cases (perhaps all?) *the extension* of a property is included in a category or sort distinct from the universe of discourse; but do we want the anti-extension restricted similarly? Unrestricted anti-extensions seem to be required if we are to explain differences between the members of different sorts. Consider, for example, one way in which we explain the numeral/number distinction: "Several tokens of the Roman and Arabic numerals 'II' and '2' are inscribed on the blackboard, but the number 2 is not inscribed on the blackboard." It might be suggested, in response, that only truth and falsity are category-restricted; but then it would seem "category mistakes" are introduced only to provide a way of saving truth and falsity as properties.

But, independent of those issues, would truth and falsity partition the domain of sentence tokens used to make truth claims? If it can be shown that the Liar is, indeed, excluded from the set of tokens used to make truth claims, then perhaps the properties would partition the domain.

It might be argued by reductio that 'This is false' does not make a truth claim, for, if 'This is false' made a truth claim, it would be both true and false, and that's not possible. But why is it impossible? I assume the reason given is that truth and falsity *are properties* (satisfying an appropriate form of the equivalence thesis) that are mutually exclusive. This argument therefore seems to beg the question, and so, in a way, does the next.

This is an argument Martin (1967) presents, only modified a bit because I don't think he tries to accommodate 'This is not true'. Martin appeals to the category mistake idea to distinguish between sentences that are semantically correct and those that are semantically incorrect. Martin claims to have shown that the Liar "can never reasonably be ruled semantically correct." However, although Martin concludes from this that the Liar is semantically incorrect, he might equally have concluded that the category mistake idea is not coherent or not useful. So the argument is not persuasive. (The reader is referred to Prior [1954] for further discussion of categories and paradox.)

Another approach along these lines might be developed on the basis of the Martin-Woodruff (1975) and Kripke (1975) model. But then we need a theory explaining why 'true' and 'false'—to use the Kripke-Herzberger terminology—must be grounded, *and*, of course, a defense of category restrictions. (There is also the alternative of denying that properties, although category-restricted, must [completely] partition a category or sort.)

Although this brief survey of possibilities hardly does justice to the various alternatives, I think it succeeds in showing that the suggestion that truth and falsity be restricted to tokens that make truth claims cannot *simply* be made by the property theorist.

But perhaps more important is the question, What do we want 'true' and 'false' for? Do we need or want 'true' and 'false' to be property-ascribing?

To date, the development of the prosentential idea seems to show that 'true' and 'false' are needed to provide us with different modes of speaking—modes of speaking that establish, or contribute to, anaphoric connections required in discourse. A characteristic feature of anaphoric devices is that they keep discourse that is about extralinguistic things, about those same extralinguistic things, while at the same time maintaining connections between discourses. If that's what is needed, then property-ascribing predicates would, by comparison with inheritor constructions, introduce an unnecessary step and perhaps also contradiction. So, while I have not yet given the attention I would like to many other areas of our truth talk, I suspect it will turn out that we do not, or *should not*, want 'true' and 'false' to be property-ascribing.

Note that I am here, as in other places, talking about the *use* of the predicates 'true' and 'false'. I'm not addressing the question of what the subject of investigation is of various theories of truth. That remains a future project (now Chapter 1 of this volume).

8

Berry's Paradox

Given a list of descriptions in English which "name" integers, there will be a least integer which is not named in less than nineteen syllables. It seems that the integer is described as

(1) The least integer not described in less than nineteen syllables

Suppose we add (1) to the list. Then the candidate referent of (1) fails to satisfy the description. In failing to satisfy the description, it can no longer be the referent of (1), but if it's not the referent, it again becomes the candidate referent. This is Berry's paradox.[1]

Berry's description, like the Liar sentence ('This is false'), is usually viewed as posing a challenge to the assumption that crucial characterizing predicates such as 'refers' and 'true' are coherent and consistent. As a result, many philosophers and logicians working with the concepts of truth and reference have sought through the development of formal models to identify (and avoid) contradiction. By contrast, the view I will defend attributes the peculiarities of the Liar and the Berry description to the presence of "ungrounded inheritors." According to this account there is no contradiction, for the Berry description fails to refer, and the Liar sentence fails to express a proposition. Although this last is not a new suggestion, the first suggestion—that the peculiarities are to be explained in terms of ungrounded inheritors—avoids a recalcitrant problem that current model theorists face. Those who hold both that 'true' and 'false' are characterizing, and that the Liar sentence fails to have a truth value, should also be able to say (consistently) that the Liar sentence is neither true nor false. But they can't. The ungrounded inheritor theorist has an advantage, for that expressibility is neither required nor desired.[2] A challenge that remains is the formal iden-

---

[1] Russell's formulation (Russell 1908) has 'named' where I have 'described'.

[2] My first mention of this point was in Chapter 7.

tification of ungrounded inheritors, especially those that obstruct communication.

I will begin with a brief summary of the earlier discussions of inheritors. The reader is referred to Chapters 3 and 4 and Grover 1976 for further details.

1. Inheritors

Successful communication requires a facility for establishing connections between one piece of discourse and another: We need to have some way of communicating that we are continuing with the same topic (when this is the case) or that we are affirming, denying, or considering something that was said earlier, etc. To establish such connections, we use topic- and content-connecting devices like pronouns. Consider a circumstance where 'she' is used anaphorically in

(2) TOM: Mary will hang the picture later.
    SUE: If she does, she'll hang it crookedly.

When context makes it clear that Sue is using 'she' anaphorically, we know that Sue intends to refer to the person Tom referred to, Mary. Note that Sue refers to the person Mary, not the word 'Mary'. I have argued elsewhere that natural languages may contain anaphoric devices other than pronouns. There is deletion. Some uses of 'do' seem to qualify as pro*verbs*, and some uses of 'such' as pro*adjectives*. A central claim of the prosentential theory of truth is that 'That is true' and 'It is true' function as pro*sentences*.

If we want to make connections with some distant piece of discourse, or with some other discourse, a pronoun (prosentence, or some other kind of proform) will not always suffice, for the anaphoric relation does not usually establish connections between distant pieces of discourse. We cannot use 'it' in chapter 5 of a book to refer to something otherwise mentioned only at the beginning of chapter 1. There are a variety of expressions that can be used to establish the connections we need. My interest is in those that are similar to pronouns (and other proforms) in that they keep discourse at the "object language" level. I call such expressions *inheritors*.

What if we wish, in this place, chapter 5, to talk about someone mentioned in chapter 1? We might say something like

(3) The carrier who delivered Joan's parcel killed Jim.

or

(4) The carrier referred to in chapter 1 killed Jim.

Donnellan (1966) has drawn our attention to the fact that definite descriptions may function in a variety of ways. My concern is with a possible non-attributive use of descriptions like 'The carrier referred to in chapter 1'.[3]

When we want to talk about something mentioned at another time, or in another place, and a pronoun won't suffice for the job, an alternative available to us is to use a definite description, as in (3) and (4). But if we want to make it clear that we are making connections with some other piece of the discourse, not any kind of definite description will do. Descriptions that contain expressions like 'referred to', 'been talking about', and 'just mentioned' will do the trick, however, for they direct us to linguistic acts. Such definite descriptions are appropriately classified as inheritors, for they are similar to anaphoric pronouns in that they establish connections with other parts of a discourse while keeping the discourse at the "object language" level. Consider the use of 'she' in (2). 'She' refers to Mary, not the word 'Mary'. And the anaphoric relation connecting 'she' and 'Mary' is no part of the propositional content of Sue's response to Tom. Similarly, if 'The carrier referred to in chapter 1' is used as an inheritor in a sentence such as (4), then (4) is about a person (Bill, if the carrier is Bill) and not about pieces of language. The work done by a description in locating an antecedent expression from which a referent is inherited is not part of what is said when a description is used as an inheritor. We can think of that locating work as being done off to the side, in a "working column" perhaps.

Successful use of inheritors requires that they be connected to expressions that acquire their referents "independently"—as a proper name does, for example, perhaps through some causal chain, or as a definite description used attributively does. If a nominal (or sentential) inheritor has as its antecedent something that can in principle supply a referent (or propositional content), it will be said to be *grounded*.

I have shown in chapter 4 that ungroundedness can arise in a va-

---

[3] This possibility was suggested to me by some of Kaplan's work on demonstratives.

riety of different ways. In the following examples, I will italicize the inheritors.

(5) FAY: *The person you are going to refer to* is someone I know.
BURT: No *she* is not.

Assume that both 'The person you are going to refer to' and 'she' are inheritors: Each should acquire its referent (if any) from the other; yet each lacks a referent. Circles of inheritors can be quite small, as in

(6) *The person I am now referring to* is coming to dinner.

A language has nominal inheritors universally available if, for any given nominal (or nominalizable) expression an inheritor can be constructed that has the expression as its antecedent.[4] This includes the possibility that an inheritor is its own antecedent, as in (6). Inheritors can be modified, as in 'The carrier not referred to in chapter 1'. A modified nominal inheritor acquires as its referent (if any) the result of applying some function to the referent of the antecedent.

"Paradoxical" expressions can be constructed when inheritors are both universally available and modifiable. This point can be illustrated in a sketchy review of the ungrounded inheritor account that I have given of the Liar sentence. Suppose α is a sentential inheritor, and suppose we write as a suffix its antecedent. Then in affirming $\alpha_{'snow\ is\ white'}$ we affirm that snow is white. If inheritors are modifiable by negation, then affirming that $\sim\alpha_{'snow\ is\ white'}$ will be affirming that snow is not white. We can now envisage a situation in which an inheritor is its own antecedent. This might be represented by α . The form of the Liar is then $(\sim\alpha)$.[5] The arrow indicates that $(\sim\alpha)$ is the antecedent of α. (This is its form, if we accept the prosentential construal of 'This is false' as a modified prosentence.) On the face of it, an attempt at affirming the Liar would seem to be not merely affirmation of contradiction, but "affirmation" of incoherence, for we have all-in-one-breath both $\sim\alpha$ and $\sim\sim\alpha$. However, because α is only an inheritor and ungrounded, $(\sim\alpha)$ is simply a sentence that fails to express a proposition.

---

[4] See Chapter 4.

[5] In Chapter 4 I use $\sim\alpha_{\sim\alpha}$ to give the form of the Liar sentence. This is not an accurate picture because it does not show that the subscripted α has $\sim\alpha$ as its antecedent. The arrow is needed.

In the next section, I will show why I think the Berry description contains an ungrounded (modified) inheritor.

2. Berry's Paradox

Suppose we have a list of descriptions that pick out integers. There will be a least integer that is not described in less than nineteen syllables. Suppose we add to the list

(1) The least integer not described in less than nineteen syllables

What is the status of (1)?

We don't have to have something as complex as (1) to generate a "paradoxical" expression with 'refers'. Suppose we had just a two-element domain $\{1, 2\}$. What is the referent of (7)?

(7) The integer to which I am not now referring

On the assumption that the referent is either 1 or 2, it would seem that (7) would have to refer to the other also. My view construes (7), not as embodying contradiction, but as a non-referring ungrounded inheritor: 'not' modifies the inheritor 'The integer to which I am now referring'. This suggestion, that the peculiarities of (7) can be accounted for in terms of an ungrounded inheritor, can be made more explicitly another way:

Suppose our language has added to it a sufficient variety of pronouns so that they are universally available. In particular, suppose 'this' is an anaphoric pronoun that has the largest nominal expression it is contained in as its antecedent. Suppose also that $\sim$ is a function which yields 2 when applied to 1, and 1 when applied to 2. Then the inheritor reading of (7) can be represented by

(8) $\sim this$

This takes us to the familiar $(\sim\alpha)$, only this time the inheritor in question is nominal. It is clear that (8) lacks a referent, for the antecedent of 'this' is (8) itself, and (8) does not acquire a referent independently.

The Berry description is more complex, for what's in question is not just one antecedent but a set of antecedents. In order to provide an anaphoric pronoun analogue of (1), I will continue to assume that pronouns are universally available. '$That_1, that_2, \ldots that_n$' will be used as anaphoric pronouns that in the present context have as their antecedents, in order, the less than nineteen-syllable descriptions of integers on the original list. An anaphoric pronoun rendering of my inheritor interpretation of (1) is

(9) The least {not{$that_1$, $that_2$, . . . , $that_n$, $that_{n+1}$}}

'$That_{n+1}$' has (9) as its antecedent. (I have assumed that (9) satisfies the syllable restriction. This could be guaranteed were (9) abbreviated by 'the least {not $that_{\{n+1\}}$}'.) 'Not' denotes a function that, applied to a set of integers, yields the complement, and 'the least' denotes a function that, applied to a set of integers, yields the smallest member of the set. '$That_{\{n+1\}}$' abbreviates {$that_1$, $that_2$, . . . $that_{n+1}$}, with '{$n+1$}' indicating that a set of antecedents is in question.

Like '$that_{\{n+1\}}$', 'integer described in less than nineteen syllables' inherits from a set of antecedent expressions. If this fact is not recognized, each of (9) and (1) will be taken to embody contradiction. For suppose we mistakenly assume '$that_{n+1}$' denotes an integer m, then (9) will denote something else. But then '$that_{n+1}$' would denote this other integer. Because '$that_{n+1}$' is an inheritor, however, it refers only if it can acquire a referent from (9). But (9) does not acquire a referent independently, because what the referent of (9) is depends on what the referent of '$that_{n+1}$' is. '$That_{n+1}$' is ungrounded, and (9) fails to have a referent. That's the problem with the Berry description: The phrase 'integer described in less than 19 syllables' should inherit from a set of antecedents, but because one of the antecedents happens to be the Berry description itself, there's an ungrounded inheritor. The Berry expression fails to refer.[6]

I have used anaphoric pronouns not just to help articulate the view I am presenting, but to make another point also. '($\sim\alpha$)', (8), and (9) show that seemingly paradoxical expressions can be constructed *without* the use of terms like 'true' and 'refers'. This shows that we must look further than models of 'true' and 'refers' in seeking explanations of the peculiarities of the "semantical paradoxes." The ungrounded inheritor account is a gesture in that direction, and one that promises a uniform treatment of the semantical and logical paradoxes.

---

[6] Is there a problem with my claim that the Berry expression does not refer? If it does not refer, an expression such as '$\exists x(x = BE)$' where 'BE' abbreviates the Berry expression, will contain a nondenoting term. I claim there is not a problem because I reject the inference from " 'a' does not refer" to '$\sim\exists x(x = a)$'. My reasons are given in §7 of Chapter 7.

3. Variations on Berry

It will occur to the reader that other versions of the Berry paradox may pose more significant challenges for the ungrounded inheritor account. I will examine one case involving the concept of an ungrounded inheritor. My main point will be to show that although there are indeed many things that can go wrong when inheritors are universally available, the cases considered, to date, provide no reason to believe that inconsistency threatens.

Use of a pronoun can be unsuccessful for a variety of reasons. A pronoun, even though it is grounded, may fail to have a referent because its antecedent fails to supply a referent. This happens with 'The king of France is bald, and *he* is wise'. Another problem arises when there is no unique candidate for the antecedent of a pronoun. Yet further difficulties occur when inheritors employ descriptions to locate antecedents. In a case in which a description—rather than an anaphoric relation—locates an antecedent, it can happen that no object satisfies the description. Consider using 'The carrier referred to in chapter 8' when there is no chapter 8. In another case, no antecedent is located because the descriptive part of the inheritor contains a contradiction.

In the case of (10), a required set of antecedents fails to be identified.

(10) The least integer not described in a less than 50-syllable description that contains no ungrounded inheritors.

If we continue to assume that an inheritor reading can be represented through the use of anaphoric pronouns, (10) has the form, for some n, of

(11) The least {not{$that_1$, . . . , $that_i$, . . . , $that_n$}}

As with (9), (11) can be abbreviated as 'The least {not $that_{\{n\}}$}'. The anaphoric pronouns of (11) are supposed to have as their antecedents the less than 50-syllable descriptions of integers that contain no ungrounded inheritors.

(11) contains an anaphoric pronoun '$that_i$' just in case the pronoun has as its antecedent a less than 50-syllable description containing no ungrounded inheritors. Will one of the '$that_i$' have (11) as its antecedent? Suppose (11) contains less than 50 syllables. If (11) were the antecedent of one of the pronouns in (11), (11) would contain an ungrounded pronoun. So (11) can't be an antecedent. But if

(11) were not an antecedent, all the pronouns in (11) would be grounded, and so (11) should be included among the antecedents. Clearly the descriptive condition on antecedents cannot be satisfied. So (11) contains pronouns that don't have antecedents. It fails to refer.

CHAPTER

9

On Two Deflationary
Truth Theories *

At one time, debates about truth centered on questions concerning the "nature of truth." Then Ramsey (1927) observed that " 'it is true that Caesar was murdered' means no more than that Caesar was murdered, and 'It is false that Caesar was murdered' means that Caesar was not murdered." Such observations have led philosophers to question the assumption that truth has a nature that must be theorized about. So there are now two schools of thought concerning truth: Some philosophers argue that truth is to be analyzed in terms of either epistemic or metaphysical concepts (as in "Truth is a relational property connecting language with the world");[1] and other philosophers argue that truth is not a substantive relational property. The former are said to advocate a *substantive* analysis of truth, and the latter a *deflationary* analysis. The development of deflationary theories has meant that substantive theorists must not only give an account of the nature of truth but also show that a substantive truth property is needed. On the other side, deflationists (who claim the truth predicate need not have an explanatory role) must either provide some other account of the role of the truth predicate or show the truth predicate is redundant. My project is to provide a comparison of two deflationary theories that claim a role for the truth predicate: the *disquotational theory of truth*[2] and the theory of which Nuel Belnap was a co-founder, the *prosentential theory of truth*.

* I thank Jerry Kapus and Anil Gupta for helpful comments on an early draft of this paper.

[1] For example, Field 1972. For other suggestions see Dummett 1976, especially pp. 115–26 and Putnam 1981, pp. 49–56.

[2] This is the theory that has been generally ascribed to Leeds (1978), Horwich (1982), Soames (1984), and Williams (1986).

A Preview

The disquotational and prosentential theories are similar in that both claim the truth predicate has utility in providing us with certain kinds of expressibility. There is some agreement about the expressibility provided, because both claim the truth predicate makes available generalization with respect to sentence positions. However, there are differences in their "formal" analyses of this role of the truth predicate. Disquotational theorists utilize first-order quantifiers and an explicit truth predicate in their analyses, while prosentential theorists appeal only to propositional quantifiers. This suggests a difference in the "level" of the truth predicate, for the disquotational analysis of generalization seems to treat 'true' syntactically as a metalinguistic predicate, while the prosentential analysis seems to have 'true' operating at the level of the object language. I argue these differences are not as significant as they might first appear.

I will also address some questions that disquotational theorists have left open. Rather than speculating as to how the theory's proponents might answer these questions, I will show that an available option for disquotational theorists is offered by the prosentential theory.

1. The Disquotational Theory

The disquotational theory seems to have been inspired by Quine's (1970) remarks about the truth predicate. The account of truth provided by the theory is also said to connect in some way with Tarski's work. I do not know whether Quine subscribes to what is now being recognized as the disquotational theory. But because his brief remarks (pp. 10–13) provide insight others do not provide, I will often rely on Quine's remarks in describing the theory. The key claims of the disquotational theory seem to be the following:

1.1. The truth predicate is a device of disquotation, of semantic ascent and semantic descent. For example,

> Truth is useful, we may say, as a device of (what Quine calls) *disquotation*. (Leeds, 1978)

> It is helpful . . . to focus on something that the truth predicate is good for—namely, what W. V. Quine has called "semantic ascent." (Soames 1984, p. 412)

Soames gives as an example of semantic ascent, the move from 'Snow is white' to "The sentence 'Snow is white' is true."

1.2. The truth predicate is said to have utility in providing a way of generalizing with respect to sentence positions. For generalization with respect to sentence positions can be achieved via quantifiers binding variables in nominal positions. The truth predicate and semantic ascent facilitate this. Soames illustrates the necessary moves in the following passage:

> The importance of semantic ascent is illustrated by cases like (3), in which we want to generalize.
> (3) a. Snow is white → (Grass is blue → Snow is white)
>   b. The earth moves → (The sun is cold → The earth moves)
> . . .
>
> . . . if one wanted to get the effect of asserting all of them, one would have to quantify, replacing sentences with variables. In English such quantification is most naturally, though not inevitably construed as first order and objectual. Thus, if the variables are taken to range over sentences we need a metalinguistic truth predicate. Semantic ascent gives us
> (4) For all sentences x, y (x is true → (y is true → x is true)).
> (Soames 1984, p. 413)

1.3. Disquotational theorists connect their theory in various ways with either Tarski-style truth definitions or the so-called T-sentences of Tarski. Soames thinks that Tarski-style truth definitions legitimize our use of the truth predicate; so defined, "the resulting truth predicate is just what is needed for metatheoretical studies of the nature, structure, and scope of a wide variety of theories." (Soames 1984, p. 425) And Williams (1986) says, "We can agree that the "disquotation" schema 'x is true in L iff p' captures something important about truth. Perhaps in conjunction with some additional conventions to cover cases like 'Everything he told you was true,' where 'true' is used in connection with statements not directly quoted, it fixes the extension of the truth predicate for language L."

1.4. Soames's talk of "a metalinguistic truth predicate" and the fact that " 'Snow is white' is true" is assumed paradigmatic, both suggest that disquotational theorists think of the truth predicate as functioning syntactically like a metalinguistic predicate.

1.5. The disquotational treatment of the relevant generalizations seems to suggest that the truth predicate also functions semantically as a metalinguistic predicate. However, *the* disquotational view on this point is not clear, for consider Quine's explanation of the truth predicate's role in semantic ascent: "The truth predicate is a reminder that, despite a technical ascent to talk of sentences, our eye is on the world. By calling the sentence ['Snow is white'] true, we call snow white." (Quine 1970, p. 12) There is a suggestion here, and in other places, that sentences containing the truth predicate are *really* about extralinguistic things. If that is the case, the truth predicate would function in a way different from (other?) metalinguistic predicates.

1.6. According to disquotational theorists, the concept of truth does not have an explanatory role; it does not require analysis in terms of either substantive metaphysical or epistemic relations. This view is expressed in claims like the following:

> Truth is a useful notion, but it is not the key to what there is, or how we represent the world to ourselves through language. (Soames 1984)

> To explain the utility of disquotation, we need say nothing about the relations between language and the world. (Leeds 1978)

2. The Prosentential Theory

Because I can provide only a brief review of the prosentential theory, I will give special emphasis to those parts of the theory that are most relevant to this discussion.[3] The principal claim of the prosentential theory is that the predicates 'true' and 'false' provide prosentential constructions. Prosentences are like pronouns (and other proforms[4]) in that they can be used anaphorically; however, whereas pro*nouns* are atomic and occupy positions nouns occupy, pro*sentences* tend to be nonatomic and occupy the positions that sentences occupy.

---

[3] The reader is referred to Chapters 3, 4, 6, and 7 for further introductory details.

[4] Included among *proforms* are pronouns, proverbs, proadjectives, and prosentences.

My review of the theory will show that the prosentential analysis of sentences containing the truth predicate carries implications regarding both the utility of the truth predicate and how this utility is to be explained.

2.1. A key claim of the prosentential theory is that 'That is true' and 'It is true' function as prosentences. I will illustrate what this can mean in a particular case. When Alan says, 'If that is true, then, ...' in

> MARY: Chicago is large.
> ALAN: If that is true, then it probably has a large airport.

Alan says, in effect, "If Chicago is large, then ..." For in the simple cases, part of the role of a proform ('that is true') is to "stand in" for its antecedent sentence (Mary's 'Chicago is large').[5] A reason for using the anaphoric 'that is true' (rather than 'Chicago is large') is to make clear that Alan is entertaining what Mary has said, rather than saying something on his own initiative. Anaphoric devices establish such connections. More generally, prosentences (and other proforms) are useful when we need to establish connections between different parts of a discourse. Such facts also explain how it is that 'that is true' can be used to express agreement.

2.2. Prosentences can be modified, as in 'That is false' and 'That may be true'. Because 'That is false', in a given context, can be used to assert the contradiction of an antecedent sentence, it can be used to express disagreement. Thus, in

> MARY: Chicago is large. ALAN: That's false.

Alan utilizes the anaphoric overtones of 'That is false' in expressing his disagreement with Mary.

2.3. The prosentential account of the role of the truth predicate in generalization goes roughly as follows: Suppose we want to generalize with respect to the component sentences in

> (1) If Eva says that the reactor is unsafe, the reactor is unsafe.
>
> If Eva says the guidelines have been satisfied, the guidelines have been satisfied.

---

[5] Though I call the sentence (or noun) with which a proform is connected its antecedent, this does not mean that the antecedent has to occur before the proform.

In English we would normally say something like

> (2) Everything Eva says (about the safety of the reactor) is true.

Our claim that 'true' has a prosentential role in (2) is based partly on the observation that there are paraphrases of sentences like (2) in which 'true' occurs in a prosentence. In (3), for example, 'true' occurs in the bound prosentence 'it is true'.

> (3) For everything Eva says (about the safety of the reactor), it is true.

This bound use of 'it is true' has an analogue in formal languages. Consider, for example,

> (4) For any p (if Eva says that p then p)

(3) and (4) say roughly the same thing. In fact, this pair of sentences illustrates our point that bound prosentences function much as bound propositional variables function in formal languages;[6] what this means, among other things, is that the truth predicate provides the expressibility that propositional variables provide us with in formal languages.

I have ignored, in (4), the suggested qualifying clause "about the safety of the reactor." On the assumption that the quantifiers are interpreted substitutionally and we have a quotation functor,[7] I could incorporate the qualification, as follows:

> (5) $\forall p$(If (Eva says that p & Qp is about the reactor's safety) then p)

where 'Qp' stands for " 'p' ".

2.4. It can be seen that the *syntax* of the prosentential truth predicate is a little different from the syntax of those predicates we typically classify as metalinguistic predicates; for we usually think of metalinguistic predicates as combining with terms to form closed sentences. By contrast, in the case of primitive sentences, the prosentential truth predicate combines with terms to form prosen-

---

[6] I refer to variables that occupy sentential positions as *propositional variables*. This is only a grammatical categorization, based on the sentential position of the variables.

[7] See Chapter 10 for one suggestion regarding the consistent use of propositional quantifiers and quotation, and quantification in and out of quotes; also Kripke 1976 for further suggestions.

tences; furthermore, prosentences might reasonably be said to be "bound" by their antecedents.

2.5. There are also *semantic* differences between the prosentential truth predicate and predicates we typically classify as metalinguistic. One difference is that the prosentential truth predicate is only a part of a prosentential construction—so it is, in a sense, an "incomplete symbol." Another difference is that the prosentential truth predicate seems to function at the level of the object language. This is something I need to say a bit more about.

What is in question is the semantic content of sentences containing the truth predicate. Many other truth theories assume that a sentence containing a truth predication, e.g., 'That is true', is about its antecedent sentence ('Chicago is large') or an antecedent proposition. By contrast, the prosentential account is that 'That is true' does not say anything about its antecedent sentence (e.g., 'Chicago is large') but says something about an extralinguistic subject (e.g., Chicago).

In order to see how the sentence 'Chicago is large', itself, need not feature in what is said, it will be helpful to consider the way pronouns function. Consider

(6) The balloon rises when it is filled with helium.

If we are to understand what is said, we must understand that the words 'the balloon' and 'it' are linked. (In this case, syntactical considerations lead us to the linkage.) However, the fact that we must see that there is a link between two expressions does not mean that when we use 'it' we actually *refer* to the words 'the balloon'. Nothing is said in (6) about either the words 'the balloon' or the linking. Similarly, even though a prosentence may be linked with an antecedent expression, we speak only of extralinguistic objects (e.g., snow or Chicago) when we use 'That is true'.

Because we usually talk of such things as balloons and snow at the level of the object language, it seems appropriate to characterize truth predications and modified truth predications as also functioning, so to speak, at the level of the object language.

2.6. The prosentential theory has assumed that truth does not have an explanatory role[8] and that truth does not thereby need to be an-

---

[8] This is not to deny that the truth predicate may be utilized in our explanations. We frequently need the expressibility that the truth predicate provides.

alyzed in terms of either substantive epistemic or metaphysical concepts. What the prosentential theory does require is a theory of anaphora. Such a theory is needed to explain the linguistic and logical aspects of anaphora in order to explain the semantic and pragmatic features of the utility of prosentences more adequately. A formal theory of the logic of prosentences may also reveal possible options regarding the syntax, semantics, and role in inference of prosentential constructions in potentially useful formal languages.

3. Generalization—A Comparison

The quantifiers used by the two deflationary theories, in their analyses of generalization, are clearly different. In the one case the bound variables occupy the positions nouns occupy, and in the other the variables occupy the positions sentences occupy. Quine's followers may hold this difference to be critical, for Quine has argued that quantification that involves bound propositional variables is incoherent if a domain-and-values interpretation is given. Such a response by "Quine's followers" would be too hasty, however. For even if Quine were right about such propositional quantifiers, it has not been shown that the propositional quantifiers employed by the prosentential theory must be given a domain-and-values interpretation. Indeed, I will be discussing a version of the prosentential theory according to which the propositional quantifiers are interpreted substitutionally. For it is this version of the prosentential theory that is most similar to the disquotational theory. Let us look at some of the details.

3.1. Soames's example (in §1.2, above) suggests the following as a disquotational analysis of (3):[9]

    (7) For every x, if Eva says x, then x is true.

if we ignore the qualifying clause "about the safety of the reactor."[10] The quantifiers are interpreted objectually with the variables ranging over a domain of closed sentences. (So that there is no confusion between the prosentential and disquotational analyses, I am using 'x', 'y', etc. as variables occupying nominal positions; I reserve 'p',

---

[9] Though disquotational theorists make much of the utility of 'true' for generalizing, they give few examples. Note also that though both Quine and Soames give examples, their analyses are different.

[10] Another possibility is "For every x, if Eva says that x is true then x is true."

'*q*', etc. for use as variables that occupy sentential positions.) Because (7) has instances like

(8) If Eva says "the reactor is unsafe," then "the reactor is unsafe" is true.

"semantic descent" is needed to return such instances to direct speech versions of the instances in (2) above. That is, to restore an instance such as (8) to

If Eva says "the reactor is unsafe," then the reactor is unsafe.

Note that the disquotational evaluation of sentences like (7) and (8) requires a domain of sentences, D, and an extension for the truth predicate.[11] In the event that the truth predicate can occur in sentences in D, we might suppose that a Tarski-style truth definition[12] is used to determine an appropriate extension for 'true' in a given context.

By contrast, for the prosentential theory, I assume the propositional quantifiers are interpreted substitutionally. So, associated with each quantifier will be a set of closed sentences that I call its *substitution range*, *SR*. We must suppose the sentences of *SR* mapped into $\{1,0\}$. In the event that bound propositional variables occur in the sentences of *SR*, we should use a "propositional Tarski-style truth construction" to determine an appropriate mapping for a given use of a quantifier. By a *propositional Tarski-style truth construction* I mean a construction similar to a Tarski-style truth construction, except that propositional quantifiers (substitutionally interpreted) and quantification in and out of quotes are featured,

---

[11] The disquotational theorist will need an operator that produces a that-clause ('that the reactor is unsafe') from the name of a sentence 'The reactor is unsafe' if the actual instances in (2) are to be recovered, unless that-clauses are treated as names of sentences. An alternative approach would be to adopt

For any x, if Eva says that x is true, then x is true.

as the disquotational analysis of (3), which has instances like

If Eva says that 'the reactor is unsafe' is true, then 'the reactor is unsafe' is true.

Semantic descent returns this instance to the original

If Eva says that the reactor is unsafe, then the reactor is unsafe.

[12] When I refer to Tarski-style constructions, I mean to include not only those of Tarski, but also Kripke's (1975), Gupta's (1982), etc.

rather than the truth predicate and first-order quantifiers (interpreted with a domain of sentences).

We know that propositional Tarski-style constructions are possible, because it can be shown that sentences of the form

>   For any x (. . . x . . . Tx . . .)

(hereafter, '$\forall x A(x, Tx)$') are provable, just in case sentences of the form

>   For any p (. . . Qp . . . p . . .)

(hereafter, $\forall p A(Qp, p)$') are provable.[13] Methods of evaluation, similar to those used in Tarski-style constructions to determine the extension of the truth predicate, would be used to assign values to the sentences occurring in the appropriate substitution ranges of the bound propositional variables. The value of a sentence like

>   (9) For any p, if Eva says that p then p.

could then be determined. For (9) will be assigned the value *1*, just in case all instances obtained by substituting the members of the appropriate *SR* for 'p', in 'if Eva says that p then p', have the value *1*.

It is clear that if we view the role of the truth predicate in (8) as similar to that of the bound propositional variable in (9), then even when used for generalizing, the truth predicate functions semantically at the level of the object language—such universal statements are in effect equivalent to a possibly infinite conjunction of sentences of the *object language.*

3.2. These are the two deflationist accounts of the truth predicate's role in generalization. What are we to make of their differences? The first point to be noted is that, if we compare only the assumptions of the quantifiers used in the two analyzing languages, the differences are trivial. For in the examples considered above, the disquotational theory assumes a domain of closed sentences, while the prosentential theory assumes a substitution range of closed sentences. In each case an acceptable evaluation derives from an appropriate Tarski-style truth construction.

In the one case, values of the sentences in the domain are determined by a Tarski-style construction, and in the other, values of the

---

[13] Anil Gupta confirms that it would be a relatively simple matter to systematically replace occurrences of 'x', say, by 'Qp', and 'Tx' by 'p', in his construction.

sentences in the substitution range are determined by a propositional Tarski-style construction. It follows that *for roughly the
same expressibility the two deflationary theories make the same
assumptions.*

There are differences, of course, in the underlying explanations of
the role of the truth predicate. For example, one theory talks of semantic ascent and T-sentences, and the other theory of proforms
and prosentences. I discuss these differences in the next section.
Later, I will say more about my supposition that deflationists can
appeal to Tarski-style truth constructions in their analyses of the
role of the truth predicate in generalization.

4. Metalinguistic Uses of the Truth Predicate

In our early discussions of the prosentential theory, Belnap was initially concerned that the prosentential theory may not provide an
account of 'true' compatible with supposedly metalinguistic uses in
model theoretic contexts. Because this is a concern other logicians
may share, I will say something about my response.[14] The issue is
relevant because it concerns another apparent difference between
the two deflationary theories that I have already mentioned: the
"level" at which the truth predicate functions.

4.1. I begin with the disquotational theory because the disquotational truth theorists seem to have had their eyes on the logician's
employment of the truth predicate.

I have already noted that the truth predicate of the disquotational
theory appears to have the syntax of a metalinguistic predicate—the
disquotational truth predicate combines with names of sentences to
form sentences, and first-order quantifiers are used. Given the effective intersubstitutability of '$\forall x(A(x, Tx))$' and '$\forall p(A(Qp, p))$' in Tarski-style constructions, one wonders whether the disquotational
truth predicate really behaves like a metalinguistic predicate. What
account do disquotational theorists give of the instances of their
universal sentences? In particular, what account do they give of
primitive sentences containing the truth predicate? Quine (1970) is
the only person who says anything about what is said when truth is
predicated of a sentence. He remarks (p.12): "The truth predicate is

---

[14] My response persuaded Belnap at the time. I do not know whether he is still
persuaded.

a reminder that, despite a technical ascent to talk of sentences, our eye is on the world. . . . By calling a sentence true, we call snow white." Unfortunately, Quine does not unpack the metaphors. I read Quine as saying that the truth predicate is not used to say anything about sentences. My reason is that his qualification of the "ascent to talk of sentences" as "technical" shows hesitancy; and the ascent seems canceled when he says that "by calling a sentence true, we call snow white." But then we might ask, if a logician only says something about snow when she says " 'Snow is white' is true," why does she not simply use 'Snow is white'? One reason offered for mentioning sentences is that semantic ascent is required for generalization with respect to sentence positions.[15] However, even if this were true, this explanation does not tell us *what is said* when there is "technical ascent to talk of sentences." Are sentences being talked about, or are they not? Some may claim we do not need to worry about such questions, because all we need know about the truth predicate, beyond its syntax, is its logic. Perhaps this is what those who claim T-sentences play a central role in the disquotational theory have in mind. Williams may be one such philosopher, for he says that the "disquotational schema . . . captures something important about truth." It is difficult to figure out what Williams's point is, for it is unclear what he thinks is captured. For a start, we need to be told which sentences count as instances of Williams's schema.[16] Can the sentence within quotes contain indexicals, or the Liar sentence, and on what grounds should we make these decisions? Note also that T-sentences alone do not tell us much about the logic of the truth predicate. For, as Sellars (1963) has noted, " 'Snow is white' (in our language) is true iff snow is white." is viewed with the greatest equanimity by pragmatist and coherentist [and deflationist] alike. Others may claim that Tarski-style constructions capture the logic of the truth predicate. But this view also does not distinguish among truth constructions. I believe we need to unpack Quine's metaphors so that we know how the truth predicate interacts with semantic ascent.

In sum, though disquotational theorists focus on a predicate that seems to have the syntax of a metalinguistic predicate, many questions concerning logicians' uses of the truth predicate presently re-

---

[15] Quine seems to say this, though I think only in a context where he is not considering the possibility of utilizing a substitutional interpretation. Both Leeds and Soames allow that first-order objectually interpreted quantifiers are not the only alternative.

[16] Williams does not explain 'x' and 'P'.

main unanswered. Only when these questions are answered will we be clearer about the level of the disquotational truth predicate.

4.2. For the prosentential account of the truth predicate as used by logicians, I need to talk about inheritors. The concept of an inheritor is a generic concept that includes within its domain expressions (including proforms) that function much as proforms function.

4.2.1. In my discussion of the Liar, I pointed out that proforms do not always suffice for the anaphoric tasks that we need accomplished.[17] This is true because proforms are effective only when they occur in close proximity to their antecedents. For example, we cannot normally use 'she' on page 60 to refer unambiguously to May, if we have not mentioned May since page 1. In such a circumstance, we must establish connections with what was said on page 1 in some other way. We can say, for example,

(10) The person I referred to on page 1 can pay her own way.

I claim that when 'the person that I referred to on page 1' is used in place of a pronoun, it is used in much the same way that a pronoun is used. So in (10), 'the person I referred to on page 1' is used to refer directly to May. The definite description functions as an inheritor. In calling such expressions inheritors, my point is that neither the speaker's words nor the speaker's speech act feature in the content of what is said in (10), just as neither the links between the words 'it' and 'the balloon', nor the words 'the balloon', feature in the content of

The balloon will rise when it is filled with helium.

We can think of the work done by the various parts of 'the person I referred to on page 1', in identifying the co-referential term on page 1, as being done, so to speak, in a working column off to the side.

There are also sentential inheritors. Prosentences are included, but there are other kinds of sentential inheritors. For certain combinations of definite descriptions and the truth predicate can stand in for antecedent sentences. For example, there are circumstances where something like

(11) If the last indented sentence is true, ...

must be used, because

---

[17] See Chapter 4 and Brandom 1988, §VI.

If that is true, then . . .

will not suffice for the task on hand. Let us suppose the speaker wants to acknowledge the antecedent sentence, and 'that is true' cannot be used because the antecedent sentence is not in close proximity. In such a case (11) can function as an inheritor. (Note that in the event the speaker does not know what the last indented sentence is, it might be more appropriate to use quantifiers in analyzing (11).)

According to the prosentential theory, sentences like

(12) 'Snow is white' is true.

are also inheritors. Construed as an inheritor, (12) says something about snow. In this case the antecedent sentence, 'Snow is white', rather than being picked out with a definite description, is explicitly displayed. Either way, the "semantic ascent" involved would not feature in what is said. In Chapter 3 we were grappling with the same issue when we suggested that the display format

Consider: Snow is white. That is true.

can be used to capture a sentence like (12).

4.2.2. It might be objected that "logicians do not have any use for inheritors, for they talk about languages and sentences, not balloons and snow." I agree that logicians do talk about languages. However, there is usually little point in talking about languages if there is no connection with the object languages in use. Inheritors facilitate connections between mention and "use."[18] For example, in a context where we have been talking about our proof theory, or the syntactical structure of a sentence, we often want to talk about a sentence or the structural form of a set of sentences of the object language. One reason is that tasks are often made easier if they are reduced to symbol-pushing maneuvers. It is in establishing connections between theory and/or symbol-pushing maneuvers and language in use that inheritors can be useful. For inheritors provide us with a way of displaying a sentence while in effect *using* it. Consider, again,

'Snow is white' is true

---

[18] For more details see Chapters 6 and 7.

This inheritor provides us with a way of saying that snow is white, while at the same time displaying the sentence. The antecedent sentence of the inheritor

Snow is white

alone would not do as well. When 'Snow is white' is used alone, our attention is not usually drawn to the structure of the sentence used. One place where explicit display is useful is in an explanation of the logical connectives. For example, we customarily explain disjunction using the following format:[19]

> (13) For any sentences x and y, $(x \lor y)$ is true just in case x is true or y is true or both x is true and y is true.

Why use this format? Given the prosentential account of the truth predicate, and possible intersubstitutability of '$\forall x \, (A(x, Tx))$' and '$\forall p \, (A(Qp, p))$', it might seem for the prosentential theorist that

> (14) For any p and q, $(p \lor q)$ just in case either p or q or both p and q.

should do just as well. Because (14) does not contain an explicit truth predicate, it seems more in the spirit of the prosentential theory. Why do we choose the format of (13) over the format of (14)?[20] A reason (13) is more useful is that the structure of the sentences is explicitly displayed: Implicit messages about the structure of the sentences of the object language can be conveyed through such explicit display. (14) is less effective in this regard.

Readers may wonder whether this talk of implicit messages does not ascribe a substantive role to the truth predicate in (13). It should be noted that if propositional quantification and quotation are available in the metalanguage, the implicit messages of (13) could have been conveyed without the use of an explicit truth predicate. For consider

> (15) For any p, q, and r, if Qr is a disjunction such that Qp is its first disjunct and Qq its second disjunct, then r just in case either p or q, or both p and q.

---

[19] I assume first-order objectually interpreted quantifiers, and in the interests of simplicity, an autonomous system of naming expressions in the object language.

[20] Note that, without argument, I cannot assume '$\forall x(A(x, Tx))$' and '$\forall p(A(Qp, p))$' are intersubstitutable in all contexts. Propositional attitude contexts may be an exception. For, whereas 'Everything Mary believes is true' might reasonably be represented by 'For every p, if Mary believes that p, then p,' this may not be equivalent to 'For every x, if Mary believes x, then x is true.'

(15) makes explicit the information implicitly conveyed by (13); yet it has the format of '∀p(A(Qp, p))'. The use of propositional quantifiers in (15) suggests only a prosentential role for the truth predicate (in inheritors) in (13). Accordingly, the truth predicate does not seem to have a substantive role in (13)—for it can be "hidden" in prosentential constructions.

Further checking has convinced me that similar accounts can be given of other uses of the truth predicate by logicians.[21] If I am right about all of this, the truth predicate of logicians can be construed as occurring only in prosentential constructions. It functions, so to speak, at the level of the object language. Furthermore, though logicians invariably "mention" sentences in the context of using the truth predicate, the truth predicate does not seem to have a substantive role in what is said about object language sentences. There seems to be little in common, semantically, between the truth predicate in prosentential constructions and those predicates (like 'is a proof') we usually think of as metalinguistic.

5. Disquotation with Prosentences

It may now be clear why I think a disquotational theorist has the option of adopting a prosentential explanation of the role of the truth predicate.

5.1. Quine's remark that "by calling the sentence true, we call snow white" agrees with the inheritor account of the content of sentences containing 'true'. Furthermore, my account of the way inheritors function provides one reading of what one might mean by "a technical ascent to talk of sentences." The ascent is "technical" and temporary, because its purpose is to pick out the antecedent sentence of the inheritor in question; and this work is done "off to the side" and does not feature in the content of the inheritor. Hence there is no conflict with Quine's claim that a sentence containing 'true' may be about snow. Also, the intersubstitutability of Tarski-style truth constructions that highlight an explicit truth predicate (as in '∀x(A(x, Tx))') and propositional Tarski-style truth constructions that highlight the prosentential role of the truth pred-

---

[21] Consider, for example, our use of 'true' in "There are true sentences that are not provable." This does not have to be represented formally as "There are x's such that x is true and x is not provable." We can say "There are p's, such that p and Qp is not provable."

icate (as in '$\forall p(A(Qp, p))$') is consistent with my claim that the disquotational account of generalization can derive from the prosentential account.

It should be noted that acceptance of prosentential explanations would amount to acknowledging that semantic ascent is *not required* for generalization with respect to sentence positions because prosentences provide a way of generalizing without semantic ascent. This is not to deny, however, that semantic ascent may be required for other reasons. Note, also, acceptance of prosentential explanations by disquotational theorists would bring explanations of the utility of the truth predicate in those cases where generalization is not an issue, for example, cases where the truth predicate is used to establish connections between parts of discourse in expressing agreement, etc.

The version of the prosentential theory that I have argued a disquotational theorist could endorse, is that version according to which propositional quantifiers are interpreted substitutionally. It would be another matter for a disquotational theorist to adopt a version of the prosentential theory according to which a domain of propositions is assumed. The question as to whether a substitutional interpretation suffices I leave open until we know more about the rest of language.

5.2. Without saying how such choices would be made, I assumed in §3 that deflationists can choose among alternative Tarski-style constructions for a formal account of the logical role of the truth predicate in generalization. However, deflationists cannot make such a choice without saying something about such issues as falsity, the Liar sentence (for though inconsistency is clearly a problem for substantive theories of truth, it is not so obviously a problem for deflationary truth theories), and "neither true nor false." Because disquotational theorists have not yet addressed these issues, I will make good on my claim that some understanding of the interaction of the truth predicate and "semantic ascent" can provide at least an intuitive basis upon which to choose among Tarski-style constructions.

For suppose the disquotational theorist accepted a prosentential explanation of the truth predicate. Then the prosentential account of the role of 'false' in modified prosentences would follow. So also would the following prosentential account of Liar sentences.[22] Pro-

---

[22] See Chapter 4.

forms are parasitic in the sense that they must be appropriately connected to antecedent expressions that can supply content. When a
proform is so connected, it is *grounded*. In the simplest cases, an
occurrence of a proform will be *ungrounded* if it has only another
proform as its antecedent. The truth teller ('This is true') is an example of an ungrounded prosentence; and the Liar, an example of
an ungrounded modified prosentence. Note that an ungrounded proform will not have content when its antecedent is not of a kind that
can initially supply content. Ungrounded proforms can be problematic for this reason—we sometimes need to know whether we run
the risk of uttering sentences without content. Accordingly, a disquotational theorist would find useful those Tarski-style truth constructions that show us how to utilize inheritors that may in some
circumstances be ungrounded.

On the other hand, a prosentential account of the truth predicate
does not require that Tarski-style constructions say anything about
philosophers' uses of "neither true nor false." My reasons for this
claim have to do with the role of 'not' in "neither true nor false" as
rejecting what is said.

We use 'not' or 'no' when we want to reject something. Often the
role of 'not' is that of a sentence modifier, as captured in our truth
tables—'not A' is the contradictory of 'A'—but 'not' does not always
modify. When 'not' is used as a modifier, 'That is not true' will be
a modified prosentence. Suppose 'Snow is white' is our antecedent
sentence; then 'That is not true' would be equivalent to 'Snow is
not white' and 'That is neither true nor false' would be equivalent
to the contradictory 'Snow is not white and snow is white'.

This reading of "neither true nor false" does not capture most
philosophical uses of the phrase, however. We need to consider another way in which 'not' can be used to reject something we find
problematic. One reason we need another way of rejecting what
someone says is that we cannot always reject something by asserting the contradictory, because the contradictory form may be problematic also.[23] For suppose the antecedent is 'The King of France is
bald'; we get nowhere by responding with 'The King of France is not
bald'. A better response might be (as Strawson 1950b, p. 183 points
out)

(16) There's a problem with what you say, for there is no
King of France.

---

[23] I have discussed this issue in greater detail in Chapter 7.

Or one might say, "I reject both!" or "Neither!" and use display to direct attention to that which one is rejecting.

(17) Neither! The King of France is bald. The King of France is not bald.

If it is important that parts of the discourse are connected, prosentences may be used, as in

(18) Neither! That is true. That is false.

Because the prosentences are displayed/mentioned rather than used, the truth predicate is only mentioned in such uses of "neither true nor false." And this is why I think Tarski-style constructions need not be required to explain philosophers' uses of "neither true nor false."

6. Summary

We have seen that the disquotational and prosentential truth predicates provide for generalization with respect to sentence positions from roughly the same conservative resources. In the one case a domain of sentences is assumed, and in the other a substitution range consisting of the same set of sentences.

The disquotational explanation of the truth predicate's role in generalization is that the truth predicate facilitates semantic ascent. Semantic ascent, in its turn, is said to facilitate generalization with respect to sentence positions. However, until Quine's metaphors relating the truth predicate and semantic ascent are explained, the disquotational truth predicate's role is not adequately explained.

The prosentential explanation of the role of the truth predicate is that it is used in prosentential constructions. A detour through semantic ascent is not required for generalization. However, inheritors may sometimes be used to draw attention to the syntax of the language under consideration; in this case, a prosentential theorist can with equanimity exploit the inter-substitutability of '$\forall p A(Qp, p)$', '$\forall x A(x, Tx)$'.

In conclusion, I have argued that the disquotational theory can be supplemented with prosentential explanations of the underlying role of the truth predicate; I have also demonstrated some advantages of doing this.

10

Propositional Quantification
and Quotation Contexts*

1. Introduction

In his discussion concerning the concept of truth in colloquial language, Tarski (1936) raises doubts as to whether we can sensibly quantify into quotation mark names. In this context he considers two ways of treating quotation mark names. The first treats a quotation mark name as a single word, i.e., as a syntactically simple expression. The second treats a quotation mark name as a syntactically composite expression of which both the quotation marks and the expression within the quotation marks are parts. I shall be concerned to develop this second approach in the next few pages. According to this approach, the quotation marks play the part of a functor that takes expressions in the language as input and gives a name as output. The principal doubts that Tarski has concerning such an approach are that (1) it may not be possible to give the precise meaning of such a functor and (2) there is a danger that such a functor will lead to one of the semantical antinomies, e.g., the Liar antinomy.

Rather than leave the subject where Tarski does, I shall investigate ways of coping with the problems he draws attention to. My reason is that it may be useful to have in philosophy some languages that do allow some use of a quotation functor and also allow quantification over variables that occur in the quoted expressions. I take up Dunn and Belnap's (1968) suggestion that a substitution interpretation might be used to provide an interpretation of the quotation functor.

In the following I suggest three languages. They have the follow-

* I thank Nuel D. Belnap, Jr., for his help in suggesting ways of presenting the material contained in this paper. This paper was written in response to some informal notes written by Bas van Fraassen in which he included a discussion of the above version of the Liar paradox.

ing features in common: (1) The languages are antinomy-free. (2) There is a quotation functor, Q, that gives a name at some stage or other of each well-formed expression in the language. (In the first language, each well-formed expression has a name at the initial stage.) (3) There is a set of "expression-term parameters" that also serve as names of expressions in the language. This means that relative to a given interpretation we allow the possibility that one well-formed expression may have several names. (4) Quantification into quotations is allowed. (5) I have used a substitution interpretation that has the feature that $\forall p A(p)$ will be true just in case, for each wff B belonging to the substitution range of p, $A(B)$ is true. (6) Each language contains, in addition to the above, an identity predicate and a set of predicate constants that are to be interpreted as properties of expressions.

It turns out that what we have in each of the three languages is a language that contains a hierarchy of languages. The languages are cumulative, so that the closed expressions that are in the vocabulary at the nth level also belong to the vocabulary of the $(n+1)$th level. So, intuitively, each level may be said to provide us with a language that can be used to talk "about" the language on the level below.

2. Grammar

I suppose that we have a stock of *sentence parameters*, and I shall use P and R as ranging over the sentence parameters. (Sentence parameters are "atomic sentences," "sentential constants." They are never bound.)

I suppose that for each n, $n \geq 0$, there is a denumerable stock of (bindable) *propositional variables* with index n. I use p^n and q^n as ranging over the propositional variables of index n.

I suppose that for each n, $n \geq 1$, there is a stock of *expression-term parameters* (i.e., "atomic" terms that upon interpretation denote expressions) with index n. I use M^n, and N^n as ranging over the expression-term parameters of index n. (Because I do not work with any other kinds of term parameters, I use "term parameter" for "expression-term parameter.")

I suppose that we have a stock of *n-ary predicates*. I use F and G as ranging over them.

The purpose of the indices emerges in the description of the languages, but, roughly, indices on propositional variables are used to restrict the substitution range of the variable, while indices on terms are used (in the second two languages) to restrict possible assignments of the denotation.

Terms and *sentences* are defined as follows:

(1) A sentence parameter or a propositional variable is a sentence.
(2) A term parameter is a term.
(3) If X is either a term or a sentence, then QX is a term.
(4) If T_1 and T_2 are terms, then $T_1 = T_2$ is a sentence.
(5) If $T_1, \ldots, T_n$ are terms and F is an n-ary predicate, then $F(T_1, \ldots, T_n)$ is a sentence.
(6) If A and B are sentences, then $\sim A$, $A \& B$, and $\forall p^n A$ are sentences.

An occurrence of variable p^n in an expression X is said to be a *bound occurrence* of p^n in X if it is an occurrence in a well-formed part of X of the form $\forall p^n A$; otherwise it is called a free occurrence. A sentence or term is said to be *closed* if all occurrences of variables in the sentence or term are bound occurrences. It follows from this that p^n in $Qp^n = M$ is a free occurrence of p^n; and p^n in $\forall p^n (Qp^n = M)$ is a bound occurrence. We use *expression* as a generic term to refer to terms and sentences, and *closed expression* to refer to closed terms and sentences.

In the following A, B, and C range over sentences. Instances where their range is restricted to closed sentences are made explicit. Similarly T_1 and T_2 range over terms, and X and Y range over expressions. "V" is used to refer to the set of closed expressions.

3. Hierarchies

In this section I introduce some concepts that will be used in providing interpretations of the languages that are being presented. In particular I wish to talk of the "rank," "grade," and "order" of an expression; and also the "vocabulary" of a certain rank, grade, or order. I use *level* as a generic term that includes the three concepts of rank, grade, and order as species.

An occurrence of an expression X in Y is said to be *extensional* providing X does not, in that occurrence, lie within the scope of a Q. (I assume that QX lies within the scope of Q.) Otherwise it is said to be a *nonextensional* occurrence. I also talk of "extensional contexts" and "nonextensional contexts." Sometimes it is convenient to make explicit the nonextensional context of X in Y, in which case we use $Y(Q(X),X)$. I first define "rank."

The *rank of an expression* X is said to be zero if there are no propositional variables occurring in extensional contexts in X; and it is $\max(n_1, \ldots, n_k) + 1$, where $n_1, \ldots, n_k$ are the indices on variables that have extensional occurrences in X.

I define the *grade of an expression* and the *order of an expression* inductively as follows:

(1) The grade of a term parameter M^n is n; and similarly for its order.

(2) The grade of a sentence parameter P is zero; and similarly for its order.

(3γ) The grade of a propositional variable p^n is $n + 1$.

(3σ) The order of a propositional variable p^n is n.

(4) If the grade of an expression X is n, then the grade of QX is $n + 1$ and similarly for its order.

(5) The grade of n-ary predicate sentence $F(T_1, \ldots, T_n)$ is max (grade $T_1, \ldots$, grade T_n); and similarly for its order.

(6) If the grades of T_1 and T_2 are n and m respectively, then the grade of $T_1 = T_2$ is $\max(n, m)$, and similarly for its order.

(7) If the grades of A and B are n and m respectively, then the grade of $A\&B$ is $\max(n, m)$, and the grade of $\sim A$ is n; and similarly for their order.

(8γ) If the grade of A is m, then the grade of $\forall p^n A$ is $\max(n + 1, m)$.

(8σ) If the order of A is m, then the order of $\forall p^n A$ is $\max(n, m)$.

I now introduce the notion of a vocabulary. I use V_α^n ($\alpha = \rho$, γ, σ) to refer to the vocabulary of the nth rank, grade, or order. V_α^n is defined as the set of closed expressions whose rank, grade, or order (according as $\alpha = \rho$, $\alpha = \gamma$, or $\alpha = \sigma$) is less than or equal to n.

Some examples:

Expression	Rank	Grade	Order
p^0	1	1	0
$\forall p^0(p^0)$	1	1	0
M^1	0	1	1
Qp^0	0	2	1
QM^1	0	2	2
$\forall p^0(Qp^0 = M^1)$	1	2	1
$\forall p^1(QQp^1 = M^3)$	2	4	3

It follows from these definitions that the difference between V_ρ^n and V_ρ^{n+1} is that the latter has, in addition to all the closed expressions of V_ρ^n, closed expressions that contain some extensional occurrences of at least one propositional variable p^n. The situation in the case of the grade and order vocabularies is more complex. (1) The $(n + 1)th$ level will have a new stock of propositional variables. In the case of V_γ^{n+1}, the new variables have an index n, as was the case for V_ρ^{n+1}, and in the case of V_σ^{n+1}, the new variables have an index $n + 1$. (2) The quotation functor provides for the $n + 1th$ level a set of names of those expressions that are of level n. (3) A new set of term parameters provides additional names of the expressions belonging to the nth level. These three features of the $(n + 1)th$ level have the effect of producing a new set of closed expressions which together with the closed expressions of the nth level constitute the vocabulary of the $(n + 1)th$ level.

4. Semantics

I give three semantics, i.e., three kinds of mappings of the closed terms into closed expressions of the language, and the closed sentences into $\{t, f\}$. These mappings ("interpretations") are determined by an "assignment," i.e., a mapping of the term parameters into closed expressions, and the closed atomic sentences into $\{t, f\}$.

A mapping I is said to be an *assignment* iff it maps the term parameters into V, and the closed atomic sentences into $\{t, f\}$. Given that I is an assignment, I is always a *rank assignment*; I is a *grade assignment* iff I maps the atomic terms of grade n into V_γ^{n-1}; I is an *order assignment* iff I maps the atomic terms of order n into V_σ^{n-1}. I use "α-assignment" ($\alpha = \rho, \gamma, \sigma$) as varying over these.

For $\alpha = \rho, \gamma, \sigma$, and for I an α-assignment, *the α-interpretation I_α* based on I is defined as the (unique) function satisfying the following conditions:

(1) I_α is an extension of I; i.e., for a closed expression X in the domain of I, $I_\alpha(X) = I(X)$.

(2) If X is QY, then $I_\alpha(X) = Y$.

(3) If X is $T_1 = T_2$, then $I_\alpha(X) = t$ iff $I_\alpha(T_1) = I_\alpha(T_2)$.

(4) If X is $\sim A$, then $I_\alpha(X) = t$ iff $I_\alpha(A) = f$.

(5) If X is $A \& B$, then $I_\alpha(X) = t$ iff $I_\alpha(A) = I_\alpha(B) = t$.

(6) If X is $\forall p^n A(p^n)$, then $I_\alpha(X) = t$ iff for each closed sentence $B \in V_\alpha^n$, $I_\alpha(A(B)) = t$. (By $A(B)$ we mean the result of putting (closed) B for every free occurrence of p^n in $A(p^n)$.)

The last and crucial clause, (6), in effect defines V_α^n (for $\alpha = \rho, \gamma, \sigma$), as the α-substitution range of the variable p^n. We therefore sometimes speak of the "rank-substitution range," etc., of p^n or of $\forall p^n A$; or of the "order-instances," etc. of $\forall p^n A$.

I now have the task of showing that for every α-assignment I there is a unique extension I_α satisfying $(1\alpha)–(6\alpha)$. It will be helpful to have the following terminology: The *depth of an occurrence of a quantifier* in an expression is said to be zero if that occurrence is nonextensional; and otherwise it is equal to the number of quantifiers within the scope of which the quantifier lies. The depth of an expression X with rank i is defined as $d_1 + \ldots + d_k$, where $d_1, \ldots, d_k$ are the depths of the quantifiers in X with index $i–1$. ($i–1$ will be the largest index on any propositional variable that has an extensional occurrence in X.)

The *length of a closed expression* X is defined as the number of connectives, predicates, and operators that occur in extensional contexts in X. As QY always occurs in nonextensional contexts, the length of $T_1 = T_2$ is 1 no matter how complex either of T_1 or T_2 happen to be. Note that the substitution of any closed expression for a propositional variable in a nonextensional context in a closed expression X does not increase the length of X.

THE I_ρ UNIQUENESS THEOREM

For every ρ-assignment I, there is a unique extension I_ρ of $I
satisfying $(1\rho)–(6\rho)$

The justification of this claim employs a triple induction. The induction is on the rank, depth, and length of expression. Clause (3ρ) relies on an induction on length. The rank and depth remain constant; in fact, they are both zero. In clause (4ρ) the induction is on length. The rank and depth remain unchanged. In clause (5ρ), the induction is again on length; the depth either decreases, or if it increases, the rank of the sentence is lowered. In the case of (6ρ) we distinguish the following cases: (1) There is just one extensional occurrence of a quantifier with index n, and the rank of X is $n + 1$. In this case an induction on rank is required because we lose control over both the length and depth of the sentence. (2) Either the rank of the sentence is $n + 1$ and there is more than one extensional occurrence of a quantifier with index n; or the rank is greater than $n + 1$. Then we require the induction on depth. We lose control over the length of the sentence and the rank remains unchanged.

These inductive moves are made possible by the fact that sentences B that yield the rank-substitution instances $A(B)$ are of lower rank than $\forall p^n A(p^n)$.

THE I_γ UNIQUENESS THEOREM

For every γ-assignment I, there is a unique extension I_γ of I satisfying (1γ)–(6γ)

That I_γ is a mapping can be established in a similar manner, i.e., by using the induction on rank; or alternatively it may be justified by arguments similar to those that will be used for I_σ.

In the case of I_σ the situation is complicated by the fact that clause (6) is circular because $\forall p^n A(p^n)$ could itself be in its own σ-substitution range. In order to establish that the circle is not vicious, I consider another interpretation $I_{\sigma'}$:

For I an order-assignment, the σ'-*interpretation* $I_{\sigma'}$, based on I, is defined as the (unique) function satisfying the following conditions:

$(1\sigma')$ $I_{\sigma'}$ is an extension of I; i.e., for a closed expression X in the domain of I, $I_{\sigma'}(X) = I(X)$.

$(2\sigma')$–$(5\sigma')$ are like (2σ)–(5σ).

$(6\sigma')$ If X is $\forall p^n A(Q(p^n), p^n)$, then we distinguish the following two cases: (1) The order of X is n. Then $I_{\sigma'}(X) = t$ iff for some parameter P, $I_{\sigma'}(A{\sim}(P\&{\sim}P)) = t$ and $I_{\sigma'}(A(P\&{\sim}P)) = t$. (2) The order of X is greater than n. Then $I_{\sigma'}(X) = t$ iff, if for all $B \in V_\sigma^n$ for some parameter P, if $I_{\sigma'}(B) = t$ then $I_{\sigma'}A(Q(B), \sim(P\&{\sim}P)) = t$, and if $I_{\sigma'}(B) = f$, then $I_{\sigma'}(A(Q(B), P\&{\sim}P)) = t$.

THE $I_{\sigma'}$ UNIQUENESS THEOREM

I first show that $I_{\sigma'}$ is well and uniquely defined. This requires an induction on the order of X, the number of quantifiers in extensional contexts in X, and the length of X. In clause $(6\sigma')$ (1) I decrease the number of quantifiers without increasing order. (Note that if the order of X is n, all occurrences of p^n in X are extensional.) In $(6\sigma')(2)$ the induction on order is required to determine the truth or falsity of B (the order of B is less than the order of X); and then I use an induction on the number of extensionally occurring quantifiers.

THE $I_{\sigma'}$ EXTENSIONALITY LEMMA
*If $I_{\sigma'}(B) = I_{\sigma'}(B')$ and A' is the result of replacing all
or some of the extensional occurrences of closed B in closed A by
closed B', then $I_{\sigma'}(A) = I_{\sigma'}(A')$*

The lemma is proved by means of an induction on the number of replacements made. A strong induction is also used on the number of extensionally occurring functors in A within whose scope a replaced occurrence of B lies.

Similarly, there is an I_σ EXTENSIONALITY LEMMA. These lemmas are in effect replacement theorems for the order language. They establish an interesting result, showing that quantification into a non-extensional functor has not disturbed the property of extensional connectives: that sentences with the same truth value may be replaced in extensional contexts without disturbing the truth value of the sentence in which the replaced sentences occurred.

THE $I_{\sigma'}$ SUBSTITUTION LEMMA
$I_{\sigma'}(\forall p^n A(p^n)) = t$ *iff for each closed sentence $B \in V_\sigma^n$, $I_{\sigma'}(A(B)) = t$.*

We show first that if $I_{\sigma'}(\forall p^n A(p^n)) = t$ then for each $B \in V_\sigma^n$, $I_{\sigma'}(A(B)) = t$. *Case (1)*. The order of $\forall p^n A(p^n)$ is n. Then $I_{\sigma'}(A(P\&\sim P)) = t$ and $I_{\sigma'}(A\sim(P\&\sim P)) = t$. For each $B \in V_\sigma^n$, $I_{\sigma'}(B) = t$ or f. If t, then $I_{\sigma'}(B) = I_{\sigma'}(\sim(P\&\sim P))$ and so by the $I_{\sigma'}$ Extensionality Lemma, $I_{\sigma'}(A(B)) = I_{\sigma'}(A(\sim(P\&\sim P)))$. If f, then $I_{\sigma'}(B) = I_{\sigma'}(P\&\sim P)$ and again by the Extensionality Lemma, $I_{\sigma'}(A(B)) = I_{\sigma'}(A(P\&\sim P))$. Therefore for each $B \in V_\sigma^n$, $I_{\sigma'}(A(B)) = t$. *Case (2)*. The order of $\forall p^n A(p^n)$ is greater than n. If $I_{\sigma'}(\forall p^n A(p^n)) = t$ then for each $B \in V_\sigma^n$, if $I_{\sigma'}(B) = t$ then $I_{\sigma'}(A(QB, \sim(P\&\sim P)) = t$; and if $I_{\sigma'}(B) = f$, then $I_{\sigma'}(A(QB, P\&\sim P)) = t$. We again use the extensionality lemma to show that for each $B \in V_\sigma^n$, $I_{\sigma'}(A(QB,B)) = t$.

In the second part of this lemma, we have to show that if for each $B \in V_\sigma^n$, $I_{\sigma'}(A(QB,B)) = t$ then $I_{\sigma'}(\forall p^n A(p^n)) = t$. Among the B's are $P\&\sim P$ and $\sim(P\&\sim P)$, so this case is trivial.

THE I_σ UNIQUENESS THEOREM
*For every σ-assignment I, there is a unique extension I_σ of I
satisfying (1σ)–(6σ)*

Existence: The second lemma guarantees that $I_{\sigma'}$ satisfies (1σ)–(6σ).

Uniqueness: We can show by an induction on order, number of extensional quantifiers, and length, that for any I_σ satisfying (1σ)–(6σ), $I_\sigma = I_{\sigma'}$. For example, suppose that by $6\sigma(2)$, $I_{\sigma'}(\forall p^k A(Q(p^k), p^k)) = f$ in virtue of $I_{\sigma'}(B) = f$ and $I_{\sigma'}(A(Q(B), P\&\sim P) = f$. By the induction on order, $I_\sigma(B) = f$ and by the induction on number of extensional quantifiers, $I_\sigma(A(Q(B), P\&\sim P)) = f$. By the extensionality lemma for I_σ, $I_\sigma(A(Q(B), B)) = f$. So $I_\sigma(\forall p^k A(Q(p^k), p^k)) = f$ by (6σ).

5. Discussion

I point out some of the distinctive features of the languages. The language that results from V_σ and I_σ is referred to as the σ-language. For the purpose of this discussion, I consider the following version of the Liar paradox:

Let $M = `\exists p((`p' = M)\&\sim p)'$. The paradox purports to show that M is true just in case M is false.

$$\exists p((`p' = M)\&\sim p)$$
$$p \mid `p' = M$$
$$`p' = `\exists p((`p' = M)\&\sim p)'$$
$$p \equiv \exists p((`p' = M)\&\sim p)$$
$$p$$
$$\forall p((`p' = M) \to p)$$

$$\forall p((`p' = M) \to p)$$
$$(`\forall p((`p' = M)\&\sim p)' = M)$$
$$\to \exists p((`p' = M)\&\sim p)$$
$$\exists p((`p' = M)\&\sim p)$$

ρ-LANGUAGE

In terms of the above derivation, the ρ-language avoids the antinomy by never including $\exists p(`p' = M \& \sim p)$ in the rank-substitution range of p. A look at I_ρ reveals that the rank-substitution range of any propositional variable will not include any sentence that has the propositional variable in it, unless the variable occurs in nonextensional contexts. A special feature of the ρ-language is that it allows the name of an expression to occur in the expression it names. In this respect it differs from the other two languages. Another feature that should be noted is that all names of expressions belong to the 'bottom' vocabulary, V_ρ^0. In this language the level of an expression X may be said to be characterized by the rank-substitution range of the propositional variables that have extensional occurrences in X; if there are no such variables, then the level of X is zero.

γ-LANGUAGE

In the case of the γ-language, we avoid the antinomy in two ways: The first is that in this language a name is not permitted to appear in the expression it names, so that we never have $M = $ '$\exists p(('p' = M)\& \sim p)$'. Second, the grade-substitution range of p will not include sentences that contain p. This language in effect combines the restrictions of the other two languages. The reason for presenting it is that such a system may be useful when one comes to developing more complex languages involving the quotation functor.

σ-LANGUAGE

As was the case with the γ-language, names of expressions cannot appear in the expressions that they name. For this reason the antinomy is avoided. A special feature of the σ-language is that the order-substitution range of a propositional variable p does include sentences that have extensional occurrences of p in them; but it does not include sentences containing nonextensional occurrences of p: e.g., $\forall p^n(p^n)$ is in the substitution range of p^n but $\forall p^n(Qp^n = M)$ is not. For this reason $\exists p(('p' = M) \& \sim p)$ is not in the order substitution range of the variable p occurring in it. This is the only language with quantifiers on level zero.

In these last two languages, there is some sense in saying that it is the quotation functor that takes us from one level to the next, because the level of the name of an expression must always be greater than the level of the expression named.

We note that the γ-language is the only language that does not allow any self-reference. In the ρ-language, as I have mentioned before, names can occur in expressions they name. This is one kind of self-reference. In the ρ-language, we have another kind of self-reference: Variables can occur in formulas that belong to the substitution range of the variable in question. Therefore my results show that, although unrestricted self-reference leads to inconsistency, partial self-reference need not.

11

Quantifying in and out
of Quotes*

1. Logic as an Organon

Logic is many things: a science, an art, a toy, a joy, and sometimes a tool. One thing the logician can do is provide useful systems, systems that are both widely applicable and efficient: Set theory has been developed for the mathematician, modal logic for the metaphysician, Boolean logic for the computer scientist, syllogistics for the rhetorician, and the first-order functional calculus for us all.

It is in this spirit that we should like to discuss the combination of quotation with quantifiers bearing the substitutional interpretation, for use by the logicians themselves or indeed by any practicing metalinguist. We do not think that substitutional quantifiers are everywhere useful for the obvious reasons about cardinality and the lack of names; but when it comes to quotes, substitutional quantifiers are just the ticket. And one of the principal sources of their usefulness is the incredible ease with which they can be explained: Given an appropriate substitution-range for the variable α, $\ulcorner[\exists\alpha](\ldots\alpha\ldots)\urcorner$ is true just in case some substitution instance of $\ulcorner(\ldots\alpha\ldots)\urcorner$ is true, and similarly for the universal quantifier. No fuss, no bother. If someone understands the context $\ulcorner(\ldots\_\ldots)\urcorner$ whenever the blank is filled by a closed expression (of the appropriate sort), then he or she automatically understands substitutional quantification into this context. For example, if someone understands quotation of expressions without variables, then he or she is bound to understand substitutional quantification into quotes. This is, we think, in contrast to Quine's (1940) mechanism of quasi-quotation, which appears to require a certain degree of sophistication for its mastery. And similarly for Kaplan's (1969) Frege-inspired account.

* This article was co-authored with Nuel D. Belnap, Jr.

There is some evidence (which we give later) that substitutional quantification into quotes is the formal analog of an intuitive idea that people naturally come to once variables and quotes have been made available. But despite this there is still the question whether there are any occasions in which it would be particularly useful to quantify into quotation contexts. We argue that quantification in and out of quotes *is* a useful technique to have in both formal and informal contexts. We make our account of quantification in and out of quotes mostly formal, partly to show that a rigorous account can be given of the practice, and partly so that restrictions necessary to avoid paradox can be made explicit. But concepts and techniques introduced in formal contexts can often be fruitfully employed in less formal discussions; for example, philosophers have used variables and domain-and-values quantifiers (especially nested quantifiers) to say things that might otherwise not have been said, or if said, said more cumbersomely. Similarly, it would seem that logicians and philosophers might find substitutional quantification with quotes to be a useful adjunct of English.

So a major task of the paper is to give a rigorous account of these devices, and the second task is to show in some detail how language containing them might be used. Beyond this, our considerations drive us to make some remarks about truth and meaning.

In the languages we discuss, a pair of quotes (left and right) is treated as a quotation functor taking expressions (not necessarily well formed) as input, and producing as output a name of the input expression. That is, a quotation mark name has two parts: (1) the quotes and (2) an expression that is named. This means that a quotation name is "non-extensional" in the sense that the denotation of the whole does not depend on the denotation of its parts (the quotes and the expression within the quotes). As indicated earlier, we also allow (substitutional) quantifiers to bind variables that occur both in and out of quotes.

1.1. CHARITY

We conjecture, albeit with great hesitation, that although the methodology of quantification into quotes has not been explicitly worked out in the way that, say, the quasi-quote method has been articulated by Quine, still various logicians have in fact implicitly used this method from time to time, doubtless without conscious formulation. As evidence we cite the following exercise from Curry 1963 (he did not envisage substitutional quantification):

The following statements appear—with some slight changes—
in reputable logical publications of the last thirty years. Bearing
in mind that in all cases except case (e) the authors were in-
tending to state general principles in which substitutions could
be made for the letters, criticize the use of quotation marks in
these statements.

(a) Consider two statements, '*P*' and '*Q*', of symbolic logic
    which are translations of the English sentences '*A*' and '*B*'.
    Then '(*P*&*Q*)' is the statement which is a translation of '*A*
    and *B*'.

(b) A statement such as "If *x* and *y* are numbers, then $x + y =
    y + x$" violates the rule about using names of things when
    speaking of those things. It should properly be written as "If
    '*x*' and '*y*' are numbers, then '$x + y = y + x$'."

(c) If '*P*' is a translation of a statement, then the negation of the
    statement is translated '$\neg P$'.

(d) If '*A*' and '*B*' are true, then '*A*&*B*' is true.

(e) If we wanted to state that Chicago lies between New York
    and Denver, we might well use C for Chicago and D for
    Denver, but to use NY for New York would be confusing.

(f) The conjunctive proposition '*p* and *q*' will be symbolized by
    '*p.q*'. The dot expresses that both propositions are asserted
    together. Hence '*p.q*' may be read 'both *p* and *q*'.

(g) For 'not-*p*' we shall write '$\neg p$'.

Our point is that, with the exception of the author of (b), who is
doubtless confused, and (e), who (as Curry says) is not trying to
make a general statement, all of these "reputable" authors *could* be
saved by a gracious application of the principle of charity: Let them
be taken to be using substitutional quantification, with, of course,
suppressed initial universal quantifiers. What they say would also
make sense if their quotes were taken as quasi-quotes; but quasi-
quotation is an extremely sophisticated device, not likely to be used
implicitly, without explicit mention of the fact and description of
the device. In contrast, there is probably a little of the substitutional quantifier in all of us, and the device is not in the least sophisticated (some would dub it naive), so that this hypothesis seems
to us to have the edge.

A similar account may be given of Fitch's (e.g., 1948) use of variables and quotes in passages like

'*fgh*' is an abbreviation of '(*fg*)*h*'.

Fitch says that his variables "stand in place of" rather than "denote" or "designate" expressions of the language he is describing, which to us sounds as if he intends to be using substitutional variables with implied universal substitutional quantification.

1.2. Why Quotes?

But why use quotes? Obviously, if quotes are going to be useful to the logician at all, they will be *especially* useful if the logician wants to display the language being talked about. For most technical (mathematical) purposes one does not, in describing a language **O**, have the slightest need for displaying any part of it, for one is never, in mathematical work, interested in the perceptual features of the object language. (Who cares that the alphabetically first variable is made by crossing a couple of diagonals?) This great lesson we learned from Curry (e.g., 1963). And we further believe that in those circumstances in which one *can* completely avoid display it is on balance probably most efficient *in fact* to avoid display.

But sometimes the perceptual features of **O** are indeed important. For one thing, one might just be interested in that level of analysis for its own sake, e.g., in the perceptual description of Chinese, or in giving a historical account of what the language of the *Principia Mathematica* looks like. But far more frequently and interestingly, one may wish to describe **O** in order to adjoin it to our language, to make it a part of the communicative apparatus we use. And for these purposes it is essential to know what **O** looks like. In these circumstances some metalinguistic technique involving display, either by the autonomous use of language or by quotation, is particularly efficient, especially as contrasted to circumlocutory description. For example, one might write

$$\text{'}(e_1 \& e_2)\text{' abbreviates '}{\sim}({\sim}e_1 \vee {\sim}e_2)\text{'}.$$

For such an abbreviative definition, display is virtually essential and certainly the only method anyone ever really uses.

So we envisage our logician with a metalanguage, **M**, and the desire to communicate concerning a certain object language **O**. One of our principal tasks is to design for him a suitable **M**. But first we face the problem of how to talk about **M**.

1.3. Our Use Language

It might make the reader uneasy if we were to use substitutional quantification in our use language (the language of this paper), so in order to avoid that source of anxiety, as well as to eliminate possible confusion, we use ordinary *domain-and-values quantification* over expressions; lowercase Greek letters will be the variables of our use language. We use *double quotes* for ordinary quotation. And we use *quasi-quotation* (Quine's corners) in the way described by Quine 1940.

What now is **M** to be like?

1.4. NOTATIONAL FEATURES OF **M**

Because the point of this paper is to explore substitutional quantification in connection with quotation, we expect **M** to come so equipped. We use *single quotes* (left and right) for the quotation functor of **M**; so that " 'a' " is used by **M** to denote "a," i.e., to denote the first letter of the alphabet. **M** uses *square brackets* for substitutional quantifiers.

We shall also be assuming that **M** has available the usual domain-and-values quantifiers. In order to distinguish these from the substitutional quantifiers, **M** systematically uses *round brackets* for domain-and-values quantifiers. Thus, $\ulcorner(\alpha)\beta\urcorner$ would be a domain-and-values quantification, and $\ulcorner[\alpha]\beta\urcorner$ would bear a substitutional interpretation. And similarly for $\ulcorner(\exists\alpha)\beta\urcorner$ and $\ulcorner[\exists\alpha]\beta\urcorner$.

1.5. SURVEY

M and **O** can be variously related; we fill in the details on this later, but for now we can put the matter quickly as follows: (1) **M** and **O** can be *completely separate*, or (2) **O** may be a *proper part* of **M**, or (3) **M** and **O** may *overlap*. We discuss these cases in turn. In §2 we discuss the case where $\mathbf{M}_2$ and $\mathbf{O}_2$ are completely separate, referring to the particular **M** and **O** of that section as $\mathbf{M}_2$ and $\mathbf{O}_2$ respectively. Then in §3 we have $\mathbf{O}_3$ a proper part of $\mathbf{M}_3$, and in §4, $\mathbf{M}_4$ and $\mathbf{O}_4$ overlap.

Because we must show both that a rigorous account can be given of a language containing substitutional quantifiers and quotes and how such languages can be used, we make the described object language in each case very like the metalanguage used to talk about it, so that, in demonstrating the ability of **M** to give the grammar and semantics of **O**, we at the same time provide an at least partially rigorous account of features present in **M**.

2. O_2 and M_2 Completely Separate

In this section we discuss the case where a metalanguage M_2 containing substitutional quantifiers and quotes is wanted in order to describe a language O_2 that is completely separate from M_2. (The situation would not materially change were we simply to treat O_2 *as if* it were completely separate.)

2.1. OCCASIONS AND PURPOSES

We sometimes find that the language we are using has shortcomings that make it unsuitable as it stands for use in talking about a particular topic. Possibly its vocabulary is not sufficiently rich; so to make the distinctions we want, we introduce new words. Or possibly the language is not as clear or as precise as we would like—ambiguities that can be tolerated or even exploited in some uses of language may be a hindrance in other cases. Providing we know what we want of our language, it is often an easy task to develop separately the piece needed, and then, if we want, we can add it to the language we are using; e.g., in chapter 1 of your book you introduce notation and concepts that you are going to use in chapter 2. But there is always the problem of making explicit what is being introduced, and showing how it is to be related to the language used. It is in accomplishing this task that substitutional quantifiers and quotes may be natural and useful devices to employ, because if an (object) language is to be used, knowing what it looks like is handy. We illustrate this point by means of O_2 and M_2.

We begin in §2.2 by describing M_2. The nature of M_2 is determined to a certain extent by O_2 because it must be adequate for talking about O_2. In §2.3 we show how M_2 can be used to give the grammar and semantics of O_2, and in the last section we discuss some special features of O_2 and M_2. In particular we indicate how O_2 may be added to M_2.

2.2. DESIGN OF M_2

We raise here the question of the design of M_2, especially with respect to its quotation functor and its substitutional quantifiers. A preliminary question, especially important because of the substitutional quantifiers, is, What is to be the *alphabet* of M_2? And consideration of this question leads one to see that the hypothesis of the separateness of O_2 and M_2 must be modified at the outset, because for one using the quotation method (or indeed any method, such as autonomy, which requires the display of characters of O_2), O_2 cannot be quite wholly cut off from M_2; at least its characters must be available in M_2 for certain purposes (though not for most usual purposes). These characters must be available in M_2 so that they can occur inside quotes, or, more generally, so that their display may be communicatively meaningful. One might say: If M_2 (e.g., English) does not already contain the characters of O_2 (e.g., Chinese), then the first thing the grammarian must do is add the characters of O_2 to the characters of M_2, presumably by the method of display. We skip this step (there are knotty problems here) and assume that O_2's characters are already available in M_2. But although the characters of O_2 must be characters of M_2, it still makes sense to say of M_2 and O_2 that they are "entirely separate," because in the cases we envisage no character of O_2 occurs in a sentence (or other distinguishable grammatical unit) of M_2 except inside quotes.

We now discuss the two special features of M_2: quotes and substitutional quantifiers.

2.2.1. QUOTES

As is well known, there can be trouble if quotes are allowed within quotes; for example, for each expression α, $\ulcorner(' \ ' = '\alpha' = '\alpha')\urcorner$ is ambiguous as to whether the middle or the rightmost occurrence of $" = "$ is to be taken as the main sign, and accordingly ambiguous as to its truth-value. But if all contained quotes are mated (which is to say that there is a one-to-one mapping from occurrences of left quotes onto occurrences of right quotes, so that with respect to corresponding occurrences the left quote occurs to the left of the right quote), the trouble is avoided. This is the move we make in §3, where the object language is a proper part of the metalanguage; but useful for M_2 is a stronger, simpler restriction. Because M_2 and O_2 are completely separate, in using M_2 to talk about O_2 we never really need to quote quoted M_2-expressions and so we can forbid *all* quotes within quotes; and whoever heard of wanting to quasi-quote quasi-quotes anyhow? But we do (later) use the facility for quoting mated quotes. The expressions allowed within quotes are baptized *quote-free* M_2-expressions; they can be generated inductively as follows: Any member of the alphabet other than a quote sign is a quote-free M_2-expression; if α and β are quote-free M_2-expressions, then $\ulcorner\alpha\beta\urcorner$ is a quote-free M_2-expression.

2.2.2. SUBSTITUTIONAL QUANTIFIERS OF M_2

We come now to the second significant feature of M_2: its substitutional quantifiers and variables.

We use

$$\text{``}e_1,\text{''} \text{``}e_2,\text{''} \ldots, \text{``}e_9,\text{''} \text{``}e_{(10)},\text{''} \text{``}e_{(11)},\text{''} \ldots,$$

as *expression variables* bearing the substitutional interpretation. Note that no one of these variables occurs as a part of another; otherwise conflicts would have arisen between obtaining the right substitution instances of a formula and allowing for nested quantifiers.

We have to be a bit careful in counting $\ulcorner[\alpha]\beta\urcorner$ well-formed when α is an expression variable and β is a formula; for we wish to satisfy the condition that $\ulcorner[\alpha]\beta\urcorner$ is well-formed only if every substitution instance of β with respect to α is well formed. (Recall that square brackets signify substitutional quantification.) This matter becomes specially sensitive because of our choice, which we now make, to define *substitution instance* in the simplest possible way: γ is a substitution instance of β with respect to α if γ is the result of putting some expression for every occurrence (without limitation) of α in β. The upshot is that we must not allow $\ulcorner[\alpha]\beta\urcorner$ as well formed unless every occurrence of α in β is protected by quotes; no other context for occurrences of α—including occurrences as part of a quantifier $\ulcorner[\gamma]\urcorner$—allows the condition above to be satisfied. Given the convention that no expression-variable is part of another, and the general restriction of occurrences of expression-variables to quote-contexts or square-bracket contexts, it suffices to require that there be no unquoted occurrence of $\ulcorner[\alpha]\urcorner$ in β.

Concerning the *semantics* of expression-variables, we discuss only their substitutional range. Because for an expression-variable we want $\ulcorner{}'\alpha'\urcorner$ to have all its instances be well-formed terms, the substitutional range of α must exclude M_2-expressions containing quotes; it must fall within the set of quote-free M_2-expressions.

There is a choice to be made at this point: Shall these variables have in their substitutional range expressions containing these very variables? In most uses of substitutional quantification, one chooses the answer "No," and the substitutional range of a variable turns out to consist only of "closed terms" or even only of variable-free terms. With this answer, where α is one of these variables, $\ulcorner'\ldots \alpha \ldots'\urcorner$ is counted always as an "open expression," ready for substitution, but not itself denoting. This answer undoubtedly simplifies some problems, but with this answer we could not use $\ulcorner{}'\alpha'\urcorner$ as a name for the variable α in question. We would either need to introduce some thoroughly opaque quotes or to solve the problem in one of several other available ways.

In order to avoid this particular complication, we explore the other choice: We let the *substitutional range of expression-variables* consist of all quote-free expressions of $\mathbf{M}_2$ whatsoever, and we count $\ulcorner'\ldots \alpha \ldots'\urcorner$ as invariably properly denoting $\ulcorner\ldots \alpha \ldots\urcorner$, even when α is an expression-variable.

2.2.3. OTHER FEATURES OF $\mathbf{M}_2$

We assume that $\mathbf{M}_2$ has *truth-functions* (ordinary English phrases interpreted in the classical way), some *grammatical* and *semantic predicates* (which ones will be obvious from the illustration), and identity ($" = "$). We also let $\mathbf{M}_2$ have a modicum of *set theory*.

Are we to have *only* substitutional quantifiers in $\mathbf{M}_2$? If $\mathbf{M}_2$ is to be used to give the semantics for a language $\mathbf{O}_2$ containing domain-and-values variables ("d-variables" for short) ranging over a certain set D_2, then the answer is no: $\mathbf{M}_2$ must be able to obtain the effect of domain-and-values variables ranging over the set of functions from the set of d-variables into the set D_2. To this extent we cannot design $\mathbf{M}_2$ independently of $\mathbf{O}_2$; but in anticipation, we use "V_2" as the name of the aforementioned set of functions, and we let "x," "y," "f," and "f_1," with maybe some subscripts, be the most general *domain-and-values variables* of $\mathbf{M}_2$, so that we can get the desired effect by "(for all f belonging to V_2)."

$\mathbf{M}_2$ has a second set of domain-and-values variables whose range is restricted to the set of quote-free $\mathbf{M}_2$-expressions. For these latter variables, $\mathbf{M}_2$ uses "a," "b," "c," "a_1," "a_2," . . . .

It is to be noticed that the bound-vs-free distinction is useful only for domain-and-values variables, and that only the presence of the latter outside quotes can give rise to an interesting distinction between closed and open sentences. For example, $\ulcorner''(a = b)'''\urcorner$ is open and by itself is neither true nor false, but true for some values of "a" and "b" while false for others. But "$('a' = 'b')'$" is closed and false; so is its vacuous quantification, "$(\forall a)(\exists b)('a' = 'b')$." Now compare: "$(e_1 = e_2)$" is ill-formed (expression-variables must never occur outside quotes), while "$('e_1' = 'e_2')$" is closed and false; but because some of its instances are true and others false, its quantification "$[e_1][\exists e_2]('e_1' = 'e_2')$" is non-vacuous and indeed is true.

2.3. Illustrative Description of O_2

In this section we illustrate the application of M_2 to the description of a language O_2. In this description it is not our purpose to reduce everything to an especially economical set of syntactical primitives. Furthermore, we use semi-English locutions of the usual sort, with a style that we trust permits ready translation into the official hen scratches of §2.2. In particular, we often suppress initial universal quantifiers, whether substitutional or domain-and-values. Because M_2 has different alphabets for each, this can cause no ambiguity and indeed is the principal reason we supplied M_2 with two alphabets. We continue, however, to indicate explicit substitutional quantification by square brackets and domain-and-values by round; e.g., "[for all e_1]" vs. "(for all f)". All of this is in accord with our design of investigating the *usefulness* of the quote-and-substitution methodology.

In advance let us say that for our illustrative purposes it suffices to suppose that O_2 comes with no more than identity, quotation, and both sorts of quantifiers, distinguished in O_2 by a difference in alphabet only. How to handle additional grammatical and semantic features should be clear to the meanest intellect.

2.3.1. general syntax

Though we shall not use these concepts, we do a bit of general syntax just to exhibit how it goes. It should be perfectly plain from the following that substitutionally quantifying into quotes provides a complete basis for the general syntax of any language O_2 not itself involving M_2's quotes.

Concatenation. $(a \frown b) = c$ iff [there are e_1 and e_2 such that] $(a = \text{'}e_1\text{'}, b = \text{'}e_2\text{'},$ and $c = \text{'}e_1 e_2\text{'})$. Hence, $\text{'}e_1\text{'} \frown \text{'}e_2\text{'} = \text{'}e_1 e_2\text{'}$; so why bother with the longer notation?

Part. a is part of b iff [for some e_1, e_2, e_3], $a = \text{'}e_1\text{'}$ and either $b = \text{'}e_2 e_1 e_3\text{'}$ or $b = \text{'}e_2 e_1\text{'}$ or $b = \text{'}e_1 e_3\text{'}$.

Character. If a has no parts, then a is a *character*.

2.3.2. grammar of O_2

We define (in M_2) the following concepts needed for understanding O_2: O_2-index, s-variable (i.e., substitutional variable), d-variable (i.e., domain-and-values variable), Q-free O_2-expression, Q-term, O_2-term, O_2-formula.

'(*)' is an O_2-*index*; if '(e_1)' is an O_2-index, then so is '(e_1*)'.

If 'e_1' is an O_2-index, then 'se_1' is an s-variable and 'de_1' is a d-*variable*.

'<', '>', 's', 'd', '*', and '$\approx$' are all Q-*free* O_2-expressions; if 'e_1' and '$_1e_2$' are such, then so is 'e_1e_2'.

If 'e_1' is a Q-free O_2-expression, then '$Q_1e_1Q_2$' is a Q-*term*.

d-variables and Q-terms are O_2-*terms*. (Note: s-variables are *not* O_2-terms.)

If 'e_1' and 'e_2' are O_2-terms, then '$<e_1 \approx e_2>$' is an O_2-*formula*; if 'e_1' is either an s- or a d-variable, and if 'e_2' is an O_2-formula such that every occurrence of '$<e_1>$' in 'e_2' is part of an occurrence of a Q-term, then '$<e_1>e_2$' is an O_2-formula. (Note: We could work out the notion of "occurrences" and the sense in which one is "part" of another as in, say, Quine 1940.)

2.3.3. SEMANTICS OF O_2

We are given a (non-empty) domain D_2. In the interesting cases D_2 can be expected to contain the set of O_2-expressions so that $\ulcorner Q_1\alpha Q_2 \urcorner$ denotes something in D_2 whenever it is an O_2-term; but we do not insist on this. In any event, D_2 induces the set V_2 of functions from d-variables into D_2; and for $f \in V_2$, we need to define denotation (in O_2) at f ("den_2f") of O_2-terms, and truth (in O_2) at f ("true_2 at f") of O_2-formulas. In the following, $f \in V_2$.

Denotation. If 'e_1' is a d-variable, then $\text{den}_2f('e_1') = f('e_1')$; if '$Q_1e_1Q_2$' is a Q-term, then $\text{den}_2f(Q_1e_1Q_2) = 'e_1'$. Also an unrelativized denotation: If 'e_1' is a closed O_2-term (in this simple case, just a Q-term), then $\text{den}_2('e_1') = \text{den}_2f('e_1')$ for an arbitrary $f \in V_2$.

Truth. '$<e_1 \approx e_2>$', if an O_2-formula, is *true$_2$* at f iff $\text{den}_2f('e_1') = \text{den}_2f('e_2')$; '$<e_1>e_2$' if an O_2-formula, is *true$_2$ at f* iff: (1) 'e_1' is a d-variable and (for every $f_1 \in V_2$) if f_1 is like f except perhaps at 'e_1', then 'e_2' is true$_2$ at f_1; or (2) 'e_1' is an s-variable and [for every e_3 and e_4], if 'e_4' is a Q-free O_2-expression and if 'e_3' results from putting 'e_4' for every occurrence of 'e_1' in 'e_2', then 'e_3' is true$_2$ at f. The unrelativized version: If 'e_1' is an O_2-formula, then 'e_1' *is true$_2$* iff (for all $f \in V_2$) 'e_1' is true$_2$ at f.

2.4. REMARKS

In this section we raise some questions concerning the relationship between substitutional and domain-and-values quantifiers, in particular drawing attention to the fact that domain-and-values quantifiers in M_2 were used to provide an account of domain-and-values quantifiers of O_2, and substitutional quantifiers of M_2 were adequate for providing an account of the substitutional quantifiers of O_2. We also discuss the "truth definition" of §2.3, and make some other miscellaneous remarks.

2.4.1. QUANTIFIERS

Because D_2 and hence V_2 may be large, and in any event we may have no names of D_2's members, nor of those of V_2, we *must* use domain-and-values quantifiers in M_2 in giving the semantics of d-variables. Substitutional quantifiers *cannot* do this job. (Recall that as logicians qua toolmakers, we are talking of languages to be really and truly used; so the model-theorists' invention of a collection of names of arbitrary cardinality moves us not an inch from this position.) Because, on the contrary, domain-and-values quantifiers can be used to give the semantics of the (substitutional) s-variables of O_2, we conclude that domain-and-values quantifiers are a necessity but substitutional quantifiers only a convenience. Note, however, that in giving the semantics of O_2's substitutional quantifiers we can also use substitutional quantifiers in M_2, as in fact we have done. This is a conclusion of some philosophical interest; it implies that the concept of substitutional quantification is *self-sustaining* and does not have to rely on domain-and-values quantification for its explanation. Their relation is then no more mysterious than that between material implication and disjunction: One can be defined in terms of the other, but not conversely; but neither is "required" in giving the truth-conditions of the other. Nor is either philosophically more "basic."

2.4.2. TRUTH-DEFINITION

The recursive legitimacy of our truth-definition needs justifying, because the truth-value of a substitutional quantification can depend on the truth-values of longer expressions: Instantiation can increase length. But in fact there is no real problem, because appeal always is made to formulas containing fewer *unquoted* expression-quantifiers. And quite generally, *one* way to avoid paradox in using both quotes and substitutional quantifiers is to require that the anaphoric occurrences of the variables, i.e., those which are distinct from the quantifying occurrence and which make cross-reference to the quantifying occurrence, occur only inside quotes, never outside quotes. (But there are others.)

2.4.3.

We note that in this enterprise of describing a new linguistic feature to be added to **M**, it is sometimes possible to produce a tool sharper than the one with which we started. For example, suppose the "or" of **M** is ambiguous as to whether it is inclusive or exclusive. This does not in the least hinder us from producing a disjunction that is unambiguously inclusive by a clause like

$[e_1][e_2]$(if 'e_1' and 'e_2' are sentences, then '$(e_1 \vee e_2)$' is true iff either 'e_1' is true but 'e_2' not, or 'e_2' is true but 'e_1' not, or both 'e_1' and 'e_2' are true).

For in this particular context the ambiguity of "or" is rendered harmless: Either way the "or" is interpreted leads to the same truth-conditions for the newly introduced disjunction sign.

2.4.4. TRUTH-PREDICATE

The role of the truth-predicate in our account of O_2 needs more discussion completely independent of quotes and substitutional quantification than we can at present give it. But a few comments are in order: First, although we speak of a "definition of truth," clearly we are not performing the speech act, that is, explaining the meaning of "truth." Rather, for §2.3 to work, one must already understand the general concept of truth—especially its pragmatic force; for we will not be understood unless we are understood as giving the truth-conditions of O_2-formulas. So in this case it is "truth" that is understood, while at the beginning the O_2-formulas are not understood. Second, "truth" has in these proceedings a double prescriptive-descriptive role in the sense of Massey (1970), just as "capital offence" does. Like the latter, "truth" is, in Massey's word, "preceptive."

There is a sense in which everyone knows and must know what "capital offence" means in order to render effective the listing by the legislature of those acts which are to be counted as capital offences, a listing that makes those very acts into capital offences. Just so with the use of "truth" in giving sense to new expressions: By *saying* α is true$_2$, we *make* it true$_2$.

Third, just because O_2 is by hypothesis not understood, we cannot suppose satisfaction of Tarski's "material condition" on the truth-definition; indeed, instances of schema (T), for example, " '<Q_1*Q_2 $\approx$ Q_1*Q_2>' is true$_2$ iff <Q_1*Q_2 $\approx$ Q_1*Q_2>'', are not even well formed (neither in M_2 nor in O_2).

Nor can we save the situation as Tarski does, by invoking a translation from O_2 into M_2; for we have no translation antecedently available. After the fact perhaps we could think of $\ulcorner$'α' is true$_2$$\urcorner$ as the translation into M_2 of an α in O_2, but if we did *that*, then any truth definition satisfies Tarski's Convention T, because $\ulcorner$'α' is true$_2$ iff 'α' is true$_2$$\urcorner$ (where the right side is the proposed translation of α) is a tautology. Nevertheless, and though we speak hesitatingly, we think after all that if we decide to add O_2 to M_2, we can make use of the fact that our truth-definition should satisfy Tarski's criterion of material adequacy, once the instances of the schema are expressible in our language.

Before adjoining O_2 to M_2, we gave the truth conditions of the sentences of O_2; so that for any sentence α of O_2 we understand $\ulcorner$'α' is true$_2$$\urcorner$. But if O_2 is now to become part of our language, we need to be able to do more than just mention α: we must be able to *use* α. We can explain in our use-language how this is done: The assumption is that once sentences of O_2 are used in the language formed by adding O_2 to M_2, Tarski's criterion of material adequacy on our truth$_2$ definition should be satisfied; so that, if O_2 is correctly added to M_2, then for all sentences α of O_2, $\ulcorner\alpha$ iff 'α' is true$_2$$\urcorner$ must be true in $M_2 + O_2$. (If substitutional propositional variables had been available in M_2—as they are in M_3—then we would require that "[p](if 'p' is a closed O_2-formula, then p iff 'p' is true$_2$)" be true in $M_2 + O_2$). We can now see, if only through a glass darkly, how O_2 is added to M_2: For each sentence α of O_2 $\ulcorner$'α' is true$_2$$\urcorner$ is already understood in M_2; and in terms of it, we introduce α into M_2.

2.4.5. PROOF THEORY

The semantics we have given for expression-quantifiers is obviously sensible. The question of the proof theory of expression-quantifiers, however, remains open. We conjecture that as it stands the proof theory might turn out to be complicated, that is, more complicated than that of ordinary domain-and-values quantifiers; but we also think that it would be simple were we to exclude from the substitutional range of the expression-variables any expressions containing occurrences of the letter "*e*," and quite generally, any expressions containing occurrences of expression-variables. This limitation is not likely to cause much inconvenience, and we rather suspect that it would be a useful line to take; but as we say, we leave the question open. In any event, the decision as to whether or not to limit the substitutional range of expression variables should be controlled by exclusively practical considerations; there is in this field no *philosophical* hay to be made.

2.4.6. MAKING M_2 UNIVERSAL

Should you wish M_2 to contain a name for every one of its own expressions, then you will have to add something: Say (1) names "q_1" and "q_2" of the left and right quote-signs respectively, and (2) the concatenation operator; if α and β are expression-terms (including variables), then $\ulcorner(\alpha \frown \beta)\urcorner$ is also an expression-term and denotes the result of concatenating the expressions denoted by α and β. If you further want to include the null expression in your ontology, touching quotes " " " would provide a well-behaved name for it. But we don't use this stuff.

2.4.7 APPLICATION TO PROOF THEORY

Quantifying into quotes might well prove useful in application to proof theory as well as to grammar and semantics. In the case, of course, in which one wants not just to talk about the proof-theoretical objects abstractly, but rather to explain to someone how to do proofs etc., then the method of display would appear to be all but essential, and accordingly quotes and substitutional quantification beckon.

2.4.8. NOMINAL AND REAL

In Belnap 1976 it turned out to be necessary to associate with certain variables occurring in interrogatives ("queriables," they were called) both a substitutional range and a value range; except that—and this terminological point is the only one we want to make—the former was called the *nominal* and the latter the *real* range. We now tend to prefer to contrast the "substitutional range" with the "value range."

2.4.9. QUASI-QUOTATION AND OTHER COUSINS

Quasi-quotation can be defined in our terms by using

$$\ulcorner \ldots a \ldots \urcorner = b \text{ iff } [\exists e_1]('e_1' = a \text{ and } b = '\ldots e_1 \ldots')$$

once for each variable free inside the quasi-quotes. Conversely, quantification into quotes with expression variables can be defined by quasi-quotation:

$$[e_1](\underline{\quad}' \ldots e_1 \ldots '\underline{\quad}) \text{ iff } (a)(\underline{\quad} \ulcorner \ldots a \ldots \urcorner \underline{\quad})$$

Domain-and-values quantification over expressions can quite generally be defined by substitutional quantification:

$$(a) (\ldots a \ldots) \text{ iff } [e_1](\ldots 'e_1' \ldots)$$

And because quasi-quotes can be defined using domain-and-values quantification, the truth of the reverse follows from the second definition above. But though the substitutional quantification can be defined by domain-and-values quantification over expressions, still

$$\ulcorner [e_1](\ldots e_1 \ldots) \urcorner$$

where "e_1" may be deep inside a quoted expression, cannot be replaced by a domain-and-values quantification in any *simple* way. A long story, no doubt involving concatenation, will be required.

One possibly useful device would be to define a kind of dequotation pseudo-functor, say $\ulcorner \bar{\alpha} \urcorner$, where α can be *only* a domain-and-values variable ranging over expressions, and where $\ulcorner \bar{\alpha} \urcorner$ can occur *only* inside quotes. Then one would explain $\ulcorner \bar{\alpha} \urcorner$ inside quotes as if it were α inside quasi-quotes; e.g.,

$$'\ldots \bar{a} \ldots ' = b \text{ iff } [\exists e_1]('e_1' = a \text{ and } b = '\ldots e_1 \ldots').$$

Naturally one would count "a" as free in such a context and could not use " '$\bar{a}$' " as a name of "$\bar{a}$." Then one could define

$$\ulcorner \ldots a \ldots \urcorner = '\ldots \bar{a} \ldots '$$

or conversely. This would shorten some formulations; e.g., concatenation could be defined by

$$a \frown b = '\bar{a}\bar{b}'$$

On the other hand, all of these devices are, in our judgment, more difficult to explain (and remember) than substitutional quantification into quotes.

3. O_3 a Proper Part of M_3

In this section we discuss the special features of the case when the described language, O_3, is a proper part of the describing language, M_3.

3.1. OCCASIONS AND PURPOSES

There are numerous occasions on which we wish to give a clear and rigorous description of the grammar and semantics of a piece of the language we are using. Such occasions arise when we are seeking to establish the suitability or unsuitability of our language for a particular task, as in showing that it is an appropriate language for use in the discussion of a certain topic, or in showing that it can provide a basis for the development of an extension of our language. Other situations arise where the grammar and semantics of our language are not completely understood, and in these cases any account of its grammar and semantics must be regarded as tentative, serving merely to develop a partial understanding of the structure of the piece of language under discussion. The isolation and characterization of intentional ("referentially opaque") contexts is perhaps an example of such a program of research. Sometimes we may thoroughly understand our language in the "how to" sense but still seek theoretical information about how it is articulated, how its pieces "fit together," what its "rules" are. Common to all these programs is the fact that the language talked about is one that we are familiar with, and for this reason there is some point—in giving an account of its grammar and semantics—in seeing what the language looks like. Hence quotes and substitutional quantifiers can provide a perspicuous way of presenting the analyses. In the discussion that follows, we limit ourselves to cases where O_3, the piece of M_3 talked about, is a formal language.

3.2. DESIGN OF M_3

We suppose in the first place that M_3 is an extension of M_2; their alphabets are the same, but the grammar and semantics of M_3 contains additions, as described below, the point of all of which is to give M_3 a capability of dealing with a portion of its own grammar and semantics. Some of the additions amount to giving increased power to features already present in M_2 (quotes and variables), while the rest involve the addition of new linguistic features (lambda abstraction and four new kinds of substitutional variables).

3.2.1. QUOTES

We want to illustrate in the next section how a language can use quotes to give the grammar and semantics of those very same quotes. Obviously, then, we cannot remain with the prohibition for M_1 which disallowed any trace of quotes-within-quotes. The reader will recall that the prohibition was introduced to avoid ambiguities, and that it is stronger than required; all that is needed to prevent ambiguities is that no unmated quotes occur in quotes. Fortunately, in discussing the grammar and semantics of quotes, one needs to talk about them only in pairs, so that in this case there is a happy meeting of what we can do with what we want to do. Hence the following: We suppose M_3 has the same quotes, left and right, as M_2, and we call any M_3-expression not containing unmated quote signs a *normal M_3-expression*. Then we allow $\ulcorner\alpha\urcorner$ to be a term whenever α is a normal M_3-expression; and of course $\ulcorner\alpha\urcorner$ denotes α.

3.2.2. EXPRESSIONS AND DOMAIN-AND-VALUES VARIABLES

M_3 uses the same alphabets for expression and domain-and-values variables as does M_2, but with ranges adjusted to accord with §3.2.1. Substitutional expression variables "e_1" etc., and domain-and-values expression variables "a," "b," etc. now take the set of all normal M_3-expressions as, respectively, their substitutional range and their value range. We continue to use "f," "f_1," etc. as the most general domain-and-values variables of M_3.

3.2.3. THE LANGUAGE M*

For almost immediate but temporary use, we dub as "M^*" the portion of M_3 so far described. Summary of M^*: truth-functions, a little bit of set theory, substitutional expression variables, domain-and-values expression variables, general domain-and-values variables, quotes, and at least the grammatical and semantic concepts pertinent to O_2.

3.2.4. TERM VARIABLES

We shall suppose that $\mathbf{M}_3$ uses "t_1", ..., "t_9", "$t_{(10)}$", ..., as *term variables*. Their point is to allow a nonrecursive definition of denotation. We may loosely describe their grammar by saying that outside of quotes they can occur anaphorically in all and only term positions (e.g., flanking the sign for identity), and that they may occur arbitrarily inside quotes. Further, if α is a term-variable and β is a formula not containing any unquoted occurrence of $\ulcorner[\alpha]\urcorner$, then $\ulcorner[\alpha]\beta\urcorner$ is a formula.

The *semantics* for these quantifiers depends on assuming $\mathbf{M}^*$ a thoroughly well-defined language: For α a term-variable, $\ulcorner[\alpha]\beta\urcorner$ is true (at some assignment of values to its domain-and-values variables) just in case every result of substituting some one closed $\mathbf{M}^*$-term for every occurrence (quoted or not) of α in β is itself true (at the same assignment).

It is to be noted that we do not define "true" nor even "true at" for formulas of $\mathbf{M}_3$ containing unquoted and unbound term variables. This point did not happen to arise for expression variables because they never occur both unquoted and unbound.

Also note that because no term contains an unmated quote sign, the substitutional range for term variables is a subset of the substitutional range for $\mathbf{M}_3$ expression variables. But still we cannot define term quantification as a restricted expression quantification by some such schema as

$$\ulcorner[t_1](\ldots t_1 \ldots) \text{ iff } [e_1] \text{ (if } 'e_1' \text{ is a closed } \mathbf{M}^*\text{-term, then}$$
$$(\ldots e_1 \ldots))\urcorner$$

The reason for this is that instances of $\ulcorner(\ldots e_1 \ldots)\urcorner$ can easily be ill-formed, which in any event is why we do not allow "e_1" anaphorically out of quotes. If our *use* language had what $\mathbf{M}_3$ has, on the other hand, we could properly (being charitable about dots inside quotes) say that

$$\ulcorner[t_1](\ldots t_1 \ldots)\urcorner \text{ is true iff } [e_1] \text{ (if } 'e_1' \text{ is a closed } \mathbf{M}^*\text{-term,}$$
$$\text{then } '(\ldots e_1 \ldots)' \text{ is true).}$$

Had we conceived of $\mathbf{M}_3$ as containing definite descriptions, set abstracts, or other terms containing formulas, the reader would notice that paradox would threaten (think of Richard's paradox). But the avoidance would be a straightforward consequence of our limitation of the substitution range of the term variables to terms of $\mathbf{M}^*$, hence to terms not containing even bound occurrences of these term variables. Because by assumption the terms of **M*** are already understood, no vicious circle can develop. We discuss this matter a little bit more in connection with propositional variables.

3.2.5. THE LANGUAGE M**

We let **M**** be the portion of **M**$_3$ which arises by adding term variables to **M***. The language **O**$_3$ whose grammar and semantics we shall describe will turn out to be a sublanguage of **M****.

3.2.6. PROPOSITIONAL VARIABLES

The second sort of in-and-out quantification we want is over *propositional variables*, which in **M**$_3$ consist of "p_1", ..., "p_9", "$p_{(10)}$", ... Their point will be to allow a nonrecursive definition of truth. Their *grammar* stipulates that their anaphoric occurrences outside of quotes are in all and only sentential positions (e.g., flanking "or"), and that they may occur arbitrarily inside quotes. Further, if α is a propositional variable and β is a formula not containing any unquoted occurrence of $\ulcorner[\alpha]\urcorner$, then $\ulcorner[\alpha]\beta\urcorner$ is a formula.

In designing an **M**$_3$ involving propositional quantification simultaneously in and out of quotes we must exercise a modicum of caution in order to avoid a form of the Liar paradox (Tarski 1936, pp. 161–62), and more generally, to be sure we are talking sense. For in-and-out quantification gives us the effect of cross-level quantification, so that *of course* paradox threatens. But just as elsewhere, it doesn't materialize if care is taken. What we must avoid is too much self-reference; although we by no means have to rule it out entirely (compare: set theory). The most natural way of doing this appears to be to use one of the concepts of order, rank, or grade of Chapter 10, though here we need only severely truncated versions of those hierarchical notions. The piece of the idea we need here is that we must cut down on the substitution-range of our propositional variables by excluding from this range *either* all formulas containing quoted occurrences of propositional variables ("order"; compare: simple theory of types) *or* all formulas containing unquoted occurrences of these variables ("rank"; compare: vicious circle principle) *or* both ("grade"; compare: ramified theory of types). We choose the middle way ("rank"), which is in some respects the simplest: The substitution-range of the propositional variables is confined to a group of formulas not including any formula containing an unquoted propositional variable. By this means our account of the truth-conditions of formulas $\ulcorner[\alpha]\beta\urcorner$ does not degenerate into a vicious circle.

In particular, we define the *substitution range of the propositional variables* of $\mathbf{M}_3$ to be the set of closed formulas of $\mathbf{M}^{**}$.

Before eliciting the principle, let us mention substitutional n-ary predicate variables of a sort that might occur both in and out of quotes. Clearly these are only interesting given the generation of new predicates by means of lambda abstraction or the equivalent; and also in that case we should have to be careful to avoid inconsistency. (Think of heteronomy.) But in the spirit of our treatment of term and propositional variables, what we should do in the case of n-ary predicate variables is clear: We should confine their range to n-ary predicates of $\mathbf{M}^{**}$, which by assumption are already understood. Then the threatening sentence "$[\exists H][G](H'G'$ iff not $G'G')$" would just be false; for even if $\mathbf{M}_3$ allowed in-and-out lambda-abstraction, so that "$\lambda F.(\text{not } F'F')$" was a predicate of $\mathbf{M}_3$, it would not be in the substitution-range of "G"—nor indeed in the range of its own "F" (We in fact add lambda-abstraction and substitutional predicate quantification just below.).

The general principle, then, underlying the concept of "rank," and common to all forms of in-and-out substitutional quantification, is that in introducing a new form of substitutional quantification $\ulcorner[\alpha]\beta\urcorner$ one should restrict the range of α to forms of speech (of the appropriate grammatical type) which are already semantically determined (in the way appropriate for the given grammatical type) independently of the new quantification. This principle, an analog of the "vicious circle principle" of set theory, seems to us easily applicable to new cases, transparently efficacious in avoiding paradox (and intuitively sensible), and even memorable. We recommend it. *But* we remark that confining in and out quantification to a semantically pre-determinate range is by no means the only way in which one can sensibly quantify in and out of quotes.

3.2.7. LAMBDA-ABSTRACTION

We add a soupçon of lambda-abstraction, the *point* of which is to assist with the definitions of "denotation at f" and "true at f." Its *grammar* is as follows: Let β be any $\mathbf{M}^{**}$-formula or $\mathbf{M}^{**}$-term containing at most the domain-and-values variable free. Then $\ulcorner(\lambda\alpha.\beta)\urcorner$ is a *predicate abstract* or an *operator abstract* according as β is a formula or a term: and similarly $\ulcorner((\lambda\alpha.\beta)\gamma)\urcorner$ is an $\mathbf{M}_3$-formula or $\mathbf{M}_3$-term, whenever γ is an $\mathbf{M}^{**}$-term. Note the severe limitations: no repeated abstraction, abstracts only in predicate or operator positions, and every abstraction yielding a *closed* predicate or operator.

The *semantics* are as usual: $\ulcorner((\lambda\alpha.\beta)\gamma)\urcorner$ is true at a given assignment just in case the formula β is true at the assignment that differs from the given one only by assigning α to the denotation of γ at the given assignment; and $\ulcorner((\lambda\alpha.\beta)\gamma)\urcorner$ denotes at a given assignment whatever the term β denotes at the assignment which differs from the given one only by assigning to α the denotation of γ at the given assignment.

3.2.8. PREDICATE AND OPERATOR VARIABLES

As in the case of lambda-abstraction, the *point* of including predicate and operator variables in $\mathbf{M}_3$ is to give the definitions of "denotation at f" and "true at f" for terms and sentences of $\mathbf{O}_3$. We use

$$\text{"}P_1\text{"}, \ldots, \text{"}P_9\text{"}, \text{"}P_{(10)}\text{"}, \ldots$$

as *predicate variables*, and

$$\text{"}F_1\text{"}, \ldots, \text{"}F_9\text{"}, \text{"}F_{(10)}\text{"}, \ldots$$

as *operator variables*. Both are substitutional. Outside of quotes, the former are allowed only in predicate positions; the latter, only in (one-place) operator positions. The substitutional range of the predicate variables is the set of predicate abstracts, and the substitutional range of the functor variables is the set of operator abstracts.

3.3. ILLUSTRATIVE DESCRIPTION OF $\mathbf{O}_3$

The differences between this section and §2.3 arise entirely from the fact that here $\mathbf{M}_3$ is simultaneously used and mentioned, because by hypothesis $\mathbf{O}_3$ is part of $\mathbf{M}_3$. In particular we take $\mathbf{O}_3$ to be that part of $\mathbf{M}_3$ (and indeed of $\mathbf{M}^{\ast\ast}$) involving expression variables, term variables (slightly modified), d-variables (just the ones over expressions), the concatenation operator, identity, the truth-predicate for $\mathbf{O}_2$, and (say) disjunction.

A word about term variables: In our illustration we wish to give their semantics rigorously, but the description of them in §3.2.4 permits only an informally rigorous account. For purposes of this illustrative section, therefore, we shall specify their substitution range not as just any closed $\mathbf{M}^{\ast}$-term; rather, we shall cut the range down to include only quote-terms and "concatenation terms" constructed by flanking the sign of concatenation with a pair of terms.

3.3.1. GRAMMAR OF O_3

O_3 has the same alphabet as does M_3. We introduce the various grammatical concepts needed for understanding the portion O_3 of M_3.

Indices, used in constructing variables, are '1', ..., '9', '(10)', ... (We skip the recursive bit.)

[For all e_1] 'e_1' is an *expression variable*, a *term variable*, or a d-*variable* iff [there is an e_2] such that 'e_2' is an index and, respectively, 'e_1' = 'ee$_2$', 'e_1' = 'te$_2$', or 'e_1' = 'ae$_2$'.

[For all e_1], ' 'e_1' ' is a *quote-term*. (Note: nested single quotes.)

If 'e_1' is either a term variable, a d-variable, or a quote term, then 'e_1' is an O_3-*term*; and if 'e_1' and 'e_2' are O_3-terms, then '($e_1 \frown e_2$)' is an O_3-*term*. An O_3-term is a *proper* O_3-*term* just in case it does not contain any free (i.e., unquoted) term variable. *Closed* O_3-*terms* are proper O_3-terms containing no free (i.e., unquoted) occurrences of d-variables.

We now define the O_3-*formulas*. O_3 has two predicates, one for identity and one for O_2-truth ("is true$_2$"). If 'e_1' and 'e_2' are O_3-terms, then '($e_1 = e_2$)' and 'e_1 is true$_2$' are O_3-formulas. We assume that O_3 has one connective, "or": if 'e_1' and 'e_2' are O_3-formulas, then '(e_1 or e_2)' is an O_3-formula. If 'e_1' is either an expression variable or a term variable, and 'e_2' is an O_3-formula, and every occurrence of '[e_1]' in 'e_2' is part of an occurrence of a quote term, then '[e_1]e_2' is an O_3-formula. If 'e_1' is a d-variable, and 'e_2' is an O_3-formula, and every occurrence of '(e_1)' in 'e_2' is part of an occurrence of a quote-term, then '(e_1)e_2' is an O_3-formula.

An O_3-formula is a *proper* O_3-*formula* iff it contains no free occurrences of term variables. (An occurrence of either a term-variable or a d-variable is *free* iff it lies neither within the scope of a quantifier binding that variable, nor within the scope of quotes.)

An O_3-formula is a *closed* O_3-*formula* iff it is proper and contains no free occurrences of d-variables.

3.3.2. SEMANTICS OF O_3: DENOTATION

We first use substitutional term variables in order to lay down what amounts to a nonrecursive definition in M_3 of "denotation" for a closed O_3-term a:

$den_3(a) = b$ iff $[\exists t_1](a = \text{'}t_1\text{'}$ and $b = t_1)$

This obviously satisfies the analog for denotation of Tarski's material condition of adequacy for truth. As a consequence, we have

$[t_1](\text{if 't}_1\text{' is an } \mathbf{O}_3\text{-term, then 't}_1\text{' denotes } t_1)$

and as a further consequence

$\text{' '}|\text{' ' denotes '}|\text{'}$

Note the convenience of quotes-in-quotes; but the quotes are always mated.

Were we content with denotation itself, we could stay with just term variables. But we also want "denotation of f." Of this we can give a nonrecursive definition in $\mathbf{M}_3$, using operator abstracts and operator variables ranging substitutionally over operator abstracts.

This definition has both a complicated (syntactical) clause and a perspicuous clause; we build the complicated part into the following accessory definition of the function Σ, taking a pair of expressions into an expression. (For applications think of "a" as denoting a term or formula, and "b" as denoting a particular general variable, say "f_1.")

$\Sigma(a,b) = c$ iff $[\exists e_1][\exists e_2]$ $(b = \text{'}e_1\text{'}$ and 'e_2' is the result of putting, [for each] d-variable 'e_3', 'e_1('e_3')' [for every] free occurrence of 'e_3' in a; and $c = \text{'}(\lambda e_1.e_2)\text{'})$

Thus,

$\Sigma(\text{'}(a_1 \frown a_2)\text{'}, \text{'}f_1\text{'}) = \text{'}(\lambda f_1.(f_1(\text{'}a_1\text{'}) \frown f_1(\text{'}a_2\text{'})))\text{'}$

and

$\Sigma(\text{'}(a_1 = a_2)\text{'}, \text{'}f_1\text{'}) = \text{'}(\lambda f_1(f_1(\text{'}a_1\text{'}) = f_1(\text{'}a_2\text{'})))\text{'}$

Σ then converts an $\mathbf{O}_3$-term (or $\mathbf{O}_3$-formula) with perhaps many free d-variables into a closed one-place operator abstract (or predicate abstract) fit for operating on (or being predicated of) an assignment of values to the d-variables.

One more preliminary: We let D_3—the domain of $\mathbf{O}_3$—be the set of normal $\mathbf{M}_3$-expressions and let V_3 be the set of mappings from the d-variables into D_3. In this section we assume that the range of "f" is confined to V_3.

Now the nonrecursive definition of "denotation at" is simple: For a a proper $\mathbf{O}_3$-term,

$den_3 f(a) = b$ iff $[\exists F_1](\text{'}F_1\text{'} = \Sigma(a, \text{'}f_1\text{'})$ and $b = (F_1 f))$.

Note the crucial use of "F_1" both in and out of quotes. We must *both* mention and use it. A consequence of the definition:

$$\text{den}_3 f('(a_1 \frown a_2)') = (\lambda f_1.(f_1('a_1') \frown f_1('a_2'))) f) = f('a_1') \frown f('a_2').$$

The move from left to center is by definition, and from center to right by lambda conversion.

Naturally, for a closed $\mathbf{O}_3$-term a, $\text{den}_3(a) = b$ iff (for all f in V_3) $\text{den}_3 f(a) = b$; but this is a fact, not a definition.

Now we use the concept of denotation to articulate the semantic structure of $\mathbf{O}_3$. The form this takes is like the usual recursive definition of "denotation"; except we presume you already understand "denotation," so that it is not, pragmatically, a definition. If 'e_1' is a d-variable, $\text{den}_3 f('e_1') = f('e_1')$; $\text{den}_3 f('\ 'e_1'\ ') = 'e_1'$; if '$e_1$' and '$e_2$' are proper $\mathbf{O}_3$-terms, $\text{den}_3 f('(e_1 \frown e_2)') = \text{den}_3 f('e_1') \frown \text{den}_3 f('e_2')$.

What *have* we done if we have not *defined* "denotation"? Precisely this: We have shed light on the structure and meaning of proper $\mathbf{O}_3$-terms by explaining how the denotation of grammatically more complex terms depends on the denotation of simpler ones; we have also shed light on what the denotation of the simplest terms depends upon. Clearly someone might know how to use $\mathbf{O}_3$-terms and still find this light helpful.

Truth. A nonrecursive definition of "truth" for $\mathbf{O}_3$, obviously satisfying Tarski's Convention T, can be stated in $\mathbf{M}_3$; this is possible because of the availability of substitutional propositional quantifiers whose substitutional range includes the closed $\mathbf{O}_3$-formulas:

a is true_3 iff a is a closed $\mathbf{O}_3$-formula and $(\exists p_1)(a = 'p_1'$ and $p_1)$

As a consequence we have

$'('1' = '1')'$ is true_3 iff $('1' = '1')$

which reminds one of the fact that snow is white.

If one is satisfied with unrelativized truth, one may stop here. Otherwise, predicate variables ranging over predicate abstracts allow us to define "true at":

a is true_3 at f iff a is a proper $\mathbf{O}_3$-formula and f is in V_3 and $(\exists P_1)('P_1' = \Sigma(a, 'f_1')$ and $P_1 f)$

Hence, for f in V_3,

$$\text{'}(a_1 = a_2)\text{'} \quad \text{is} \quad \text{true}_3 \quad \text{at} \quad f \quad \text{iff} \quad (\lambda f_1.(f_1(\text{'}a_1\text{'}) = f_1(\text{'}a_2\text{'})))f \quad \text{iff}$$
$$f(\text{'}a_1\text{'}) = f(\text{'}a_2\text{'})$$

We can now use the fully defined concept of "true_3 at" to throw light on the semantic structure of O_3 by exhibiting how truth-at of more complicated O_3-formulas depends on truth-at of their parts, and how truth-at of the simplest proper O_3-formulas depends on the denotation-at of their parts. As in the case of denotation, it is important to understand that we are *not* defining true-at; that has already been done. Nor are we defining the linguistic features of O_3; as part of M_3 they are by hypothesis already understood in the know-how sense. Rather, we are adding to our (a priori) stock of knowledge concerning the nature of O_3. Throughout, we suppose f is in V_3. '$(e_1 = e_2)$' if an O_3-formula, is true_3 at f iff $\text{den}_3 f(\text{'}e_1\text{'}) = \text{den}_3 f(\text{'}e_2\text{'})$; '$e_1$ is true_2', if an O_3-formula, is true_3 at f iff $\text{den}_3 f(\text{'}e_1\text{'})$ is true_2; '$(e_1$ or $e_2)$', if an O_3-formula, is true_3 at f iff at least one of 'e_1' and 'e_2' is true_3 at f; '$[e_1]e_2$', if an O_3-formula, and if 'e_1' is an expression variable {or 'e_1' is a term variable}, is true_3 at f iff every result of putting a normal M_3-expression {or a closed O_3-term} for every occurrence of 'e_1' in 'e_2' is true_3 at f; '$(e_1)e_2$', if an O_3-formula, is true_3 at f iff (for every f_1 in V_3 which is like f except perhaps at 'e_1'), 'e_2' is true_3 at f_1.

It follows that for any closed O_3-formula a,

a is true_3 iff for each f, a is true_3 at f

But again, this is no definition.

Had O_3 not contained domain-and-values quantifiers, then the semantics of O_3 could have been given using only unrelativized "truth in O_3" and "denotation in O_3." For example,

'$(e_1 = e_2)$', if an O_3-formula, is true_3 iff $\text{den}_3(\text{'}e_1\text{'}) = \text{den}_3(\text{'}e_2\text{'})$; '$[e_1]e_2$', if an O_3-formula, and if 'e_1' is an expression variable, is true_3 iff every result of putting a normal M_3-expression for every occurrence of 'e_1' in 'e_2' is true_3.

3.4. REMARKS

We defend our definitions of truth and denotation and explain how these definitions relate to the recursive truth conditions. In so doing we make some remarks about theories of truth, truth-conditions, meaning, and translation.

3.4.1. CONVENTION T AND INFINITE CONJUNCTIONS

Tarski (1936, pp. 187–88) states Convention T as follows:

A formally correct definition of the symbol 'Tr', formulated in the metalanguage, will be called an *adequate definition* of truth if it has the following consequences:

(α) all sentences which are obtained from the expression '$x \in$ Tr if and only if p' by substituting for the symbol 'x' a structural-descriptive name of any sentence of the language in question and for the symbol 'p' the expression which forms the translation of this sentence in the metalanguage;
(β) the sentence 'for any x, if $x \in$ Tr then $x \in S$' (in other words 'Tr $\subseteq S$').

Note that clause (β) mentions a single consequence the definition must have, while (α) refers to infinitely many. The reason for this disparity is entirely due to Tarski's choice of metalanguage; with the apparatus of $\mathbf{M}_3$ (and ignoring inessential grammatical differences), one can say instead that a formally correct definition of "true$_3$" is *adequate* if it has as consequences (just) the two sentences (α') "[p](if 'p' is a closed $\mathbf{O}_3$-formula, then: 'p' is true$_3$ iff p)" and (β') "[p](if 'p' is true$_3$ then 'p' is a closed $\mathbf{O}_3$-formula)," which removes the disparity. And this works quite generally whenever the closed formulas of an $\mathbf{O}$ fall within the substitutional range of "p."

Why it works can be seen from Tarski (1944, p. 344): "The general definition has to be, in a certain sense, a logical conjunction of all these partial definitions," he says, referring to the various instances of the schema

(T) *x is true if and only if p.*

Now in order to avoid technicalities, Tarski explicitly refrains from explaining what is meant by a "logical conjunction of infinitely many sentences," but it is perfectly clear how it should go, given the concept of consequence: A closed sentence α is a logical conjunction of the set of closed sentences Z provided that α is "the greatest lower bound" of Z with respect to the consequence relation viewed as partial ordering: α is to have every member of Z as a consequence, and if any other sentence has every member of Z as a consequence, then that other sentence has α as a consequence as well. So $\ulcorner[\alpha]\beta\urcorner$ is precisely a logical conjunction of all the substitution instances of β with respect to α. And that is why our definition works. To put the matter another way, the reason Tarski himself had to define "truth" recursively is that he did not have available in his metalanguage a means for formulating, nonrecursively, the infinite conjunction of all of the instances of (T). But it is precisely this which M_3 allows.

3.4.2. FORMAL CORRECTNESS AND MATERIAL ADEQUACY

Tarski (1936) canvasses the possibility of defining truth by "for all p, 'p' is a true sentence if and only if p" (p. 159), only to abandon it. His reasons are (1) the usual ones about the impossibility of sensibly quantifying into quotes and (2) paradox; but we have demonstrated that these are not good reasons. In particular, we claim that the threat of paradox from quantifying into quotes—also urged by Harman (1970) and Binkley (1970)—is no more (and of course no less) disturbing than the similar threat posed by set theory, which *everyone* uses in truth definitions.

So it would appear that our definition is "formally correct." And it also obviously satisfies Convention T and is thus "materially adequate." We conclude that it leaves nothing to be desired, as a definition of truth, that is.

3.4.3. TRUTH AND TRUTH CONDITIONS

We have shown that quantification in and out of quotes can be used to define "true in O_3" and "denotation in O_3." Definitions were also provided for "true_3 at" (satisfaction) and "denotation_3 at"; these were, however, *not* needed to define "is true_3" as in Tarski. They were rather needed to give a semantic analysis of open sentences and of the domain-and-values quantifiers.

The reader will recall that in giving the semantics of O_3 we separated the definition of the four locutions "truth," "truth at," "denotation," and "denotation at" from the theory that describes the truth conditions of sentences of the language. The other side of this coin is that, quite unlike Tarski's definition of truth via a recursive definition of satisfaction (a concept we have caught by "true at"), ours throws no light at all on the structure of the language under investigation. We believe, however, that the project of defining truth is quite independent of articulating the semantic structure of a language, at least in those cases in which the object language is either a part of or translatable into (by a pre-given translation func-

tion) a fixed portion of our metalanguage. It is only confusing to mix
these tasks together.

It will be said, we predict, that we have made some kind of philosophical mistake in even trying to define truth and denotation nonrecursively—without, that is, making reference to those features of
the language which dictate how more complex expressions are constructed from simpler ones. It will be argued that *because* our definitions of truth and denotation cast no light on the meanings of the
various grammatical structures making up O_3, therefore, although
we may have succeeded in satisfying Tarski's Convention T, still
our definition (or theory) of truth and denotation is empty, uninter-
esting, and philosophically deficient.

We grant the spirit of the remark, but its details are based on a
confusion. Especially do we agree that the concepts of truth and denotation do not become (very) interesting until they are used in a
theory of truth-*conditions* and denotation-*conditions* illuminating
the semantic structure of a language. But to ask for such a theory is
not to ask for a theory about *just* truth and denotation; it is to ask
in addition that the theory be about the generative features of the
language, explaining how the semantics of more complex expressions derive from that of the simpler ones. It is seriously misleading
to call *such* a theory a "theory of truth"; it is rather a theory of truth
and the generating features; or, for short, a "theory of truth-conditions."

What we have established is that, given adequate resources one
can have a theory of truth all by itself, a theory that in no part mentions the "insides" of sentences and how they are constructed. We
have demonstrated that the theory of truth is *separable from* and
does not depend on a theory of truth conditions. Of course, what is
separated off isn't very interesting—it was never meant to be—but
that it can be separated off is interesting.

It is to be noted that there is nothing here militating against the
suggestion of Davidson (1967) that every theory of truth-conditions
(our word for what he means) should satisfy Convention T. His
view in our language would be that the theory of truth conditions,
without our definition, should have our definition as a consequence.

3.4.4. TRUTH AND MEANING

There is therefore some point in thinking of the recursive clauses
of §3.3 as giving the *meanings* of the functors of the language, be-

cause it was in terms of these functors that the definition was broken down into its clauses; but lest it be thought this is all there is to meaning in the context of formal languages, or that this is *the only* way of giving the meanings of the functors (and hence of the sentences) of a formal language, we add the following comments:

There are many ways of "getting at" the meanings of expressions of a formal language, of which we mention four: One way is to engage in a formal (mathematical) semantic analysis, possibly by giving the truth conditions of the sentences of the language, as we did for O_3. Note that for O_3 we needed not only "truth" but also "denotation," "denotation at," and "truth at." Note also that the case of O_3 was relatively simple because O_3 was a language already understood (it was part of M_3), and so in-and-out quantification was available; therefore, we were able to define the concepts needed, *independently* of giving the semantic analysis. But apart from this we do not by any means believe that these four concepts are enough on which to found a theory of meaning.

The second way of giving the meaning of a functor is to give the role (use) that functor has in the language—in many languages its role in deductive inferences is what is important. We have not, in this paper, explored this method of characterizing pieces of our object languages, mainly because we have almost entirely neglected proof theory, but the method is discussed and defended in Curry 1963 and in Belnap 1961–62.

The third way is to provide a translation into a second formal language; e.g., the explanation of the combinators by means of their translations into the lambda calculus, or one of the familiar translations from number theory into set theory.

The fourth way, necessarily not rigorous so sometimes misleading yet intuitively helpful (indeed essential), is to provide a reading (surely *not* a "translation") of functors and sentences of the object language in a natural language familiar to us, e.g., reading the horseshoe as "if ... then ...". (This procedure of the a priori sciences is analogous to the "correspondence rules" of the empirical sciences.)

3.4.5. TRUTH AND TRANSLATION

Suppose O_3' is completely separate from M_3, but there is a "translation" mapping, i.e., a mapping Tr from O_3' into M_3 which (for whatever reason) we take as a translation (whatever that means). Suppose further the range of Tr is within the range of our substitutional propositional variables. *Then* we may define "true in O_3" by *a is true$_3$*, iff *a* is a closed **O**$_3$'-formula and $[\exists p_1]('p_1' = Tr(a)$ and $p_1)$

Obviously we satisfy Tarski's Convention T.

As before, we could use this concept of truth to give an account of the semantic structure of **O**$_3$'. Note that the preavailability of the translation function is *essential* here if the above is to serve as a definition of "true in **O**$_3$'."

Such situations arise when **O**$_3$', as a separate language, is being used to characterize certain features of **M**. In these cases we *do* have in mind some translation, and our interest is in the semantic structure of **O**$_3$': The truth definition serves merely as a means to this end.

Complications can arise: If there are translations available of only some of the sentences of **O**$_3$', then the definition above has to be modified to

> For each closed **O**$_3$'-formula *a*, if [there is a p_1] such that $Tr(a) = 'p_1'$, then [for all such p_1] *a is true$_3$'* iff *a* is a closed **O**$_3$'-formula and p_1.

This definition provides only a partial definition of "truth in **O**$_3$'." Not until the semantic structure of **O**$_3$' is given is the truth predicate completely defined. So we have again (see §2.4.4) further subtle interplay between the processes of defining truth and giving the meanings of the functors of the language.

Alternatively, if we have already available a definition of "truth in **O**$_3$" and we wish to relate **O**$_3$' to **M**$_3$ by means of a translation, then a translation function *Tr* is acceptable only if, for each closed **O**$_3$'-formula *a*,

> if $Tr(a) = 'p_1'$, then *a* is true$_3$ iff p_1

We have used both substitutional and domain-and-values quantifiers. Substitutional quantifiers must be used if we want, and can have, in-and-out quantification. Because for in-and-out quantification the substitutional range of the variables must be restricted to expressions of the use language (in this case **M**$_3$), and because **O**$_3$' is completely separate (by hypothesis), we must either use domain-and-values quantifiers or substitutional quantifiers restricted so that bound variables occur only inside quotes, to talk about expressions of **O**$_3$'. In the definitions above we happened to use domain-and-values quantifiers.

3.4.6. ONTOLOGY

Objections may be raised against our definition of "truth in O_3" independently of quotation and paradox. It has been argued that propositional quantifiers introduce entities that (philosophers and) logicians should try to do without. For example, Quine (1970) has argued that in giving an account of propositional quantification we must construe sentences as names—names of "fictitious objects" such as truth values or propositions. Because we believe that a correct account of propositional quantification must construe sentences only as sentences (see Chapter 2), and not as names (of any kind of objects), we think Quine is wrong on this point. So propositional quantifiers have not cost us anything ontological.

4. O_4 and M_4 Overlap

The case when the language we are describing overlaps with the language we are using is perhaps of the most interest, because it is likely the most common case. For example, of this kind is the introduction of new locutions by means of definitions, because the linguistic features we are introducing rarely form a complete language by themselves but rather intertwine with the language we already have. It is therefore with regret that the usual spatiotemporal considerations lead us to beg off discussing this case and enter only the opinion that quantification in-and-out may well have a place here, and that consideration of the role of the truth-predicate in this situation may well reveal some unsuspected subtleties.

In conclusion, we should like to opine that it is truly unwise to think of domain-and-values quantification as some kind of mystical paradigm, or as perhaps the only real quantification, or as *the* frame of reference (Wallace 1970), and to use various pejoratives such as "simulated quantification" or "subtle limits" to cast aspersions on substitutional quantification. For goodness sake, let it stand on its own feet as a legitimate, sensible, and even *possibly* useful device. And if it turns out not to be useful, why, then, neglect it for that reason? Not because it somehow partakes of bastardy.

UNIVERSITY OF BRISTOL

Department of Philosophy

9 Woodland Road
Bristol
BS8 1TB

Bibliography

Austin, J. L. 1950. "Truth," *Proceedings of the Aristotelian Society*, Supp. Vol. 24, pp. 111–28. Reprinted in Pitcher 1964, pp. 18–31.

Ayer, A. J. 1946 (2nd ed.). *Language, Truth and Logic*. London: Victor Gollancz, Ltd.

Barwise, Jon, and John Etchemendy. 1987. *The Liar: An Essay on Truth and Circularity*. New York: Oxford Univ. Press.

Belnap, Nuel D. 1961–62. "Tonk, Plonk, and Plink," *Analysis* 22, pp. 130–34. Reprinted in *Philosophical Logic*, ed. P. F. Strawson, Oxford: Oxford Univ. Press, 1981, pp. 132–37.

———. 1967. "Intensional Models for First Degree Formulas," *The Journal of Symbolic Logic* 32, pp. 1–22.

———. 1973. "Restricted Quantification and Conditional Assertion," in *Truth, Syntax, and Modality*, ed. H. Leblanc, Amsterdam: North-Holland, pp. 48–75.

———. 1974. "Grammatical Propaedeutic," appendix to Vol. I of A. R. Anderson and N. D. Belnap, *Entailment*, Princeton, NJ: Princeton Univ. Press, 1975.

Belnap, Nuel D., and Dorothy Grover. 1973. "Quantifying in and out of Quotes," in *Truth, Syntax, and Modality*, ed. H. Leblanc, Dordrecht: Reidel, pp. 17–47. Reprinted as Chapter 11 in this volume.

Belnap, Nuel, and Steel, Thomas. 1976. *The Logic of Questions*. New Haven: Yale Univ. Press, 1976.

Binkley, R. 1970. "Quantifying, Quotation, and a Paradox," *Nous* 4, pp. 271–77.

Blanshard, Brand. 1939. *The Nature of Thought*, vol. 2. Fourth edition, 1964. New York: Humanities Press.

Bradley, F. H. 1909. "On Truth and Coherence," *Mind* 1909, pp. 329–42. Reprinted in Bradley 1914.

———. 1914. *Essays on Truth and Reality*. Oxford: Oxford Univ. Press. (Reprinted 1964)

Brandom, Robert. 1984. "Reference Explained Away," *The Journal of Philosophy* 81, pp. 469–92.

———. 1988a. "Inference, Expression, and Induction: Sellarsian Themes," *Philosophical Studies* 54, pp. 257–85.

———. 1988b. "Pragmatism, Phenomenalism, and Truth Talk," in *Realism and Antirealism: Midwest Studies in Philosophy*, vol. 12, ed. P. A. French, T. E. Uehling, and H. K. Wettstein, Minneapolis: Univ. of Minnesota Press, 1988, pp. 75–93.

Brentano, F. C. 1904. *The True and the Evident*. Ed. and trans. R. M. Chisholm. London: Routledge and Kegan Paul.

Burge, Tyler. 1979. "Semantical Paradox," *The Journal of Philosophy* 76, pp. 169–98. Reprinted with a postscript in Martin 1984, pp. 83–117.

Carnap, R. 1946. *Introduction to Semantics*. Cambridge, MA: Harvard Univ. Press.

Chastain, Charles. 1975. "Reference and Context," in *Language, Mind, and Knowledge: Minnesota Studies in the Philosophy of Science*, vol. 7, ed. Keith Gunderson, Minneapolis: Univ. of Minnesota Press, pp. 194–269.

Chihara, C. 1979. "The Semantic Paradoxes: A Diagnostic Investigation," *Philosophical Review* 87, pp. 590–619.

Clark, R. 1970. "Concerning the Logic of Predicate Modifiers," *Nous* 4, pp. 311–35.

Cummins, Robert. 1989. *Meaning and Mental Representation*. Cambridge, MA: MIT Press.

Curry, H. B. 1963. *Foundations of Mathematical Logic*. New York: McGraw-Hill.

Davidson, Donald. 1967. "Truth and Meaning," *Synthese* 17, pp. 304–23. Reprinted in Davidson 1984, pp. 17–36.

———. 1969. "True to the Facts," *The Journal of Philosophy* 66, pp. 748–64. Reprinted in Davidson 1984, pp. 37–54.

———. 1977. "Reality without Reference," *Dialectica* 31, pp. 247–58. Reprinted in Platts 1980, pp. 131–40.

———. 1984. *Inquiries into Truth and Interpretation*. Oxford: Oxford Univ. Press.

———. 1990. "The Structure and Content of Truth," *The Journal of Philosophy* 87, pp. 279–329.

Devitt, Michael. 1984. *Realism and Truth*. Princeton, NJ: Princeton Univ. Press.

Devitt, M. Forthcoming. "Aberrations of the Realism Debate," *Philosophical Studies*.

Dewey, John. 1920. *Reconstruction in Philosophy*. New York: Holt.

———. 1931. "The Development of American Pragmatism," in his *Philosophy and Civilization*, New York: Capricorn Books, 1963, pp. 13–35.

Donnellan, Keith S. 1966. "Reference and Definite Descriptions," *The Philosophical Review* 75, pp. 281–304. Reprinted in *Readings in the Philosophy of Language*, ed. J. Rosenberg and C. Travis, Englewood Cliffs, NJ: Prentice-Hall, 1971, pp. 195–212.

Dummett, Michael. 1958. "Truth," *Proceedings of the Aristotelian Society* 59, pp. 141–62. Reprinted in Pitcher 1964 and Dummett 1978.

———. 1973. *Frege: Philosophy of Language*. London: Duckworth.

———. 1976. "What Is a Theory of Meaning?" (II), in *Truth and Meaning*, ed. Gareth Evans and John McDowell, Oxford: Clarendon Press, pp. 67–137.

———. 1978. *Truth and Other Enigmas*. Cambridge, MA: Harvard Univ. Press.

Dunn, Michael, and Nuel D. Belnap. 1968. "The Substitution Interpretation of the Quantifiers," *Nous* 2, pp. 177–85.

Dunn, Michael and Anil Gupta. 1990. *Truth or Consequences*. Dordrecht: Kluwer.

Etchemendy, John. 1988. *The Journal of Symbolic Logic* 53, pp. 51–79.

Evans, Gareth, and John McDowell, eds. 1976. *Truth and Meaning*. Oxford: Clarendon Press.

Field, Hartry. 1972. "Tarski's Theory of Truth," *The Journal of Philosophy* 69, pp. 347–75. Reprinted in Platts 1980, pp. 83–110.

––––––. 1986. "The Deflationary Conception of Truth," in *Fact, Science, and Morality: Essays on A. J. Ayer's Language, Truth and Logic*, ed. Graham MacDonald and Crispin Wright, Oxford: Blackwell, 1986, pp. 55–117.

Fine, Arthur. 1984. "The Natural Ontological Attitude," in *Scientific Realism*, ed. Jarrett Leplin, Berkeley: Univ. of California Press, 1984, pp. 83–107.

Fitch, F. B. 1948. "An Extension of Basic Logic," *Journal of Symbolic Logic* 12, pp. 95–106.

Fodor, Jerry A. 1987. *Psychosemantics: The Problem of Meaning in the Philosophy of Mind*. Cambridge, MA: MIT Press.

Frege, G. 1884. *The Foundations of Arithmetic*. Trans. J. L. Austin. Chicago: Northwestern Univ. Press.

––––––. 1892. "On Sense and Meaning," *Translation from the Writings of Gottlob Frege*, 3d ed., ed. P. Geach and M. Black, Oxford: Blackwell, 1960, pp. 56–78.

––––––. 1915. "My Basic Logical Insights," in *Gottlob Frege: Posthumous Writings*, ed. H. Hermes, Chicago: Univ. of Chicago Press, 1979, pp. 251–52.

––––––. 1918–19. "The Thought: A Logical Inquiry," trans. A. M. and M. Quinton, *Mind* 65, 1956, pp. 289–311. Reprinted in E. D. Klemke 1968, pp. 507–35.

Geach, P. 1967. "Intentional Identity," *Journal of Philosophy* 64, p. 627.

Grover, Dorothy. 1972. "Propositional Quantifiers," *Journal of Philosophical Logic* 1, pp. 111–36. Reprinted as Chapter 2 in this volume.

––––––. 1973. "Propositional Quantification and Quotation Contexts," in *Truth, Syntax, and Modality*, ed. H. Leblanc, Dordrecht: Reidel, 1973, pp. 101–10. Reprinted as Chapter 10 in this volume.

––––––. 1976. " 'This is False,' on the Prosentential Theory," *Analysis* 36, pp. 80–83.

––––––. 1977. "Inheritors and Paradox," *The Journal of Philosophy* 74, pp. 590–604. Reprinted as Chapter 4 in this volume.

––––––. 1979. "Prosentences and Propositional Quantification: A Response to Zimmerman," *Philosophical Studies* 35, pp. 289–297. Reprinted as Chapter 5 in this volume.

––––––. 1981a. "Truth," *Philosophia* 10, pp. 225–51. Reprinted as Chapter 6 in this volume.

Grover, Dorothy. 1981b. "Truth: Do We Need It?" *Philosophical Studies* 40, pp. 69–103. Reprinted as Chapter 7 in this volume.

———. 1983. "Berry's Paradox," *Analysis* 43, pp. 170–76. Reprinted as Chapter 8 of this volume.

———. 1990a. "On Two Deflationary Truth Theories," in *Truth or Consequences*, ed. Michael Dunn and Anil Gupta, Dordrecht: Kluwer, 1990, pp. 1–17. Reprinted as Chapter 9 in this volume.

———. 1990b. "Truth and Language-World Connections," *Journal of Philosophy* 87, pp. 671–87.

Grover, D. L., and Belnap, Nuel. 1973. "Quantifying in and out of Quotes," in *Truth, Syntax, and Modality*, ed. H. Leblanc, Dordrecht: Reidel, 1973, pp. 17–47. Reprinted as Chapter 11 in this volume.

Grover, D. L., J. L. Camp, and N. D. Belnap. 1975. "A Prosentential Theory of Truth," *Philosophical Studies* 27, pp. 73–124. Reprinted as Chapter 3 in this volume.

Gupta, Anil. 1982. "Truth and Paradox," *Journal of Philosophical Logic* 11, pp. 1–60. A revised version reprinted in Martin 1984, pp. 175–235.

Harman, G. H. 1970. "_____ is True," *Analysis* 30, pp. 98–99.

Heidelberger, H. 1968. "The Indispensability of Truth," *American Philosophical Quarterly* 5, pp. 212–17.

Hermes, Hans, ed. 1979. *Gottlob Frege: Posthumous Writings*. Trans. Peter Long and Roger White. Chicago: Univ. of Chicago Press.

Herzberger, Hans G. 1970. "Truth and Modality in Semantically Closed Languages," in *The Liar Paradox*, ed. R. L. Martin, New Haven: Yale Univ. Press, pp. 133–74.

———. 1982. "Naive Semantics and the Liar Paradox," *The Journal of Philosophy* 79, pp. 479–97.

Horwich, Paul. 1982. "Three Forms of Realism," *Synthese* 51, pp. 181–201.

———. 1990. *Truth*. Oxford: Blackwell.

Kaplan, David. 1969. "Quantifying In," in *Words and Objections*, ed. D. Davidson and J. Hintikka, Dordrecht: Reidel, 1969, pp, 206–42.

Kleene, S. C. 1952. *Introduction to Metamathematics*. New York: Van Nostrand.

Klemke, E. D., ed. 1968. *Essays on Frege*. Urbana: Univ. of Illinois Press.

Kneale, W. M. 1962. *The Development of Logic*. Oxford: Clarendon Press, 1962.

Kripke, Saul. 1975. "Outline of a Theory of Truth," *The Journal of Philosophy* 72, pp. 690–716. Reprinted in Martin 1984, pp. 53–81.

———. 1976. "Is There a Problem About Substitutional Quantification?" in *Truth and Meaning*, ed. Gareth Evans and John McDowell, Oxford: Clarendon Press, pp. 325–419.

Lakoff, G. 1970. "Pronominalization, Negation, and the Analysis of Adverbs," in *Readings in English Transformational Grammar*, ed. R. Jacobs and P. Rosenbaum, Waltham, MA: Ginn, 1970, pp. 145–65.

Leeds, Steven. 1978. "Theories of Reference and Truth," *Erkenntnis* 13, pp. 111–29.

LePore, Ernest. 1986. "Truth in Meaning," introductory essay in *Truth and Interpretation*, ed. E. Lepore, Oxford: Blackwell.

Lewis, David. 1972. "General Semantics," in *Semantics of Natural Language*, ed. Donald Davidson and Gilbert Harman, Dordrecht: Reidel.

Martin, Robert L. 1967. "Towards a Solution to the Liar Paradox," *The Philosophical Review* 76, pp. 279–311.

———, ed. 1970. *The Paradox of the Liar*. New Haven: Yale Univ. Press.

———, ed. 1984. *Recent Essays on Truth and the Liar Paradox*. New York: Oxford Univ. Press.

Martin, Robert L., and Peter Woodruff. 1975. "On Representing 'True-in-L' in L," *Philosophia* 3, pp. 213–17. Reprinted in Martin 1984, pp. 47–51.

Massey, Gerald J. 1970. "Is 'Congruence' a Peculiar Predicate?" (mimeograph).

McDowell, John. 1978. "Physicalism and Primitive Denotation: Field on Tarski," *Erkenntnis* 13, pp. 131–52. Reprinted in Platts 1980, pp. 111–30.

McGee, Vann. 1989. "Applying Kripke's Theory of Truth," *Journal of Philosophy* 86, 10, pp. 530–39.

Montague, R. 1970. "The Proper Treatment of Quantification in Ordinary English," in *Formal Philosophy*, ed. Richmond H. Thomason, New Haven: Yale Univ. Press, 1974, pp. 247–70.

Parsons, Charles. 1974. "The Liar Paradox," *The Journal of Philosophical Logic* 3, pp. 381–412. Reprinted with a postscript in Parsons, *Mathematics in Philosophy: Selected Essays*, Ithaca: Cornell Univ. Press, 1983, pp. 221–67; also reprinted in Martin 1984, pp. 9–45.

Parsons, T. 1970. *A Semantics for English* (mimeograph).

Partee, Barbara. 1970. "Opacity, Coreference, and Pronouns," *Synthese* 21, pp. 359–85.

Peirce, Charles S. 1878. "How to Make Our Ideas Clear," *Popular Science Monthly* 12 (January 1878), pp. 286–302. Reprinted in *Charles S. Peirce: Selected Writings*, ed. Philip P. Wiener, New York: Dover, 1958, pp. 113–36.

Pitcher, George, ed. 1964. *Truth*. Englewood Cliffs, NJ: Prentice-Hall.

Platts, Mark, ed. 1980. *Reference, Truth and Reality: Essays on the Philosophy of Language*. London: Routledge and Kegan Paul.

Pollock, John L. 1977. "The Liar Strikes Back," *Journal of Philosophy* 74, pp. 604–606.

Prior, Arthur N. 1954. "Entities," *Australian Journal of Philosophy* 32, p. 159. Reprinted in his *Papers in Logic and Ethics*, ed. P. T. Geach and A. J. Kenny, Amherst: Univ. of Massachusetts Press, 1976, pp. 25–32.

———. 1967. "Correspondence Theory of Truth," in *The Encyclopedia of Philosophy*, ed. Paul Edwards, New York: Macmillan, vol. 2, pp. 223–32.

Prior, Arthur N. 1971. *Objects of Thought*. Oxford: Oxford Univ. Press.

———. 1976. *The Doctrine of Propositions and Terms*. Amherst: Univ. of Massachusetts Press.

Putnam, Hilary. 1978a. "Realism and Reason," in Putnam 1978b, pp. 123–40.

———. 1978b. *Meaning and the Moral Sciences*. London: Routledge and Kegan Paul.

———. 1981. *Reason, Truth and History*. Cambridge: Cambridge Univ. Press.

Quine, W. V. 1940. *Mathematical Logic*. New York: Harper and Row. Revised edition, 1951.

———. 1970. *The Philosophy of Logic*. Englewood Cliffs, NJ: Prentice-Hall.

———. 1981. "Things and Their Place in Theories," in *Theories and Things*, Cambridge, MA: Belknap Press of Harvard Press, 1987, pp. 1–23.

———. 1986. "Reply to Roger F. Gibson," in *The Philosophy of W. V. Quine*, ed. L. E. Hahn and P. A. Schilpp, LaSalle, IL: Open Court, 1986, pp. 154–57.

———. 1987. "Truth," in his *Quiddities: An Intermittently Philosophical Dictionary*. Cambridge, MA: Belknap Press of Harvard Univ. Press, 1987, pp. 212–16.

———. 1990. *Pursuit of Truth*. Cambridge, MA: Harvard Univ. Press.

Ramsey, F. P. 1927. "Facts and Propositions," *Proceedings of the Aristotelian Society*, supp. vol. 24, pp. 153–70. Reprinted in his *Foundations* (ed. D. H. Mellor), London: Routledge and Kegan Paul, 1978, pp. 40–57.

Rorty, Richard. 1982. *Consequences of Pragmatism*. Minneapolis: Univ. of Minnesota Press.

———. 1986. "Pragmatism, Davidson and Truth," in *Truth and Interpretation*, ed. Ernest LePore, Oxford: Blackwell, pp. 333–55.

Russell, Bertrand. 1906–1907. "On The Nature of Truth," *Proceedings of the Aristotelian Society* 7, pp. 28–49.

———. 1908. "Mathematical Logic as Based on a Theory of Types," *American Journal of Mathematics* 30, pp. 222–62.

———. 1921. *The Analysis of Mind*. London: G. Allen and Unwin.

Sellars, Wilfrid. 1960. "Grammar and Existence: A Preface to Ontology," *Mind* 69 (276), pp. 499–533. Reprinted in Sellars 1963, pp. 247–81.

———. 1962. "Truth and Correspondence," *The Journal of Philosophy* 59, pp. 29–55. Reprinted in Sellars 1963, pp. 197–224.

———. 1963. *Science, Perception and Reality*. London: Routledge and Kegan Paul.

Soames, Scott. 1984. 'What Is a Theory of Truth?' *The Journal of Philosophy* 81, pp. 411–29.

Stalnaker, Robert. 1984. *Inquiry*. Cambridge, MA: Bradford Books.

Strawson, P. F. 1949. "Truth," *Analysis* 9, pp. 82–97.

————. 1950a. "Truth," *Proceedings of the Aristotelian Society*, supp. vol. 24, 129–56. Reprinted in Pitcher 1964 and Strawson 1971.

————. 1950b. "On Referring," *Mind* 59, pp. 320–44. Reprinted in *Readings in the Philosophy of Language*, ed. J. Rosenberg and C. Travis, Englewood Cliffs, NJ: Prentice-Hall, 1971, pp. 175–95.

————. 1965. "A Reconsideration of Austin's Views," *The Philosophical Quarterly* 15, pp. 289–301. Reprinted in Strawson 1971.

————. 1971. *Logico-Linguistic Papers*. London: Methuen.

————. 1974. "Positions of Quantifiers," in *Semantics and Philosophy*, ed. M. K. Munitz and P. K. Unger, New York: New York Univ. Press, pp. 63–79.

Suppes, Patrick. 1957. *Introduction to Logic*. Princeton, NJ: Van Nostrand.

Tarski, Alfred. 1936. "The Concept of Truth in Formalized Languages," in his *Logic, Semantics, Metamathematics: Papers from 1923–1938*, trans. J. H. Woodger, Oxford: Clarendon Press, 1956, pp. 152–278.

————. 1944. "The Semantic Conception of Truth," *Philosophy and Phenomenological Research* 4, pp. 341–76. Reprinted in *Semantics and the Philosophy of Language*, ed. Leonard Linsky, Urbana: Univ. of Illinois Press, 1952.

Walker, Ralph C. S. 1989. *The Coherence Theory of Truth*. London and New York: Routledge.

Wallace, J. 1970. "On a Frame of Reference," *Synthese* 22, pp. 117–50.

Williams, Michael. 1980. "Coherence, Justification and Truth," *Review of Metaphysics* 34, pp. 243–72.

————. 1986. "Do We (Epistemologists) Need a Theory of Truth?" *Philosophical Topics* 4, pp. 223–42.

Wilson, Kent. 1980. "Redundancy and the Prosentential Theory of Truth" (mimeograph).

————. 1990. "Some Reflections on the Prosentential Theory of Truth," ed. Michael Dunn and Anil Gupta, Dordrecht: Kluwer, 1990, pp. 19–31.

Wilson, Mark. 1982. "Predicate Meets Property," *Philosophical Review* 91, pp. 549–89.

Wittgenstein, Ludwig. 1953. *Philosophical Investigations*. Trans. G. E. M. Anscombe. New York: Macmillan.

————. 1974. *Philosophical Grammar*. Ed. R. Rhees. Trans. A. Kenny. Berkeley and Los Angeles: Univ. of California Press.

Woodruff, Peter, and Robert L. Martin. 1984. "On Representing 'True-in-L' in L," *Philosophia* 3, pp. 213–17.

Wray, David. 1987. "Logic in Quotes," *Journal of Philosophical Logic* 16, pp. 77–110.

Zimmerman, Michael J. 1978. "Propositional Quantification and the Prosentential Theory of Truth," *Philosophical Studies* 34, pp. 253–68.

Index

In an attempt to minimize redundant references, some occurrences of key terms have not been referenced. The term *prosentence* is an example: Because prosentences are explained in similar ways in several different chapters, only some of these passages have been referenced.